Ten Lectures on Construction Grammar and Typology

Distinguished Lectures in Cognitive Linguistics

Distinguished Lectures in Cognitive Linguistics publishes the keynote lectures series given by prominent international scholars at the China International Forum on Cognitive Linguistics since 2004. Each volume contains the transcripts of 10 lectures under one theme given by an acknowledged expert on a subject and readers have access to the audio recordings of the lectures through links in the e-book and QR codes in the printed volume. This series provides a unique course on the broad subject of Cognitive Linguistics. Speakers include George Lakoff, Ronald Langacker, Leonard Talmy, Laura Janda, Dirk Geeraerts, Ewa Dąbrowska and many others.

The titles published in this series are listed at *brill.com/dlcl*

Ten Lectures on Construction Grammar and Typology

By

William Croft

BRILL

LEIDEN | BOSTON

The Library of Congress Cataloging-in-Publication Data is available online at http://catalog.loc.gov
LC record available at http://lccn.loc.gov/2020033711

Typeface for the Latin, Greek, and Cyrillic scripts: "Brill". See and download: brill.com/brill-typeface.

ISSN 2468-4872
ISBN 978-90-04-36352-6 (hardback)
ISBN 978-90-04-36353-3 (e-book)

This book is printed on acid-free paper and produced in a sustainable manner.

Printed by Printforce, the Netherlands

Contents

Note on Supplementary Material

All original audio-recordings and other supplementary material, such as hand-outs and PowerPoint presentations for the lecture series, have been made available online and are referenced via unique DOI numbers on the website www.figshare.com. They may be accessed via a QR code for the print version of this book. In the e-book both the QR code and dynamic links will be available which can be accessed by a mouse-click.

The material can be accessed on figshare.com through a PC internet browser or via mobile devices such as a smartphone or tablet. To listen to the audio recording on hand-held devices, the QR code that appears at the beginning of each chapter should be scanned with a smart phone or tablet. A QR reader/scanner and audio player should be installed on these devices. Alternatively, for the e-book version, one can simply click on the QR code provided to be redirected to the appropriate website.

This book has been made with the intent that the book and the audio are both available and usable as separate entities. Both are complemented by the availability of the actual files of the presentations and material provided as hand-outs at the time these lectures were given. All rights and permission remain with the authors of the respective works, the audio-recording and supplementary material are made available in Open Access via a CC-BY-NC license and are reproduced with kind permission from the authors. The recordings are courtesy of the *China International Forum on Cognitive Linguistics* (http://cifcl.buaa.edu.cn/), funded by the *Beihang University Grant for International Outstanding Scholars*.

 The complete collection of lectures by William Croft can be accessed by scanning this QR code.

Preface

The present text, entitled *Ten Lectures on Construction Grammar and Typology* by William Croft, is a transcribed version of the lectures given by Professor William Croft in November 2010 as one of the three forum speakers for *the 8th China International Forum on Cognitive Linguistics*. William Croft received his Ph.D. from Stanford University in 1986. He is currently Professor Emeritus of Linguistics at the University of New Mexico. Croft's areas of specialty are typology, semantics, cognitive linguistics, construction grammar and evolutionary models of language change. His publications include *Typology and Universals* (2nd edition, 2003), *Syntactic Categories and Grammatical Relations* (1991), *Explaining Language Change* (2000), *Radical Construction Grammar* (2001), *Cognitive Linguistics* (with Alan Cruse, 2004) and *Verbs* (2012). Croft has held visiting positions at the Max Planck Institute for Psycholinguistics, the Max Planck Institute for Evolutionary Anthropology and the Center for Advanced Study in the Behavioral Sciences. More information about Professor Croft and his research can be found on his website: http://www.unm.edu/~wcroft.

The China International Forum on Cognitive Linguistics provides a forum for eminent international scholars to talk to Chinese audiences. It is a continuing program organized by nine prestigious universities in Beijing. The main organizing institution is Beihang University (BUAA); co-sponsors for CIFCL8 include Tsinghua University, Peking University, Beijing Foreign Studies University, and Beijing Forestry University. Professor Croft's lecture series was mainly supported by *the Beihang University Grant for International Outstanding Scholars* for 2010 (Project number: Z1057, Project organizer: Thomas Fuyin Li).

The text is published as one of the *Eminent Linguists Lecture Series*. The transcription of the lectures, proofreading of the text, and publication of the work in its present book form, has involved many people's strenuous inputs. The initial drafts were completed by the following postgraduate students from Beihang University: Chao Chen, Miaomiao Dou, Rong Han, Fan Tian, Dongfang Wang, Yue Wu, Na Yang, Zuan Zhang, Jingyuan Zhao, Xueqing Zhou. Then we editors did the word-by-word and line-by-line revision. To improve the readability of the text, we have deleted the false starts, repetitions, fillers like *now, so, you know, OK, and so on, again, of course, if you like, sort of,* etc. Occasionally, the written version needs an additional word to be clear, a word that was not actually spoken in the lecture. We have added such words within single brackets [...]. To make the written version readable, even without watching the film, we've added a few "stage instructions", in italics also within single brackets: [...]. The stage instruction describes what the speaker was doing, such as pointing at a slide, showing an object, etc. The speaker, Professor Croft, did the final revision with the assistance of Steve Pepper. The published version is the final version approved by the speaker.

Thomas Fuyin Li
Beihang University (BUAA)
thomasli@buaa.edu.cn

Yan Ding
Beijing Jiaotong University (BJTU)
a1931918@gmail.com

Basics of Construction Grammar

Thank you very much. First, I'd like to thank Professor Li for inviting me and setting up and organizing this very nice lecture series. I'm very happy to be here along with my colleagues, Melissa Bowerman and Zoltán Kövecses. As you can see from the screens the topic of my whole series of lectures is "Construction Grammar and Typology". And so I'd like to start by giving you an overview of the lectures that I will be presenting here. I hope that many of you will be able to attend most of the lectures. I know that people will be coming and going depending on their own schedules. I also appreciate the fact that you are all here at 8 o'clock in the morning.

I'm going to give you a brief outline of the lectures to give you some idea of where I'm going because the whole sequence is a kind of integrated whole. So what is the basic topic of these lectures? The syntactic theory that's associated with Cognitive Linguistics is what's called "construction grammar". This is a theory that in its modern form was first developed by Charles Fillmore at the University of California in Berkeley, and I will be describing the basics of it this morning. One particular aspect about construction grammar is that it's symbolic. So one way in which it differs from other grammatical theories or models of syntax is that it's actually not only about syntax; it's about syntax and semantics—form and meaning. Now, my contribution to construction grammar is basically to bring a typological perspective on constructions, because I believe that this provides important insights on the nature of form, meaning, and the symbolic relations you find in grammar.

The first five lectures in the series basically have a theme that you can summarize as "Syntax is simpler than you think". One of the things that many of you may know about many syntactic theories that are presented these days is that some of them are extremely complicated in terms of the syntactic structures they propose for the analysis of particular sentences in any language. The main thrust of my own argument is that in fact this is not the best way to go.

 All original audio-recordings and other supplementary material, such as any hand-outs and powerpoint presentations for the lecture series, have been made available online and are referenced via unique DOI numbers on the website www.figshare.com. They may be accessed via a QR code for the print version of this book. In the e-book, both the QR code and dynamic links are available, and can be accessed by a mouse-click.

In fact, the relationship is very simple; that is, the syntactic structure of sentences is actually extremely simple.

This morning I will be talking about the basics of construction grammar. Pretty much everything that I will tell you this morning you can find is shared with other approaches to construction grammar, such as those by Fillmore and Kay at Berkeley, George Lakoff also at Berkeley, Adele Goldberg at Princeton, as well as my own work on Radical Construction Grammar. Then, in the lecture I give this afternoon [Lecture 2], I will talk about the role of syntactic categories and constructions in Radical Construction Grammar. This is probably the most distinctive characteristic of my approach to construction grammar. While it's compatible with other kinds of construction grammar, it really is rather different, so I'll spend some time this afternoon defending it and showing you how I would respond to various criticisms that have been made.

Tomorrow morning I will use as a case study an example of the issue of parts of speech in Chinese [Lecture 3]. Obviously I'm doing this because I'm here in Beijing. However I'll actually be using mostly evidence from a paper by Elaine Francis and Stephen Matthews on Cantonese, so most of what I will be talking about is on Cantonese. But many of the aspects of the structure of Cantonese that they discuss are also true of Mandarin (to the best of my knowledge). On Saturday afternoon I will be moving on to another topic, which has to do with the internal structure of constructions—the syntactic structure of constructions [Lecture 4]. This is an argument which also continues the theme that "syntax is simpler than you think": there's actually very little internal structure to the analysis of constructions in construction grammar. It doesn't need to have any more; and in fact it's a bad idea to have additional structure.

And then, lastly, on Sunday morning, I will be talking about the syntactic space of constructions [Lecture 5]. The point here is that when we talk about constructions and we think of things like English passive or other kinds of constructions, some linguists, including some construction grammarians, have proposed that we can talk about a universal passive construction that can be described in different languages, or be described as occurring in different languages. My argument here will be that, in fact, that is not the case. It's just like the syntactic categories that I'll talk about this afternoon: grammatical constructions are language-specific. Although we can talk about their syntactic properties and compare them from one language to the next, we can't just assume that they're going to be identical.

The second half of my lectures will be covering what looks like a variety of themes: meaning, form, verbalization and evolution, but in fact they are all interrelated. They all touch on another basic principle accepted by many construction grammarians, what we call in Cognitive Linguistics the "usage-based model". I will be talking about how the usage-based model can be adapted by taking the perspective of verbalization: in other words, how speakers take a particular experience they want to communicate to the listener and actually express that experience using the grammar of their language. This perspective gives you—again that's probably the most interesting thing to me—it gives you a rather novel view of how to look at meaning and the relationship between meaning and form. It also touches on the model of language change that was referred to in the introduction.

In the first lecture, which is on Sunday afternoon here at Beihang University, I will be talking about grammar and verbalization of experience using a model that was originally proposed by Wallace Chafe [Lecture 6]. I will be elaborating that model and arguing that this model of verbalization actually allows us to talk about what kinds of constructions you do find in the world's languages. And then the heart of the second half of my presentation has to do with a particular way of looking at the relationship between form and meaning—and in particular conceptual categories—that I have been working on for a while. It started a long time ago actually, but it is partly in the book I wrote on Radical Construction Grammar. However, much of what I'll be presenting is based on research I've done since then. So in the first talk of the lectures that will be held in other universities here in Beijing, I'll be talking about typological universals and the semantic map model [Lecture 7]. The semantic map model is basically about how to represent conceptual structure, or relationships between conceptual structures, in typology. Once I introduce that, I will use it to bring insights, I hope, into various aspects of the representation of meaning and form in Cognitive Linguistics.

So these two talks here on Tuesday are actually very closely related to each other. I'll be talking about semantic maps and a statistical technique called multidimensional scaling which essentially allows us to analyze very complex data that you collect in cross-linguistic comparison on the nature of categories, and it leads to some very interesting conclusions, I think, about the nature of grammatical categories and conceptual categories [Lecture 8]. On Wednesday morning, I'll be drawing those conclusions by looking at a model which I call "exemplar semantics" that allows us to rethink the relationship between form and meaning in language [Lecture 9]. There are also aspects of exemplar semantics, a certain kind of usage-based approach, that leads you to the kind of evolutionary model that represents another strand of my research [Lecture 10].

Ok, so that's the overview. You can see that the lectures kind of fall into two halves. The first half is either based on or built on the work I did in the book on Radical Construction Grammar; it's basically an outline of the approach. The second half shows some consequences based on research I've done since I published that book.

This morning I'm going to talk about the basics of construction grammar. They are concepts that you can find shared across different approaches to construction grammar. This has its roots in the classic work by Fillmore from the late 1980s and also by other linguists who do not call themselves construction grammarians who worked at the same time or in parallel. By the way, for those of you who are following the slides in your handout packet, the overview I just gave you is not there in the packet, as you have surely all noticed. Now I start with what's in the packet. I've made a few minor changes to the slides, mainly just corrections of errors and things like that, so basically what's up here is what you have in your packet.

I'm going to start by looking at the basic organization of linguistic knowledge that non-construction grammarians assume people have in their heads, some kind of mental representation of grammatical knowledge. The model that is quite widespread is obviously associated with generative grammar, but also with a number of its offshoots including theories like Lexical Functional Grammar, Head-driven Phrase Structure Grammar—non-transformational theories—and also with Ray Jackendoff's recent work in which he has stopped being a Chomskyan generative grammarian and is developing a different theory. The model that they all have is a componential model, which I will describe on the next slide.

Construction grammar is actually very different. If there is any one thing that makes construction grammar distinctive, it's the way that it essentially abandons this componential model that the other syntactic theories use. However, I don't want to overstate the differences between construction grammar and the componential models. At least in the way componential models are actually set up, they actually do share some properties with construction grammars. There is some sense in which construction grammar takes certain qualifications of the componential model and takes them to their logical conclusion.

So what does the componential model look like? You may have seen these things if you've taken introductory courses in formal syntax [Figure 1]. You have different components, such as the phonological component, the syntactic component and the semantic component, all of which are self-contained. That is, you study phonology in the phonological component; you examine syntax in the syntactic component; you examine semantics in the semantic component. And in fact, as all of you know—I think this is a problem and I won't be surprised if it is true here in China as well as in United States, in

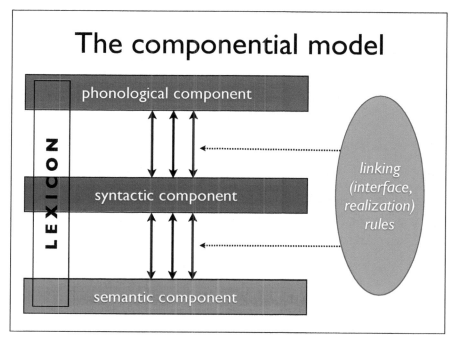

The componential model

phonological component

LEXICON

syntactic component

semantic component

linking
(interface,
realization)
rules

FIGURE 1

Western Europe and in Australia—the way that we teach linguistics in university is based on the componential model. You take a class in phonology; you take another class in phonetics; you take another class in syntax; you take another class in semantics, and so on. And then when you are done, you become a linguist, a specialist in linguistics.

Now, there is one exception that all of the advocates of the componential model are willing to acknowledge, and that is that the lexicon actually combines features from all these different components. So, for example, if you have a word like *take*, a verb, it has a phonological form "take"; it has syntactic characteristics—the fact that it combines with a subject or an object, or maybe some kind of oblique phrase—and it has a semantics which we can represent in whatever way we want; I'm not so concerned with that right now. That is how you link the different components in the traditional componential model. It's obvious that every time you speak, you're producing sounds, the sounds form words (lexical items) that are organized into syntactic structures and utterances, and there is a meaning that the speaker is trying to convey.

But that turns out not to be enough, because you have all sorts of syntactic structures that I would call constructions, and these syntactic structures

The componential model

- Each qualitatively different type of grammatical structure is independent

- The most important regularities are self-contained within each component

- The lexicon links together information in each component, but is arbitrary and associated with individual lexical items

- Nevertheless, linking (interface, realization) rules are required, e.g. rules of semantic interpretation/syntactic realization

FIGURE 2

systematically convey certain meanings. You use an intransitive construction if you want to express one kind of meaning and a transitive construction if you want to express another kind of meaning. So what are the systematic relations in meaning? They can't just be captured only by the words and the sentence and whatever syntactic traits you attribute to them. You have to have some kind of rules that relate, say, the syntactic structure to the semantic structure. Nowadays, these rules are called "linking rules"; sometimes they're called "interface rules"; sometimes they're called "realization rules", the realization of meaning in syntactic form. Well, these rules essentially say that there are other ways in which we have to link these separate components than just the lexicon. So there's some sense in which these components are not as self-contained or independent or autonomous from each other as you might think.

This next slide [Figure 2] summarizes the main points I just made, which is that each qualitatively different type of grammatical structure is independent. This is the idea that when you look at phonology, you don't have to worry about syntax; when you look at syntax, you don't have to worry about phonology or worry about semantics; when you look at semantics, you don't have to worry about syntax, let alone phonology. In particular, there is the claim that if you want to understand the nature of language, the best thing to do is to isolate

Constructions in Western traditional grammar

Correlative Comparative Sentences in Latin (Gildersleeve and Lodge 1895)

Sīc dē ambitiōne quōmodo dē amīca   queruntur
so of ambition   as   of sweetheart they.complain
'They complain of ambition as they do of a sweetheart.'

- a complex syntactic structure (correlative conjunctions, etc.)

- with a particular meaning (comparison)

- and particular grammatical and semantic constraints (type of conjunction, mood of clause; specialized meanings, etc.)

FIGURE 3

phonology from syntax, isolate syntax from semantics. Look at them by themselves, and you'll find general principles or universal properties of each type of linguistic structure.

Now, as I said, the lexicon links together information in each component, but the assumption is that the lexicon is arbitrary. So there is nothing terribly interesting about the fact that the English word *take* has the phonological structure that it does and has the meaning that it does, and has the syntactic behavior that it does. Nevertheless, as I already mentioned, linguists that use the componential model require linking rules, interface rules or realization rules, such as rules of semantic interpretation or syntactic realization. So, in fact, not everything that's interesting about syntax and semantics can be done by ignoring the other. In short, that second bullet point is actually not entirely true; not all the important regularities are self-contained.

Now, "construction" as a notion is found in traditional grammatical analysis in the western grammatical tradition [Figure 3]. I just picked out at random an example from a 19th century grammar of Latin. Many grammars were of course written in the 19th century, long before the advent of structuralism and generative grammar and all these other 20th century syntactic theories. So what did they do when they were faced with the kinds of facts of languages that we are interested in? Well, they actually divided syntactic structures into categories which they called constructions. So for instance, this particular grammar isolates a particular kind of construction that they call a correlative comparative sentence or construction. I give you an example from this particular grammar book of this kind of construction. The translation is "they complain of ambition as they do of a sweetheart"; I can't remember the source.[1]

So what is a construction in a traditional Western grammar? It is a complex syntactic structure. If you look at the sentence and the morpheme gloss, you see the word *sīc* "so" and the word *quōmodo* "as". These are what are called correlative conjunctions. And of course, the correlative conjunctions combine two different phrases here. There is a particular meaning associated with the construction; the name of the construction tells us that it involves comparison—between their complaint about ambition and their complaint about a sweetheart. The construction also has particular grammatical and semantic constraints: there's only a subset of conjunctions that can be used in this kind of construction; there are limits on the mood of the clause, a grammatical category of Latin; and there are specialized meanings for these different conjunctions and other things that characterize this construction.

So that is what you find if you go to the pre-construction grammar notion of a construction in the Western grammatical tradition. I'm sorry, I don't know if there is anything equivalent in the Chinese grammatical tradition. Now, this notion of construction, this traditional notion, is denied by Chomsky, and he's been fairly consistent about this view at least in the last twenty or thirty years. I have two quotations here on the screen and in your book about that [Figure 4]. One is from *Lectures on Government and Binding* from thirty years ago where he says, "a central element in the work discussed here, as in recent work from which it evolves, is the efforts to decompose such processes as 'passive', 'relativization', etc., into more fundamental 'abstract features'." He calls these processes 'passive' and 'relativization' because in generative grammar, these constructions are created through a transformational rule, or set of rules, although we think of them more as constructions rather than the output of those rules.

In more recent work, in *The Minimalist Program*, 1993, Chomsky describes Universal Grammar and says it "provides a fixed system of principles and a finite array of finitely valued parameters. The language-particular rules reduce the choice of values for these parameters. The notion of grammatical construction is eliminated, and with it, construction-particular rules." For him, a construction-particular rule is like the rule that creates relative clauses. So in both of these cases, he is arguing that you don't need constructions; you can

---

1   SEN., E.M., 22, 10 (Seneca the Younger, *Epistulae morales ad Lucilium*).

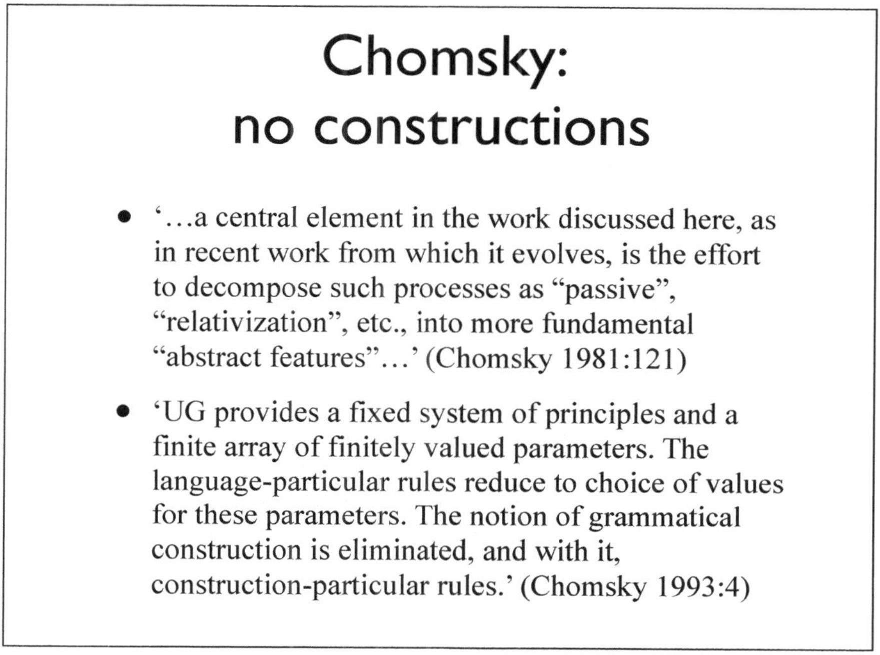

Chomsky:
no constructions

- '...a central element in the work discussed here, as in recent work from which it evolves, is the effort to decompose such processes as "passive", "relativization", etc., into more fundamental "abstract features"...' (Chomsky 1981:121)

- 'UG provides a fixed system of principles and a finite array of finitely valued parameters. The language-particular rules reduce to choice of values for these parameters. The notion of grammatical construction is eliminated, and with it, construction-particular rules.' (Chomsky 1993:4)

FIGURE 4

come up with something more abstract and then you don't need constructions any more.

Now the main challenge to this work is from what are called "idioms" in the western grammatical tradition, and this is the starting point for the research by Fillmore and Kay and O'Connor, a great paper from 1988 which I recommend to all of you. And there is another paper from linguists, actually in a different grammatical tradition—Nunberg, Sag and Wasow—also talking about idioms. They make some very insightful points, some of which I will talk about right now, and others I will talk about in Lecture Four.

One point they make is that you have what are called idioms in English, things like "pull strings". "Pull strings" means to use influence in order to obtain something you want, like a job. And they describe these as "idiomatically combining expressions". That's their term for it [Figure 5]. And the crucial thing, the point that they make is that *pull* plus *strings* is compositional, it is just not predictable from abstract rules. So in other words, we need a construction specific rule, that is, we take a very specific view of constructions [and the rule that produces the construction], so that "pull strings" is by itself an idiomatic construction. To quote their words, "by convention [that is, a convention of English], *strings* [in "pull strings"] can be used metaphorically to refer to personal connections when it is the object of *pull*, and *pull* can be used

Idioms and constructions

- Most "idioms", such as *pull strings,* are idiomatically combining expressions (Nunberg, Sag & Wasow 1994); they are compositional but not predictable from "abstract" rules

- 'By convention...*strings* [in *pull strings*] can be used metaphorically to refer to personal connection when it is the object of *pull*, and *pull* can be used metaphorically to refer to exploitation or exertion when its object is *strings*' (Nunberg et al. 1994:496)

FIGURE 5

Idioms and constructions

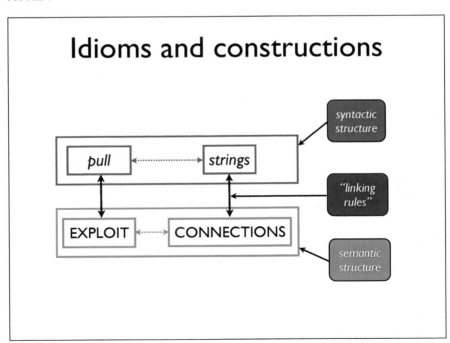

FIGURE 6

metaphorically to refer to exploitation or exertion when its object is *strings*". In other words, you can say what *pull* means in this idiom and you can say what *strings* means in this idiom. The words just don't mean the same thing that they do elsewhere, like pulling a cart, or using strings to tie a package.

This is the notation I'm going to be using in various forms in the rest of this morning's lecture. Let's look at "pull strings" using the componential model [Figure 6]. Everything is color-coded: blue represents syntactic structure; red represents those meanings that you find only in this combination, that is, the semantic structure of this construction. The horizontal boxes represent the semantic structure and the syntactic structure. Then you have, so to speak, "linking rules". That was what Nunberg, Sag and Wasow described in that quotation: that *pull* in combination with *strings* means exploit, and *strings* in combination with *pull* means connections.

Now, the insight that Fillmore, Kay and O'Connor presented is that some of these so-called "idioms" are actually schematic. They aren't just concrete words like *pull* plus *strings*. They are more schematic syntactic categories that are combined in special ways, and have their own rules about their syntax and semantics, and maybe even about the phonology and the pragmatics. So the classical example they have is "X let alone Y", the "let alone" construction, which was the focus of the analysis of their paper [Figure 7]. There are two examples at the bottom of the slide, both from their paper: "Max won't eat SHRIMP, let alone SQUID". What that means, if you are not familiar with the construction, is two things; one is that Max won't eat shrimp, and two, I am saying that the fact that Max eats shrimp is actually pretty significant, and that he is even less adventurous in food than somebody who eats squid would be.

The second sentence shows that you can have this kind of parallelism within these two clauses where you have two elements being contrasted: so "Max won't TOUCH the SHRIMP, let alone CLEAN the SQUID". So now we are comparing touching the shrimp to cleaning the squid, and saying that Max won't do the first thing, and that's, you know, a pretty strong statement, since it's more surprising than if he wouldn't want to clean the squid.

One point they make here which I have on the second bullet point on the slide is that the syntactic and semantic and other details about the "let alone" construction—contrary to Chomsky's claim—cannot be derived from more general facts about English conjunctions; or from English focus constructions represented by the accents on *shrimp* and *squid*, or more specifically focus constructions with multiple paired foci, so *shrimp* and *squid* are paired foci with *touch* and *clean*; or from what are called negative polarity items because this "let alone" construction always occurs within a negative clause context.

Idioms and constructions

- Some "idioms" are schematic and have their own rules governing their syntax and semantics (and even phonology and pragmatics)

- X let alone Y (Fillmore et al. 1988) is similar but not identical to other more general constructions including: conjunctions, focus constructions with multiple paired foci, and negative polarity items

Max won't eat SHRIMP, let alone SQUID.
Max won't TOUCH the SHRIMP, let alone CLEAN the SQUID.

FIGURE 7

Even though its properties cannot be predicted from these more general grammatical categories and constructions of English, the "let alone" construction is still quite systematic in terms of its semantic interpretation [Figure 8]. First, you have to have two propositions to compare: "Max does not eat SHRIMP", "Max does not eat SQUID". They are in what is called the same scalar model. Then there has to be some way that you and I can say that "Max not eating SHRIMP" is a more informative or surprising statement than "Max does not eat SQUID". The propositions must have the same polarity; in this case they must both be negative. And then the first conjunct, "Max not eating SHRIMP", is the more informative proposition in the scale. (As I mentioned before, at least from a American cultural perspective, not eating SHRIMP is more informative than not eating SQUID; there are lots of people that don't eat squid, and there are fewer people around that don't eat shrimp.) And then you can generalize this to an example like "Max won't TOUCH the SHRIMP, let alone CLEAN the SQUID": you can determine the semantic interpretation looking at those combined foci [that is, not touching shrimp is more informative than not cleaning squid].

Fillmore, Kay and O'Connor's paper was very important because it showed that there is a lot of regularity in the "let alone" construction that could not be predicted from general grammatical principles as Chomsky claimed. And

Idioms and constructions

- *X let alone Y* also has a systematic semantic interpretation ranking paired propositions on aligned scalar models

  - The propositions (*Max not eat shrimp, Max not eat squid*) must be in the same scalar model

  - The propositions must have the same polarity

  - The initial, full conjunct denotes the proposition that is stronger or more informative on the scale (Max not eating shrimp is more informative than Max not eating squid)

  - Generalizable to multiple paired foci

FIGURE 8

yet it was regular and systematic, and therefore most linguists interested in linguistic theory would say that you need to be able to explain it; you can't just ignore it or pretend it's some arbitrary fact like "pull strings". Even "pull strings", as Nunberg, Sag and Wasow showed, is systematic within its own extremely narrow domain: basically *pull* combined with *strings*, and *strings* combined with *pull*.

They were not the first to observe this fact. It was just that other linguists didn't draw the conclusions that Fillmore *et al.* did: that these facts force us to rethink the nature of grammar and syntactic structure. Ellen Prince, for example, an American linguist who did much work on pragmatics and who sadly just passed away a couple of weeks ago, focused her attention on looking at the pragmatic structure of particular English constructions, including the so-called "cleft" constructions [Figure 9]. Here are two examples that she collected and published in a paper from 1978 (so we are talking about something done over 30 years ago). Look at the two examples: "It is against pardoning these that many protest" (the It-cleft) and "What you are saying is that the President was involved" (the WH-cleft). I'm not going to go into detail here. My main point is just to show that there are antecedents to construction grammar, at least among American and English speaking linguists.

It-cleft and WH-cleft (Prince 1978)

It is against pardoning these that many protest.
(*Philadelphia Inquirer,* February 6, 1977)

What you are saying is that the President was involved.
(Haldeman, Watergate tapes)

- WH-clefts allow adverbs and prepositional phrases, *It*-clefts allow verb phrases or sentences

- In WH-clefts, the subordinate clause information is in the hearer's consciousness, while the *It*-cleft has two subsenses, 'stressed focus' and 'informative presupposition'

FIGURE 9

Prince showed that there are certain syntactic differences between these two different kinds of cleft constructions: that's what the first bullet point tells you. They allow different kinds of units: adverbs and prepositional phrases for WH-clefts, verb phrases and sentences with It-clefts. In WH-clefts, the clefts also differ in their pragmatics. So, in WH-clefts the subordinate clause information is in the hearer's consciousness already, whereas the It-cleft has two subsenses, which I won't go into now, but they are different from the WH-cleft. In other words, these two cleft constructions differ in both their syntax and their semantics. But they are also quite systematic in that, if you find such clefts in naturally occurring discourse, you can draw some conclusions about their grammatical behavior and their semantic interpretation.

Another kind of construction is in a great paper by Anna Wierzbicka, an Australian linguist, comparing constructions in English that have *have* plus some kind of verb form [Figure 10]. As you can see from the example at the top, which is taken from the title of her paper, you can "have a drink" in English, but you cannot "have an eat". She wanted to explore why this is the case. First, she argues that the expression that comes after the indefinite article *a* is actually not a noun, but a verb, a kind of bare verb (infinitival form). So it's not your ordinary noun, to begin with; you cannot infer that just because it comes after

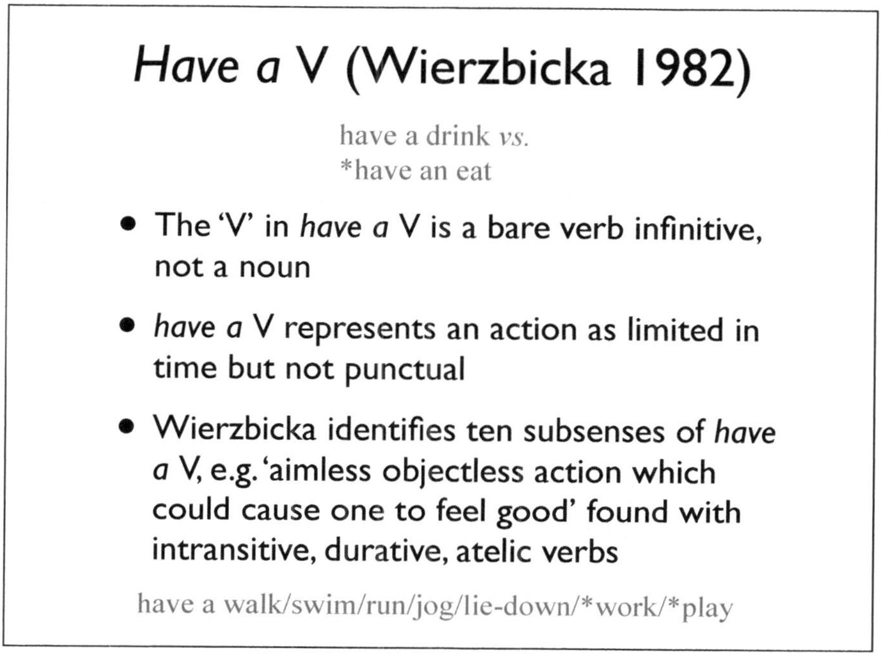

Have a V (Wierzbicka 1982)

have a drink *vs.*
*have an eat

- The 'V' in *have a* V is a bare verb infinitive, not a noun

- *have a* V represents an action as limited in time but not punctual

- Wierzbicka identifies ten subsenses of *have a* V, e.g. 'aimless objectless action which could cause one to feel good' found with intransitive, durative, atelic verbs

have a walk/swim/run/jog/lie-down/*work/*play

FIGURE 10

an indefinite article, it's a noun in the same sense that other phrases with an indefinite article have nouns.

More generally, she said that "have a V" represents an action as limited in time but not punctual in the aspectual sense, not occurring at a point in time. In fact, it is much more complicated than that. And that's what a lot of these people working on constructions tend to discover: that you think that there is one construction like "have a V", but in fact, Wierzbicka identifies ten subsenses of "have a V". One example is what she calls aimless objectless action which could cause one to feel good. And she points out that it is restricted with verbs that have certain kinds of semantic properties. They are intransitive; aspectually they are durative and atelic. So you can say "have a walk", "have a swim", "have a run", "have a jog", "have a lie-down", but you can't say in this meaning "have a work" or "have a play", as those verbs do not fit the description.

Lakoff [Figure 11]: this is more of a prototypical cognitive linguist doing this kind of research. About at the same time as Fillmore and his colleagues were working on the "let alone" construction, Lakoff published a detailed analysis of *there*-constructions. He again took what started out as one construction and ended up with 15: 11 types of what he called "deictic *there*-constructions" and 4 sub-senses of what he called the "existential *there*-construction". I'm giving

---

There-constructions (Lakoff 1987)

Central: There's Harry with the red jacket on.
Perceptual: There goes the bell now!
Paragon: Now there was a real ballplayer!
Delivery: Here's your pizza, piping hot!

- Lakoff identifies eleven subsenses of the Deictic *There*-construction and four subsenses of the Existential *There*-construction

- Each one has distinctive syntactic and semantic properties

Central: There's a fox in the garden.
Strange: There's a man been shot.
Ontological: There is a Santa Claus.

FIGURE 11

you some examples of the deictic *there*-constructions at the top and the existential *there*-constructions at the bottom. And in the very long appendix to his 1987 book, he shows that each construction has distinctive syntactic and semantic properties.

Again the details are not here. My main point is to show you that linguists working in different grammatical traditions, like Ellen Prince, Anna Wierzbicka, George Lakoff, and also Ray Jackendoff, have all proposed that we have to acknowledge the existence of constructions, patterns of grammatical structure that are systematic, have systematic syntactic properties and semantic properties. And you can't just derive them from abstract general principles of syntax. So the Jackendoff examples are more recent. Examples include what he calls the "time-*away*" construction [Figure 12]. This is a particular use of *away*, but it's actually *away* in a special combination. So he points out that in a sentence like "Bill slept the afternoon away", *sleep* is an intransitive verb, but it takes what looks like a direct object "the afternoon". In "Fred drank the night away with a bottle of Jack Daniels", you get this construction with transitive verbs like *drink*, but you can't use the transitive object. You have to express the transitive object as a *with*-phrase, "with a bottle of Jack Daniels".

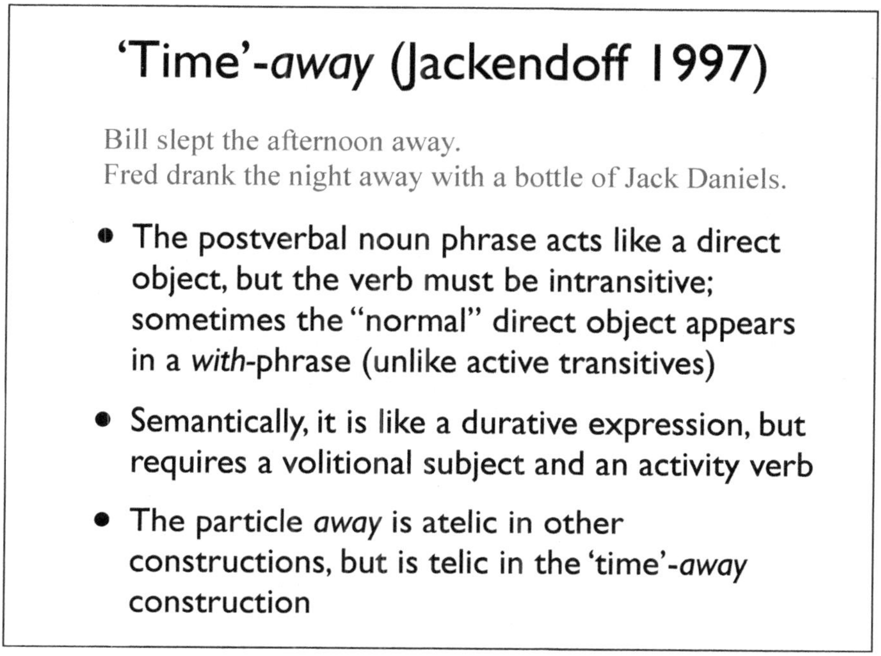

'Time'-*away* (Jackendoff 1997)

Bill slept the afternoon away.
Fred drank the night away with a bottle of Jack Daniels.

- The postverbal noun phrase acts like a direct object, but the verb must be intransitive; sometimes the "normal" direct object appears in a *with*-phrase (unlike active transitives)

- Semantically, it is like a durative expression, but requires a volitional subject and an activity verb

- The particle *away* is atelic in other constructions, but is telic in the 'time'-*away* construction

FIGURE 12

Semantically, these are durative expressions. So they talk about some events that take place over time. But they have an additional constraint that the subject must be a volitional agent and the verb describes an activity. There is something quite striking about the particular particle *away*, which is that if you look at other constructions in English that use the particle *away*, it has an atelic meaning, it denotes an unbounded, ongoing process. But in this particular construction it describes a bounded process, bounded by the time interval described by this direct object, "the afternoon" or "the night". So this is definitely a property of the construction that cannot be predicted from other uses of *away*.

Now, some linguists—not Fillmore *et al.*, but some other linguists—have proposed what we might call an "Enhanced Componential Model" [Figure 13]. So we're back to this original slide; there are autonomous components here. You allow the lexicon to cross these components, but now we also allow for constructions of the type I've just described. So constructions also have form and meaning, and they also have linking rules. But we aren't going to get rid of the componential model yet. At least that's the view of many linguists who work in this area. So, many syntacticians nowadays acknowledge that we have

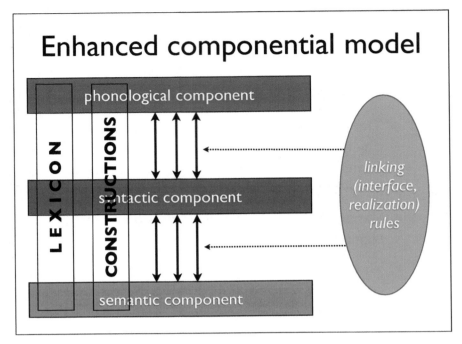

FIGURE 13

to account for constructions in this sense. But they are still unwilling to get rid of the componential model. But what constructions show us is that these different components are not so self-contained and there are many important regularities that cannot be captured by looking at just syntax, just semantics, or just phonology. General linking rules are not going to do it for you because the rules of semantic interpretation, the syntactic constraints, are particular to the individual constructions, like the word, the meaning of the word *away* that we just saw.

Now, Fillmore *et al.* and others have pointed out that if we propose that we need constructions for analyzing grammatical structures, then suddenly this little thing we added to the componential model is actually better than the componential model in describing any kind of syntactic or grammatical or lexical structure. So the way to look at this is to think about constructions not in a traditional grammatical sense, but in a much broader sense as any kind of pairing of form and meaning. And these pairings of form and meaning, which include the lexicon, vary in certain essential parameters [Figure 14]. The two parameters we are going to look at are complexity, whether there's more than one or just one formal element; and schematicity, whether we are talking

The syntax-lexicon continuum

Construction type	Traditional name	Examples
complex, schematic	**syntax**	[Adj N], [Sbj *be* Verb-*en by* Obl]
complex, substantive verb	**subcategorization frame**	[Sbj *consume* Obj]
complex, substantive	**idiom**	[Sbj *pull strings*]
complex, bound	**morphology**	[Noun-*s*], [Verb-Tns]
atomic, schematic	**syntactic category**	[Dem], [Num]
atomic, substantive	**word/lexicon**	[*after*], [*wilderness*]

FIGURE 14

about some general category defined by the construction or a specific word like *pull* in "pull strings", or *away* in the "time-*away*" construction.

So if you are talking about what your traditional grammarians call syntax, what you are looking at are constructions that are complex: they consist of more than one element. They are also schematic: those elements cover classes of words like the ones we would call adjective and noun (for now at least). Many linguists, in describing the syntactic behavior of lexical items like a verb like *take*, called these subcategorization frames. These things go under new names nowadays. But basically, a subcategorization frame consists of a schematic, complex construction—for example, it describes something that has a subject and an object—but the verb itself is substantive: it's a particular verb, not the general category of transitive verb. Idioms like "pull strings": these are complex but substantive. Each individual word is specified and it only has the meaning if those two words are combined in the right way. Those are the kinds of idiomatically combining expressions that Nunberg, Sag, and Wasow talked about.

But you can go even further than that. We can move away from things that we traditionally call syntax into morphology. So in morphology, we can talk about something which is complex and morphologically bound. So we have the schematic category "noun" which combines with an inflection for plurality in English. And that too is a construction in this sense, it's a pairing of form and meaning. It just happens to be that the morphemes are bound instead of free, and they may be schematic or they may be substantive. We can even talk about atomic units. We can talk about syntactic categories in the traditional sense. They are atomic—they're not complex, it's just one element—but these are schematic. The syntactic category covers a large class of words. I will be talking a lot more about those later [Lectures 2–3 and 7–9]. And finally, words, the lexicon, can also be described as very special kinds of constructions. They are atomic, just one word. But they are also substantive. They are not schematic at all. So you have words like *after* and *wilderness*. In other words, a word like *after* or *wilderness* is a construction just as much as the attributive adjective construction or the passive construction is a construction in this generalized sense.

All these points were made by Fillmore, Kay and O'Connor in their classic 1988 paper; that's another respect in which I think of this paper as being very far-sighted. The first major publication on construction grammar really laid out all the most important principles. The principle here is that if you allow constructions into your model of grammatical analysis, then you can now describe all kinds of grammatical structures in the same way, as a pairing of form and meaning that can be complex or atomic, can be fully schematic, partially schematic or fully substantive. So the constructional model now looks different [Figure 15]. We don't have components any more. Instead we have constructions, including the lexicon as a special class of constructions. And each construction now has phonological properties, syntactic properties and semantic properties. So the point that I've just made is that the constructional model provides a uniform representation of all grammatical structure. The constructional model retains distinctions between different types of grammatical information. When you put them all together, you can still distinguish between properties of a construction's form and properties of the construction's function in particular.

The constructional model now has to capture those regularities that used to be captured within components and it does this by taxonomic relations between constructions [Figure 16]. So for example, if you have a regular grammatical expression like "tie strings", and then you have idiomatic constructions like "pull strings" or "kick the bucket," they all have in common that they have a verb form followed by a direct object. The way we capture the fact that they all have this in common is that we have a superordinate or schematic construction, the verb-object construction, that captures this fact, that all these constructions share this property in common. We'll see this is not the only way

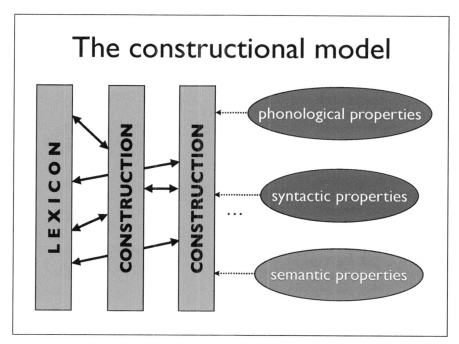

FIGURE 15

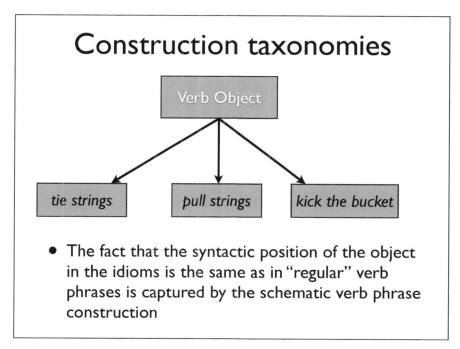

FIGURE 16

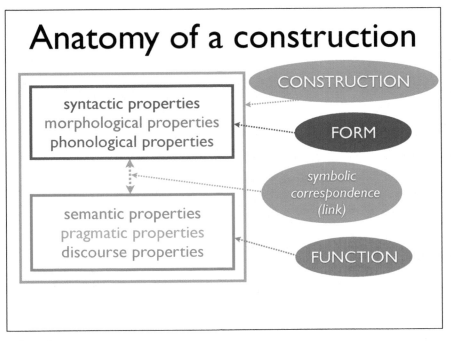

Anatomy of a construction

syntactic properties
morphological properties
phonological properties

CONSTRUCTION

FORM

symbolic correspondence (link)

semantic properties
pragmatic properties
discourse properties

FUNCTION

FIGURE 17

to capture generalizations. But the point here is that this is one way in which you do this in construction grammar.

Although I'm going to say in my lectures the constructions are pretty simple, they still have internal structure [Figure 17]. If we look at a construction, we can see that we have to make a very important distinction between the properties of the construction's form—syntactic, morphological and phonological properties—and the properties of the construction's function or meaning—semantic properties, pragmatic properties and discourse properties. And crucially, these things are paired. So constructions are what Langacker called symbolic units, pairings of form and meaning.

Now let's compare how form and function are done in the componential model to how it's done in the construction grammar model [Figure 18]. I've used labels here that obviously don't have much to do with cognitive linguistic approaches to grammar: it's the traditional generative approach, where we have phrases like noun phrases, verb phrases and then we have some kind of pseudo-logical representation of meaning like predicate and argument and quantifier and so on. In the componential model, these two kinds of structures are separated into syntactic and semantic components. Then you have to create linking rules that tell you that you interpret the intransitive clause in terms

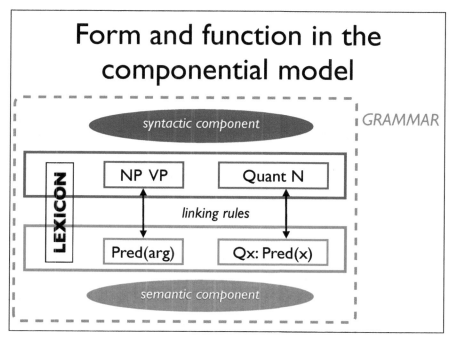

FIGURE 18

of a predicate applied to an argument, a quantifier modifying a noun (as quantification). And that's the grammar.

In the constructional model, you can see we still have the same units, but now they're paired as individual constructions linked to their meanings [Figure 19]. I will go quickly over this; it repeats the kind of things I've said before.

Comparing the two [Figure 20], on the left you have a typical generative representation. The first thing to notice is that it's only syntactic structure. The second is that it's a complex structure even here. The kind of box notation on the right represents the constructional model and here the thing to notice is that you have some kind of description of the construction's form and of its meaning, for example simple intransitive sentences like "Heather sings": again, syntactic structure and semantic structure. And the construction as a whole is a pairing of those two.

Now I'd like to introduce some terminology—some of this terminology is mine, some of this is Fillmore and Kay's—so that we can talk about these basic parts of a construction in the rest of the lectures [Figure 21]. Parts of the syntactic form of a construction, we'll call "elements"; parts of the semantic form or the semantic part of the construction, the meaning, we'll call "components". So we have elements for syntax, components for semantics, and then the term

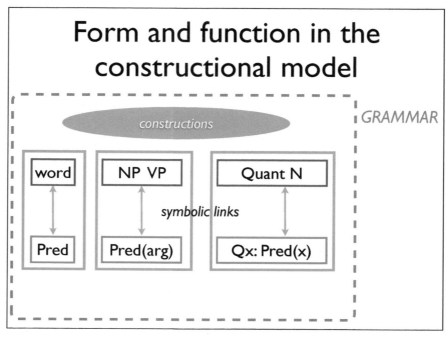

FIGURE 19

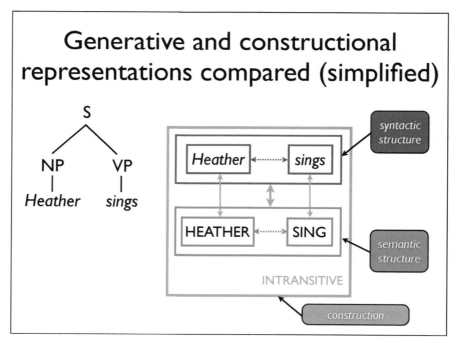

FIGURE 20

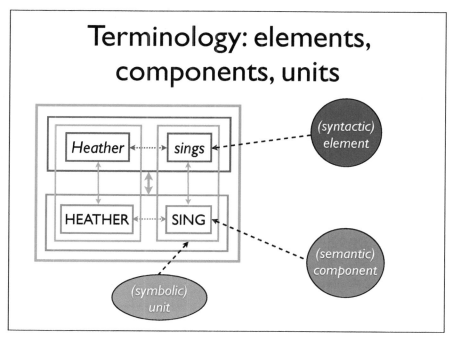

FIGURE 21

"unit" (which is actually from Langacker) for any particular pairing of form and meaning.

You can also have an exploded diagram of a construction [Figure 22]. This is very similar to what you find in Langacker's Cognitive Grammar. Instead of having the box, the *Heather* and *sing* inside the box which represents a unit is split out. Now we can describe the relationship between each individual element and the construction as a whole and between the two elements; (above) and the same down here (below) for the components.

This reveals a very important distinction, that between "roles" and "relations" (this terminology was introduced by Fillmore and Kay) [Figure 23]. A role is what an element does as a part of the whole construction. So you can say that *Heather* is the subject in the intransitive construction. A relation is a relation between two different elements in a single construction; it's a relationship between two parts of the construction. And that's the sense in which we say *Heather* is the subject of the verb *sings*.

Now you will notice, of course, that grammarians use the same term "subject" to describe a role and a relation. This is not always the case; in this particular example it is true. I put this example in here to essentially warn you that some grammatical terminology is ambiguous in the sense that it describes both a role and a relation, and you have to ask yourself when you are looking

Exploded diagram of a construction

	Intransitive Construction	
Heather		sings
HEATHER		SING
	Predicate(Argument)	

FIGURE 22

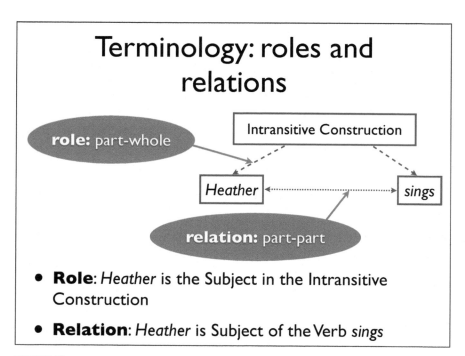

Terminology: roles and relations

role: part-whole

Intransitive Construction

Heather ← → sings

relation: part-part

- **Role**: *Heather* is the Subject in the Intransitive Construction
- **Relation**: *Heather* is Subject of the Verb *sings*

FIGURE 23

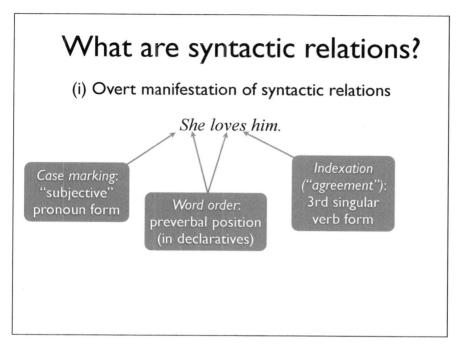

FIGURE 24

at a particular description of a grammatical construction, is the author talking about a role or about a relation? As we'll see, this will turn out to be very important because I will say that we should not be talking about relations at all, only roles [Lecture 4].

Then what is this notion of syntactic relations, this relation between parts? People sometimes ask me about this question because when you talk to more generative oriented syntacticians or some European syntacticians, then you'll see that they actually don't talk about syntactic relations. They talk about several different kinds of things, and I want to clarify that here [Figure 24]. The first thing that they talk about is what grammatical properties actually identify a syntactic relation? In the sentence "She loves him", how do we know that *she* is a subject of *love*, and *him* is the object of *love*? Well, for *she*, we can look at the case marking, it has a special pronoun form in English. We can also look at the verb. You can see the verb has indexation which is also called agreement, third singular form. And you can also look at the word order. The subject occurs before the verb in English in declarative sentences. So that's one thing you can talk about.

Another thing you can talk about with syntactic relations is how you represent them [Figure 25]. There's been a long debate, several decades long, in Western syntactic analysis about whether it is better to express the relationships

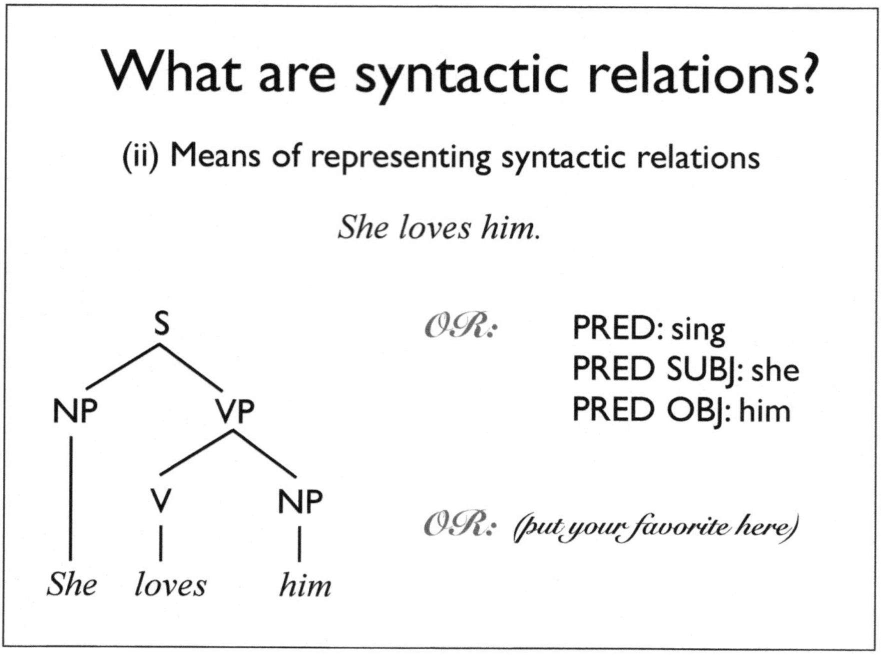

What are syntactic relations?

(ii) Means of representing syntactic relations

She loves him.

OR: PRED: sing
       PRED SUBJ: she
       PRED OBJ: him

OR: (put your favorite here)

FIGURE 25

in terms of what's called constituent structure (left), or in terms of some kind of functions or dependencies (right), or pick your favorite one. I don't particularly care because I'm going to be getting rid of these anyway.

So I'm just going to talk about syntactic relations in the abstract [Figure 26]. The relationship between *she* and *loves* is indicated by a dotted arrow between *she* and *loves* in this diagram. And as I said, I'm not particularly concerned whether we represent that relation in terms of constituency or dependency. Right now, for looking at this in terms of syntactic structure, I'm not yet concerned about how it is expressed: with special forms of pronouns, agreement on the verb or word order. We will come back to that.

However, you can allow for constructions to be nested [Figure 27]. If you have a sentence in English like "That blonde girl is my niece", that's the equational construction. But the parts of the equational construction are themselves constructions. So you have an equational subject which has the form with a demonstrative followed by an adjective and ending with a noun and then an equational complement which has a similar structure. You have the equational subject and complement constructions embedded inside the equational construction as a whole, as well as of course the equational verb "to be."

What are syntactic relations?

(iii) The abstract syntactic relation itself

She loves him.

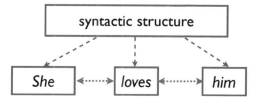

FIGURE 26

Nesting of constructions

- Constructions may be nested in other constructions (both compressed and exploded diagrams are given below)

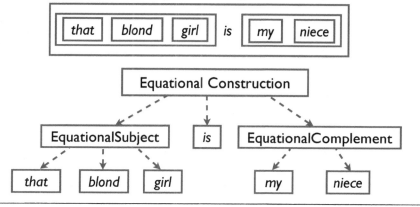

FIGURE 27

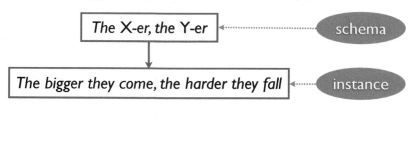

Construction taxonomies

- Construction grammar captures generalizations and idiosyncrasies via a construction taxonomy

- For example, there is a construction [*The X-er, the Y-er*], and also an idiomatic instance of it, *The bigger they come, the harder they fall*

The X-er, the Y-er ············· schema

The bigger they come, the harder they fall ·········· instance

FIGURE 28

Constructions can form taxonomies [Figure 28]. So one of the things you can say is that with another construction discussed by Fillmore, Kay and O'Connor, what they call "the X-er, the Y-er"—a comparative correlative construction in their terms, you have a general construction which can be used with a lot of different words. Then you also have a specialized construction, like the English idiom, "The bigger they come, the harder they fall" (basically, who are prouder or more powerful, if they fall, they tend to fall farther, so to speak). So that's obviously in the form of "the X-er, the Y-er" construction. So this is a more general construction, a schema (this is following the work by Bybee and Langacker and so on). And the more specific construction is an instance.

Then you can develop fancy taxonomies in multiple levels in order to capture the relationships and generalizations about the syntactic structure of English [Figure 29]. We'll come back to this in the later lectures [Lectures 5 and 7–9].

So constructions may have multiple parents [Figure 30]. This is another important thing. If you're talking about a particular sentence like "I didn't sleep", if you look at the way English forms sentences, clauses, you can talk relatively independently about how English combines a verb or predicate with its arguments—subject and object and oblique—from how a verb expresses negation. We can represent this—and construction grammarians do this all the

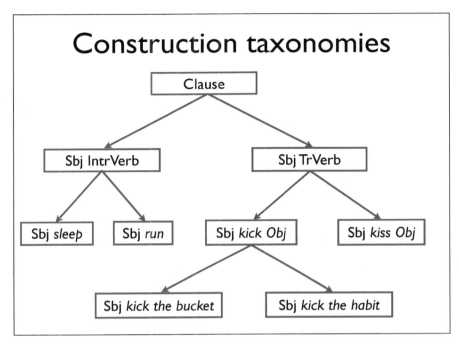

FIGURE 29

Construction taxonomies

- Constructions may have multiple "parents" that specify independently varying properties of the construction

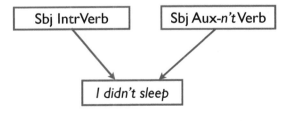

FIGURE 30

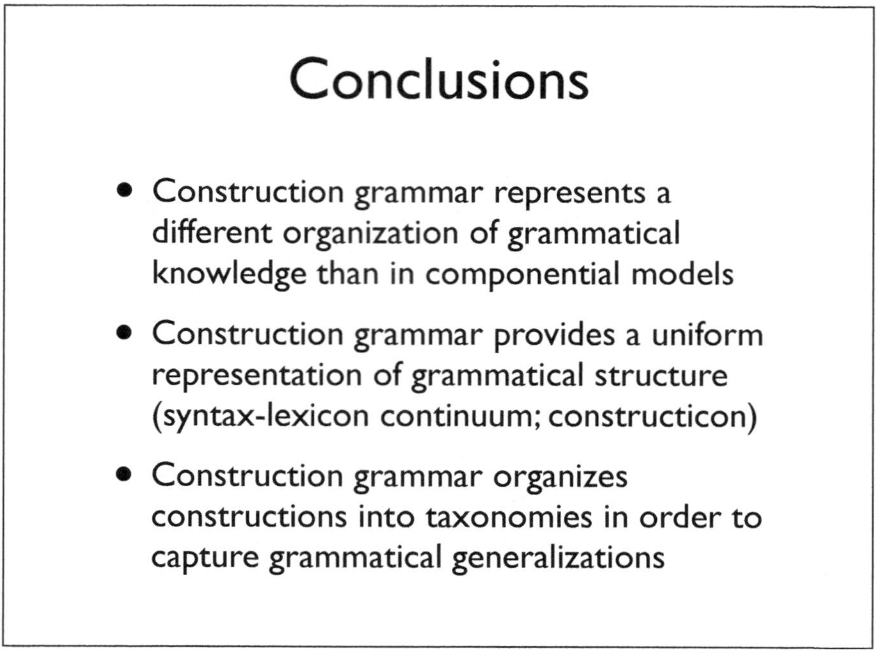

Conclusions

- Construction grammar represents a different organization of grammatical knowledge than in componential models

- Construction grammar provides a uniform representation of grammatical structure (syntax-lexicon continuum; constructicon)

- Construction grammar organizes constructions into taxonomies in order to capture grammatical generalizations

---

FIGURE 31

time—in terms of a particular sentence like "I didn't sleep", inheriting some grammatical properties from one construction—the construction for intransitive verbs—and some grammatical properties from another construction—a construction that describes how we form declarative negative sentences in English. Combine the two and you get "I didn't sleep".

So, to conclude, as a brief introduction [Figure 31]: construction grammar represents a different organization of grammatical knowledge than in componential models. Construction grammar provides a uniform representation of grammatical structure. This is the syntax-lexicon continuum. Some construction grammarians use the term "constructicon" to describe this. And then construction grammar organizes constructions into taxonomies in order to capture grammatical generalizations. So I said at the beginning of the lecture that there are certain things that all construction grammar theories have in common. It's basically these three points that I've presented here on the concluding slide.

And that's the end of what I have to say about constructions this morning. It's a general introduction. If you come back this afternoon [Lecture 2], I'll start talking about some more specific things about how Radical Construction Grammar differs from the kind of generic view of construction grammar that I've presented here this morning. So thank you very much.

Radical Construction Grammar: Categories and Constructions

Thank you very much for coming back. This afternoon I'm going to talk about Radical Construction Grammar, and the basic assumption that it makes. So I'll start to just quickly review the basic ideas that I've described this morning [Figure 32]. Basic construction grammar is what I described this morning and it's pretty straightforward. Grammatical knowledge is represented as constructions, pairings of form and meaning. An example of that is what you see at the

"Basic" construction grammar

X is Adj-*er than* Y:
value of X on Adj scale is greater than value of Y on Adj scale

- Grammatical knowledge is represented as constructions: pairings of form and meaning

- Constructions may be complex or atomic (single words or morphemes), schematic or substantive (or anything in between)

- Constructions can be organized into taxonomic hierarchies

X is Adj-*er than* Y
|
X is *larger than life*

FIGURE 32

All original audio-recordings and other supplementary material, such as any hand-outs and powerpoint presentations for the lecture series, have been made available online and are referenced via unique DOI numbers on the website www.figshare.com. They may be accessed via a QR code for the print version of this book. In the e-book, both the QR code and dynamic links are available, and can be accessed by a mouse-click.

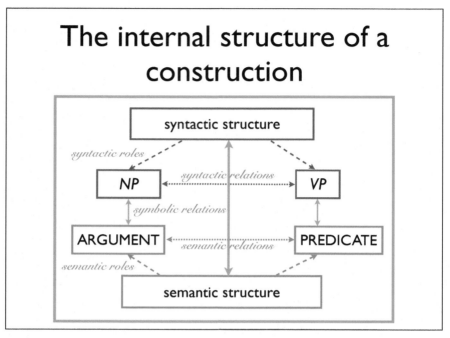

The internal structure of a construction

FIGURE 33

top of the slide: so the English comparative construction has a description that you see there on the top and then down here is a summary of its meaning.

Constructions may be complex or atomic—that is, single words or morphemes are atomic—and schematic or substantive or anything in between. And then constructions can be organized into taxonomic hierarchies, as with the example down there on the bottom. So that's just a review of the basic principles that I told you are common to all different types of construction grammar.

And then another quick review here is the internal structure of a construction [Figure 33]. This is the exploded diagram. An important thing to note is that you have a construction here and its parts and the role that each part plays in the whole construction. Syntactic relations is what goes between the two elements. We're going to be talking about syntactic roles today, this afternoon. I'll talk about syntactic relations tomorrow [Lecture 4]. Symbolic relations are the relations that link the elements to their meanings and also the whole structure. I won't be talking too much about that today. So the important thing is this notion of a syntactic role.

Ok, now I told you about Radical Construction Grammar and someone asked me at the end of the morning lectures [Lecture 1] what makes it different from other kinds of construction grammars. And basically, one way of looking at it is what Radical Construction Grammar does not have. So first there are no syntactic categories—those are the roles I just described—independent of the constructions that define them. That's what I will be talking about this afternoon, in Lecture Two, and tomorrow morning [Lecture 3]. There are also no syntactic relations, so those we can do without entirely. We have only syntactic roles, those part-whole relations, and I will be talking about that tomorrow afternoon [Lecture 4]. And then there are also no universal formal construction types. I alluded to this this morning. That's going to be Lecture Five; that's Sunday morning. So these are the principles I'm going to be arguing for, or rather arguing against today.

So what do we use instead? Because after we get rid of all this stuff, we have to have something to capture grammatical structures and grammatical generalizations. So syntactic role categories are defined by semantic maps over conceptual spaces which constrain them. This is Lectures Seven and Eight; these are the lectures on Tuesday that I mentioned before. So I'm afraid you'll have to wait; I hope some of you will be still here on Tuesday to hear about that. Symbolic relations allow syntactic roles to be related to one another semantically; that's what we use instead of syntactic relations, and I will talk about that tomorrow afternoon [Lecture 4]. And then the syntactic space defines and constrains the continuum of formal construction types. So constructions may vary across languages. But again, there are limits to that variation, or at least some kinds of constraints on them; and I'll talk about that on Sunday.

So today we are going to focus on syntactic categories. The issues I'm going to go into here have to do not just with what counts as a syntactic category or how you define them in a grammatical analysis, but also how you defend them, how you decide that they actually exist in a language. So most of what I'll be talking about today has to do with what's called syntactic argumentation: how you construct arguments to support a linguistic analysis. And this is what I'll be mainly criticizing.

In the Western linguistic tradition, syntactic argumentation is originally about what's called the distributional method. Syntactic categories, that is, word classes, like noun, or count noun, or classifier, but also classes of larger units, like phrases, subjects and so on, clauses, relative clause, adverbial clause, are determined by the distributional method. You'll see what that is in a moment. The distributional method is a term that was used in the linguistic theory called American structuralism from the 1930s and 40s. It's not dead; it continues on with new names. They're referred to typically as tests, or criteria, or arguments, or evidence for syntactic categories. So you might see tests for defining a direct object or criteria for deciding whether or not Mandarin

Syntactic categories and the distributional method

(1a) *Jack is **cold**.*   (3a) **Jack is **dance**.*
(1b) **Jack **colds**.*   (3b) *Jack **dances**.*
(2a) *Jack is **happy**.*   (4a) **Jack is **sing**.*
(2b) **Jack **happies**.*   (4b) *Jack **sings**.*

	[Sbj *be* __]	[Sbj ____-TNS.PERS]
Adj: *cold, happy*, **etc.**	✓	*
Verb: *sing, dance*, **etc.**	*	✓

FIGURE 34

has adjectives, arguments for or against the existence of adjectives and so on [Figure 34].

So this is a simple example. This is how you distinguish between adjectives and verbs in English. Instead of doing it in a verbal description, I've given you the actual kinds of examples that are really necessary to establish this fact. The first example you see is the word *cold*. You can see that it's used with the copula *be*: "Jack is cold". You cannot use it without a copula, and you cannot inflect it. So (1b) is unacceptable: "Jack colds". And then *happy* works the same way: "Jack is happy" is what you have to say with a word like *happy*. On the other hand, words like *dance*, you don't use them with a copula; you use them without the copula, as in (3b): "Jack dances." And you have to inflect it. The same is of course true for *sing*.

That's the distinction between a verb and an adjective in English, which we can describe in terms of its distribution. So our criterion means: you've got one particular construction, you have a particular role in that construction, which I've left blank here: [Sbj *be* __]. And then you have some words that can fit in that role, and other words that can't fit in that role. And then likewise, you have another construction, and then you have an empty role here: [Sbj __-TNS.PERS], which is essentially inflection and no copula, just the subject. And then you have words that can't occur in that construction and other words that can occur in that construction. So you have a contrast here. And this is what's described as a difference in syntactic distribution or syntactic behavior, or you would call these two constructions "tests" or "criteria" or "arguments" to establish the verb-adjective contrast in English.

So that's how the method works. And basically every serious syntactician uses this method. There is really no other way to define categories. Now I've already said this, but I will have to say it again: all these things—tests, criteria, arguments, and evidence and so on for syntactic categories or other syntactic constructs, those are really just constructions. So if we go back to [Figure 34], these things that are the tests and the distributional patterns: they are constructions. The distribution is a particular role in that construction. So you start by assuming that there are constructions here. You can't use the distributional method without assuming the existence of these two constructions, for example. You can't define verb and adjective in English without assuming already the existence of two different constructions—a copula construction and a simple inflected predicate construction. Now the thing is, and this is an important point—actually I did not really make this point clear in my book *Radical Construction Grammar*; it's something that came out later in discussions. In fact, when you look at these non-construction grammars that use this method of syntactic argumentation, they are implicitly assuming the existence of constructions because they use this in their method, they just don't use the name. We'll see an example of that later. Instead they use all the other names: "tests", "criteria", "arguments", "evidence".

So what's the standard view of syntactic categories? How would you do this? This is kind of what you've learned in an *Introductory Linguistics* and certainly in an *Introductory Syntax* class. So we find constructions that identify the syntactic categories that we believe to exist, like verb and adjective in English. There's a further assumption that there is a small number of large word classes for the major parts of speech. So we should in principle be able to find things like noun, verb and adjective, or subject and object, or whatever you are looking for. Another assumption that's made is that we can differentiate major classes like verb from subclasses like transitive verb and intransitive verb. A fourth assumption that's made is that these classes are cross-linguistically valid, if not found in all languages. So for instance once we've identified adjectives in a language like English, we can then move on to a language like Mandarin, or Cantonese, and then say this language has adjectives, or this language does not have adjectives.

The last point is actually the most crucial one, and this is something I've talked a little bit about in the book: that these word classes are the basic

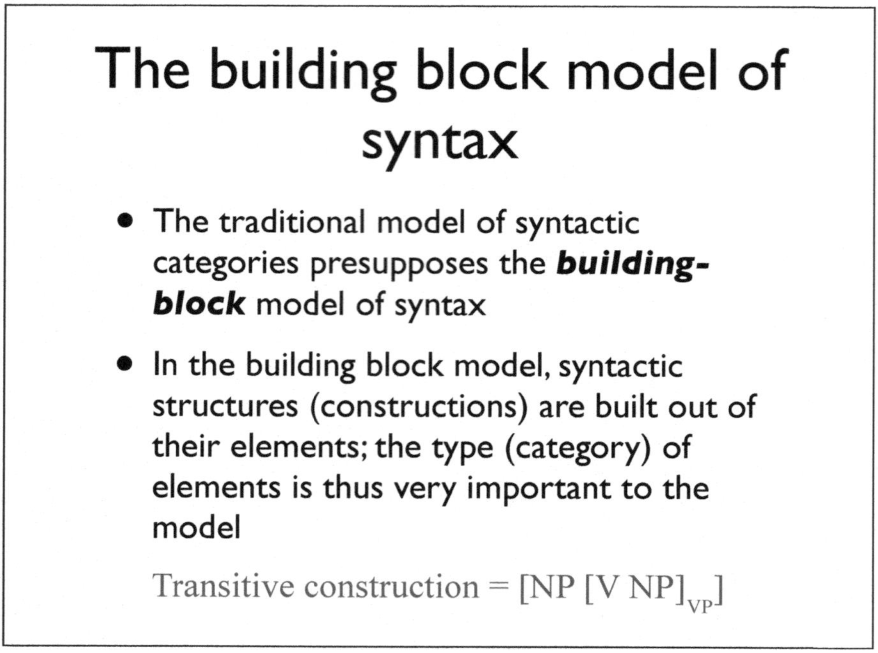

The building block model of syntax

- The traditional model of syntactic categories presupposes the **building-block** model of syntax

- In the building block model, syntactic structures (constructions) are built out of their elements; the type (category) of elements is thus very important to the model

Transitive construction $= [\text{NP} \ [\text{V NP}]_{\text{VP}}]$

FIGURE 35

building blocks of larger syntactic constructions, larger syntactic structures, including constructions. And that's why all these assumptions on [Figure 35] are so important to so many syntacticians; it's because of that last point. This is the building block model of syntax. And what I'm going to say is: this is a very deeply rooted assumption about how you analyze syntactic structures. I would imagine that most of you assume it or at least were taught to assume it. It's a model that goes way back earlier than generative grammar, so I'm not just criticizing generative grammar here or even American structuralism. This goes way, way back. And that's why I emphasize it because, of course, I'm going to tell you that it's wrong, and so I will have to try to persuade you about why this is the wrong way to look at syntax. This might be difficult, as you'll see when I discuss other linguists who I've criticized in print about this.

So this traditional model of syntactic categories like noun, verb and adjective presupposes the building block model of syntax. In the building block model, syntactic structures, i.e. constructions in our view, are built out of their elements. So this transitive construction here is built; you take the NP category, combine it with a verb and then you take that and combine it with another NP—this is for English—and you end up with an English transitive construction. So in other words, if these are the building blocks of syntax, then it's really

What is being described?

(1) *Jack kissed **Janet**.*
(2) ***Janet** was kissed by Jack.*
(3) *The old man walked with **a cane**.*
(4) **A cane** *was walked (with) by the old man.*

- Two tests/criteria for the Direct Object category

	[Sbj Verb ___]	[___ *be* Verb-PASS...]
Direct object: *Janet*	✓	✓
Oblique: *a cane*	*	*

FIGURE 36

important to know what type each building block is. It is important to know that this is a verb, and not an adjective, for example, because you can't build it if it is an adjective.

So what's wrong with this picture? Basically, everything that I told you before. So the first point, which I'll be spending a lot of time on today, is that we can't use just any construction to identify word classes. The second point is that words—or for that matter, phrases—do not form large distributionally uniform classes, nor can we differentiate major classes from subclasses. Instead, word classes are language-specific, and therefore they cannot be used to posit some kind of cross-linguistic category as adjective that you would find in both English and some other language. And basically the bottom line is that the building block model of syntax doesn't work. These are strong statements. But I hope to be able to show you why this is really the better way to look at language.

So what's being described? Here is an example, a different example; it's from my book [Figure 36]. Looking at the direct object, you have these expressions in boldface—"Jack kissed Janet"—in this construction, the object, and then in the passive construction the same object can be made into the subject of the passive construction. "A cane", however, in this construction, doesn't occur as

What is being described?

(1) *Jack weighs **160 pounds**.*
(2) **160 pounds** was weighed by Jack.*

- The two tests don't match. The usual strategy is to pick one test as the "real" test, in this case, the Passive (i.e. *160 pounds* is not a direct object)

- But that doesn't explain why *160 pounds* doesn't need a Preposition in the Active clause

- Most important: what is being described is NOT something about a **category** "Direct Object", but something about the Passive **construction**

FIGURE 37

an object. It has to have the preposition "with"—"the old man walked with a cane"—and then you cannot make it the passive subject. So that looks fine. We have two tests for the "direct object" category, and the direct object works, it fills this role here and fills this role here, and "a cane" doesn't work in either of these constructions.

So the traditional solution here is to call the first thing a direct object and the second an oblique phrase. The only trouble is, this doesn't always work [Figure 37]. So you can say "Jack weighs 160 pounds" and it looks like it fits the active construction, but "160 pounds was weighed by Jack" is unacceptable. In other words these two tests match in the examples on the previous slide: "Janet" fits both of them, "cane" fails both of them. But in the case of "160 pounds" they don't. "160 pounds" fits the first test, the active construction, but it doesn't fit the role of the second construction.

So what do linguists do in this case? This is a fact about English and we cannot deny this fact. So what do linguists do when they see this? The usual strategy is, if you have two constructions that don't match, you pick one of these constructions and say this gives you the real answer to the question. Is "160 pounds" the direct object of "weigh" or not? In this case the usual strategy is to take the second sentence as the one that tells you what is a true direct object in English, and then, since "160 pounds" is not acceptable, then you say

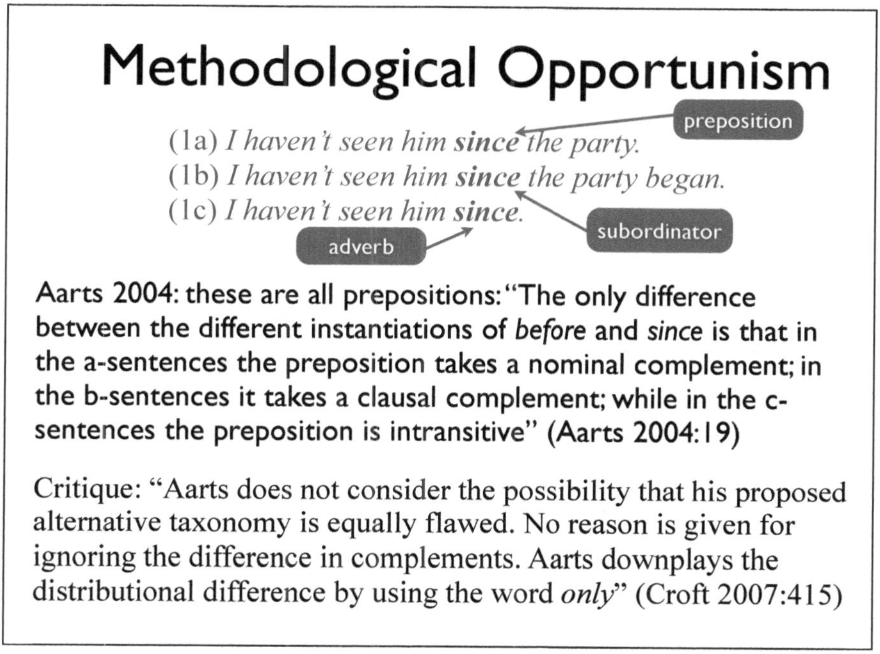

Methodological Opportunism

(1a) *I haven't seen him **since** the party.*   preposition

(1b) *I haven't seen him **since** the party began.*

(1c) *I haven't seen him **since**.*

adverb   subordinator

Aarts 2004: these are all prepositions: "The only difference between the different instantiations of *before* and *since* is that in the a-sentences the preposition takes a nominal complement; in the b-sentences it takes a clausal complement; while in the c-sentences the preposition is intransitive" (Aarts 2004:19)

Critique: "Aarts does not consider the possibility that his proposed alternative taxonomy is equally flawed. No reason is given for ignoring the difference in complements. Aarts downplays the distributional difference by using the word *only*" (Croft 2007:415)

FIGURE 38

that it's not a direct object. A little problem comes up though, which is that "160 pounds" is still acceptable in the first sentence. And now we have no explanation for why, because it's supposedly not a direct object.

But more important, and this is the crucial point here, is that this fact I've just given you—a very simple fact about English—is not really telling you something about the category "direct object". And we'll try to figure out why it is or it isn't. If you decide that the passive sentence is your true test for a direct object, what you are really doing is you are telling me something about the passive construction except you are pretending it's about direct objects; since you decided a direct object is defined by that passive construction, you are really telling me something about the passive construction. And that's really a very important point. That's why this is a talk about construction grammar.

In my book I described this as "methodological opportunism". This is the first of a series of examples where I take analyses that have been published by other linguists. In this particular case, I actually wrote a comment or critique of the analysis and the author was able to respond to me, and then I was able to respond later on in another publication [Figure 38].

So the example that he looked at is the English word *since*. Now the traditional grammatical analysis of *since* is that the sentences you see on the screen illustrate three different categories. The first one is a preposition because it

governs a direct object: "since the party". The second one is a subordinator because it introduces a subordinate clause: "since the party began". And the third
is an adverb because it modifies a verb and there's nothing following it. That's
the traditional analysis, three categories. Now, a linguist named Bas Aarts who
works on the syntax of English wrote a paper discussing the nature of categories and he used this example and he took the position that there was actually
just one category here which he called "preposition". He wrote:

> The only difference between the different instantiations of 'before' and
> 'since' is that in the a-sentences, [*he had more than one example,*] the
> preposition takes a nominal complement, or a noun phrases; and in
> the b-sentences, it takes a clausal complement, while in the c-sentences
> the preposition is intransitive.
>
> AARTS 2004:19

So in my critique, I said,

> Aarts does not consider the possibility that his proposed alternative [to
> the traditional analysis] is equally flawed. No reason is given for ignor-
> ing the difference in complements. Aarts downplays the distributional
> difference by using the word 'only' (right up here [Figure 38], 'the only
> difference') as if that was unimportant.
>
> CROFT 2007:415

Aarts didn't like this and he said in response: "what we have ... are prepositions that can take different types of complements or no complement." (Aarts
2007:439) And essentially he is repeating his original analysis, he isn't actually telling us something new. So in the continuation of my criticism, I said
(I'm talking about these two different analyses) that Aarts' analysis is what you
call a "lumping" or "lumper" analysis: one side lumps formatives together; all
these different uses of *since* are one category. And the other splits them; the
traditional analysis splits *since* into three different categories. And I quote myself (Croft 2001:32) saying "there is no a priori way to resolve the question: the
lumper overlooks the mismatches in distribution, and the splitter overlooks
the generalizations."

So what I am saying is not only that Aarts is wrong in lumping the three
categories together. I am also saying that the traditional analysis that splits
them apart is wrong. So they are both wrong. Now Aarts, in responding to me,
said: "it's not clear what exactly is meant by a mismatch in distribution if we

Methodological Opportunism

(1a) *I haven't seen him **since** the party.*
(1b) *I haven't seen him **since** the party began.*
(1c) *I haven't seen him **since**.*

(2a) **Joan is really **into** she flies in a balloon.*
(2b) **Joan walked **into**.*
(2c) **Randy looked **down** the bird looked up at him.*
(2d) *Randy looked **down**.*
(2e) *Randy walked **down** the hill.*

(3a) *She slept **while** I ate lunch.*
(3b) **She slept **while** my lunch.*
(3c) *I ran **back**.*
(3d) **I ran **back** my office.*

(Croft 2010:343)

FIGURE 39

adopt the lumping strategy [that's his own strategy], unless one insists that the prepositions cannot introduce clauses and one denies the possibility that prepositions can be intransitive."

Well, that may be true for *since*—*since* allows all three of these, but if you look at other prepositions, so-called prepositions, you'll see that some of them can't introduce clauses or they can't be intransitive [Figure 39]. So if you take *into*, you can say "Joan ran into the room", but you can't say "Joan is really into she flies in a balloon", or "Joan walked into". Or take *down*. You can say "Randy walked down the hill", the last example. You can also say "Randy looked down". But you can't say "Randy looked down the bird looked up at him". So the distributional pattern that Aarts uses to say that there is just one preposition *since* doesn't work for other prepositions.

And then if we go beyond prepositions, there are some words like "while" that do not allow a nominal complement. So you can say "she slept while I ate lunch", that's a clause. But you can't say "she slept while lunch", or "while my lunch". Then you have an adverb form like "I ran back", that's fine. But you can't say "I ran back my office". So if you start looking at not just a word like *since*, but also *into*, *down*, *while*, and *back*, you will see that in fact Aarts simply is

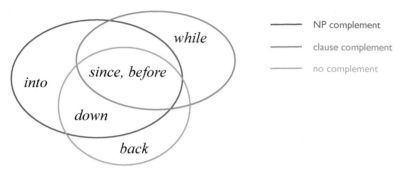

A genuine distributional analysis

while

since, before

into

down

back

——— NP complement

——— clause complement

——— no complement

- Neither lumping (Aarts) nor splitting (traditional); there are no large classes with uniform behavior
- The generalizations are defined by **constructions**

FIGURE 40

incorrect to say that there is no difference here. These words don't all act the same way. In any careful analysis of what an English speaker knows about their language, we'll have to recognize this fact.

So here is a genuine distributional analysis—it looks better on the screen because it's got three colors there [Figure 40]. This is a genuine distributional analysis. It doesn't lump, and it doesn't split. Each of these circles here—blue, red, and green—shows you both what is in common for each of these words and what is different about each of these words. The generalizations here are defined by constructions. So these ovals describe different constructions— color coded, so the blue is the words that take a noun phrase complement; the red takes a clausal complement, and then the green takes no complement. You'll see all these words behave in many different ways, but they do share properties: *since, before, down* and *back* can all be adverbs; *since, before* and *while* can all take a clausal complement, and so on. So you can see here, we've got three categories defined by three constructions, but the categories are not the traditional three categories because they overlap. I also do not lump them all together like Aarts did. But this analysis does acknowledge that *since* and *before* can occur in all three constructions.

So what's the Radical Construction Grammar view? Well, the pattern I've just showed you where the three constructions don't match, this is actually the normal state of affairs. If you look carefully at any kind of linguistic category, and a range of constructions that are supposed to be possible with words of that category, and you look at every word in that category, you'll discover that in fact the words don't all act alike. They occur in a lot of constructions, but not all of them, and different words will occur in different constructions in ways like we just described in that simple example. And if you add some kind of exception features or special subclasses and so on, these are just essentially patches or hacks to avoid this fact.

And here is a crucial point, the distributional analysis presupposes the constructions used to set up the syntactic categories. That was the whole point that I've made, emphasizing that distributional analysis presupposes the existence of these constructions. But the building block model of syntax claims that constructions are built out of these word classes. So the constructions are used to define the word classes and then linguists turn around and say that the word classes are the building blocks to create the constructions. In other words, it's a circular argument. And that's the problem. The way to avoid this circular reasoning is to say that constructions are basic and categories are derived. We don't have prepositions as an independent category from constructions; instead we have constructions like noun phrase complement, clausal complement or no complement. And those constructions define categories. But the categories don't exist independently of the constructions because the categories were defined by the constructions. I'm afraid it's the only way that makes sense, really. It takes a long time to take this view, took me a while to figure this out and clearly from the discussions I've had, in print, in lectures I've given, it's very difficult for many people to consider this as an alternative way to look at syntax. So it may take you a while to see this. But I hope you will be able to see this.

You can find the same problem in another language. Aarts is a specialist in English and of course I am a native speaker of English, so it's easy to give you these examples. Now let's look at a language that probably nobody in this room knows, though some of you may have looked at it [Figure 41]. This is a language spoken in the northwest coast of the United States: Straits Salish. Here we've got two different constructions: predication and determination. And then we have words which I'll describe with semantic labels, action words like *sing*, object words like *chief*, and property words like *afraid*. And you'll see that it looks like in this language you have the same construction for all three classes of

The problem in another language

Straits Salish	Predication	Determination
Action words	t'iləm=lə=sxʷ	cə t'iləm=lə
	'you sang'	*'the (one who) sang'*
Object words	si'em=lə=sxʷ	cə si'em=lə
	'you were a chief'	*'the (one who) was a chief'*
Property words	sey'si'=lə=sxʷ	cə sey'si'=lə
	'you were afraid'	*'the (one who) was afraid'*

- Jelinek & Demers: no Noun/Verb distinction
- van Eijk & Hess, on Lillooet and Lushootseed: Noun/Verb distinction, because of Possessive, Aspect inflections
- Jelinek & Demers: '["Nouns"] have the same syntax as any other predicate'

FIGURE 41

words and predication. They all take those clitics =*lə* and =*sxʷ*, and likewise in determination they all seem to look the same.

So one article came out many years ago, about 15 years ago, that was arguing that this language makes no distinction between nouns and verbs because words denoting actions, objects and properties all behave the same way. They are in the same distribution. A couple of other linguists, working on two closely related languages, said that there is a noun/verb distinction. And that's because they looked at other constructions besides the two listed on the screen and found differences. Jelinek and Demers responded and simply said: "nouns have the same syntax as any other predicate." So again it's kind of like Aarts, they simply assert that these words are all alike. It's the same problem we saw with English *since*, but just a different language.

There's actually another problem here which I mentioned and it will become important later. The semantics of the word in the determination construction—the one on the right—is actually different. So when you combine it with an action word, it means the person who sang, the one who sang. It doesn't refer to an action, it refers to a person. With an object concept, of course, it just means really the chief. And then a property word also refers to a person, the one who was afraid. So there is a semantic shift. And that's often ignored by people who look at the syntactic analysis.

Now there's another problem here. Jelinek and Demers, when they said there is no noun/verb distinction, they concluded that this language has only verbs. Well, how do they know that? In English, we have nouns and verbs, or at least that's what we all call them. But how do we know that in Salishan, it has only one category here, according to them. Why do we call it verb? Why don't we call it noun? Why don't we call it something totally different?

Now I've given you this example because of the debate about nouns and verbs in this language and other languages as well as the debate about adjectives in Chinese which I'll talk about tomorrow. Well, there is a best solution for this. Many linguists, especially many typologists who look at lots of different languages every day have come to this conclusion for grammatical relations but not for parts of speech. And that conclusion is in this long quotation by Matthew Dryer. It's worth reading the whole thing. It's a very good paper of his.

> The search for the understanding of the similarities and differences among grammatical relations [so this is things like subject and object, or ergative and absolutive] in different languages will be impeded if we make the mistake of thinking of grammatical relations as crosslinguistic categories, and will be more successful if we bear in mind that grammatical relations are unique to every language. [so that's one of my points before; he goes on to say] The similarities among languages regarding grammatical relations can be explained directly in terms of functional and cognitive principles that underlie language and which cause languages to be the way they are.
>
> DRYER, "Are grammatical relations universal?", 1997

I completely agree with that statement, to the point where I say this is also true for noun, verb and adjective, not just subject and object. And I find it quite striking, that even typologists who have to deal with this crosslinguistic variation all the time, also have difficulty extending Dryer's conclusion to parts of speech.

Well, if we go back to Aarts, now we'll look at the problem from a crosslinguistic perspective. So before, I looked just at English and showed you some problems with Aarts's analysis. Then we looked at another language, Straits Salish, and showed you some problems there with that analysis. So now let's look at German [Figure 42]. This is the one example in Aarts's paper that's not from English. This is a phrase that means "a man who speaks several languages".

The crosslinguistic problem

German: *ein   mehrere Sprachen **sprechender**   Mann*
a.NOM several   languages speaking:MNOM.SG man.MSG

English: ***this*** *box/**these*** *boxes; **that*** *chair/**those*** *chairs*

"One can say that English has only two adjectives, *this* and *that*. If
we take this option, we still have no basis for saying why
agreement with the following noun is the criterion for adjective
class membership…Or one can say there is an English Adjective
class, which includes *thin* and *utter* but not *this* and *that*. If we
take the latter option, then we have no syntactic basis for
assuming that the English Adjective class is the same as the
German Adjective class." (Croft 2007:417)

FIGURE 42

So he's talking about the form that's in bold: *sprechender*. He says it has clear
adjectival properties. So "clear adjectival" means he doesn't think there is any
dispute about the category. And then he explains in parentheses, "It occurs
before a noun with which it agrees in case and number." Well let's go back to
English. If you look at English, no word agrees in case. The only words that
agree in number in English are *this* and *that*. You have "this box" and "these
boxes", "that chair", "those chairs".

So I wrote in response to Aarts: "one could say that English has only two
adjectives *this* and *that* because they are the words in English that agree in
number, just like the words in German." And then I said, "if we take this option,
we still have no basis for saying why agreement with the following noun is
the criterion for adjective class membership." But then I suggest another thing:
"One could say that there is English Adjective class, which includes *thin* and
utter [these are the words that Aarts discussed] but not *this* and *that*. If we take
the latter option, then we have no syntactic basis for assuming that the English
Adjective class is the same as the German Adjective class."

Now I didn't say this in my response, but the reason that we think that
English adjectives *thin* and *utter* are just like the German ones, is semantic
not syntactic. They denote property concepts. They are not deictic terms like
this and *that*. So my point here was that if we take a criterion like does the

word agree in number with the noun as our criterion for being an adjective in German?, then we ought to use the same criterion in English. But when you do that, the only words that fit that criterion in English are *this* and *that*. Do we want to call them adjectives or not? So Aarts in response said:

> As for the perceived problem that the English and German adjective classes are not the same, if the aim is to arrive at a universally valid definition for adjectives, as Croft suggests, then the same aim might be expected to apply to constructions as syntactic primitives, in Croft's sense. But given the idiosyncrasies of constructions cross-linguistically, this is unlikely to be achieved.
>
> AARTS 2007:441, fn. 2

That is my point. My point is you can't compare the words in German and English. It's either based on semantics, or just based on historical tradition that we call them adjectives in both German and English. It's not based on the syntax of the two languages. And of course as you know already, I said that one of my points about Radical Construction Grammar is that constructions are not the same across languages. So of course I agree with that point that Aarts makes.

Ok, now, here is another response. Aarts is a linguist who analyzes English. So he's working on one language. As I said there are a lot of typologists who look at many languages, myself included of course. Two of them had a discussion about nouns and verbs in a language called Munda, Evans and Osada [Figure 43]. Again I wrote a critique of their analysis, and they responded to it. My critique was that you can't just use any old construction because basically what you do is: you already decided in advance whether a language has nouns or verbs, and then you just find a construction that distinguishes them. Or if you already decided in advance that the language doesn't have a noun/verb distinction, then you just find another construction which doesn't distinguish them. That doesn't really tell you much of anything about nouns and verbs. So they responded that although the exact criteria that linguists use differ from language to language, "the distributional tests are not a random grab bag [they exaggerated a little bit from what I said] ... some properties of members of a particular class turn out to be excellent predictors of other properties, so that one can set up chains of dependencies between properties ..." (Evans and Osada 2005:452).

Well, I agree with a lot of what they say, but they actually hide something here, these things called "properties": these are constructions, because they are "just properties, tests, criteria" of the distributional method, and the distributional method is defined as constructions. So when they talk about one

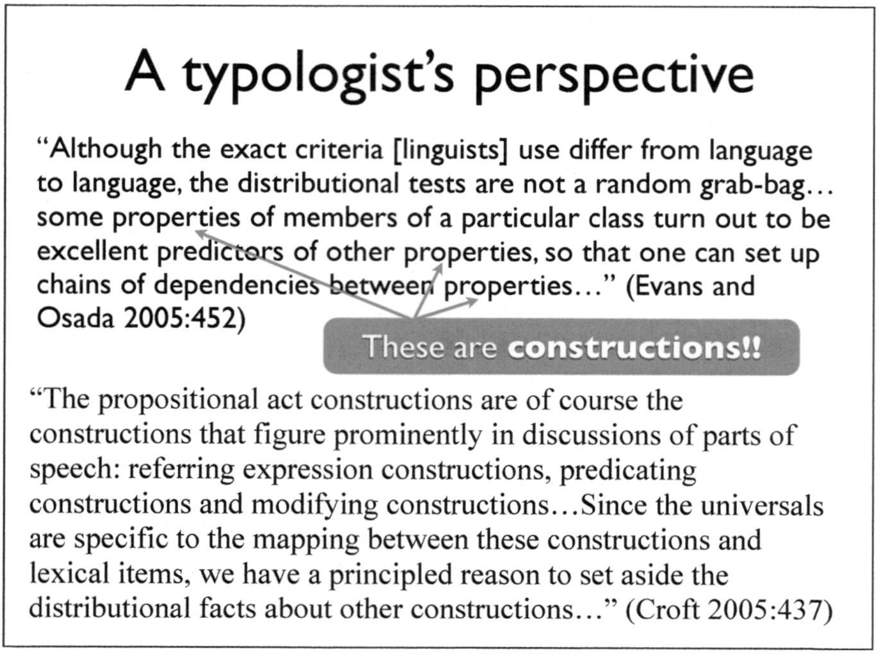

A typologist's perspective

"Although the exact criteria [linguists] use differ from language to language, the distributional tests are not a random grab-bag... some properties of members of a particular class turn out to be excellent predictors of other properties, so that one can set up chains of dependencies between properties..." (Evans and Osada 2005:452)

These are **constructions!!**

"The propositional act constructions are of course the constructions that figure prominently in discussions of parts of speech: referring expression constructions, predicating constructions and modifying constructions...Since the universals are specific to the mapping between these constructions and lexical items, we have a principled reason to set aside the distributional facts about other constructions..." (Croft 2005:437)

FIGURE 43

property predicting another property, what they are really telling you about is one construction predicting something about another construction. So it's a fact about constructions; once again, this is why I am a construction grammarian.

So in my critique here, I point out that when you are looking at parts of speech like noun, verb and adjective, as Evans and Osada were doing, these authors use certain constructions that are called propositional act constructions: predication, modification, reference. I'm going to talk about that again tomorrow with Cantonese [Lecture 3]. So I say the propositional act constructions are of course the constructions that figure prominently in discussions of parts of speech: referring expression constructions, predicating constructions, and modifying constructions. Since the universals are specific to the mapping between these constructions and lexical items, the supposed word classes, we have a principled reason to set aside the distributional facts about other constructions. I'm kind of jumping ahead here, but my point is: what Evans and Osada are talking about are constructions. Some constructions are good predictors of other constructions. But there are lots of constructions in a language, zillions of them. How do you pick the ones that you want to study? The ones where you think there are going to be some interesting universal relationships, a prediction or implication?

Distributional analysis and universal syntactic elements

- Distributional analysis is independent of the assumption of universal syntactic elements as building blocks of grammar

- The assumption of universal syntactic elements must be reconciled with language-internal and crosslinguistic diversity

- The ancillary hypotheses to save the assumption are implausible and result from methodological opportunism

FIGURE 44

Well, you look at the constructions themselves and the kind of functions they perform. Reference, predication, and modification are fundamental ways in which you package information in a clause, so you might guess that they would be interconnected. And things like transitive versus intransitive, that's a fact about argument structure constructions. Those are different kinds of constructions. You might not expect them to have any connection to reference, predication or modification. And in general, they don't. So you leave them out. You can just pick certain constructions, but the main thing is you have to be honest about what you are talking about. You are analyzing properties of constructions, not properties of word classes.

Ok, distributional analysis in universal syntactic elements: so this is a very important point here [Figure 44]. Distributional analysis is independent of the assumption of these universal syntactic elements as building blocks of grammar: distributional analysis has always been used to support the building block theory of grammar, but they don't depend on each other. And in fact anybody who is careful in looking at the distributional facts in languages will easily find evidence that undermines the building block theory of grammar.

So, if you are going to be one of those people, your assumptions of universal syntactic elements must be reconciled with language internal and crosslinguistic diversity. Well, my point is that you can't. So people make up

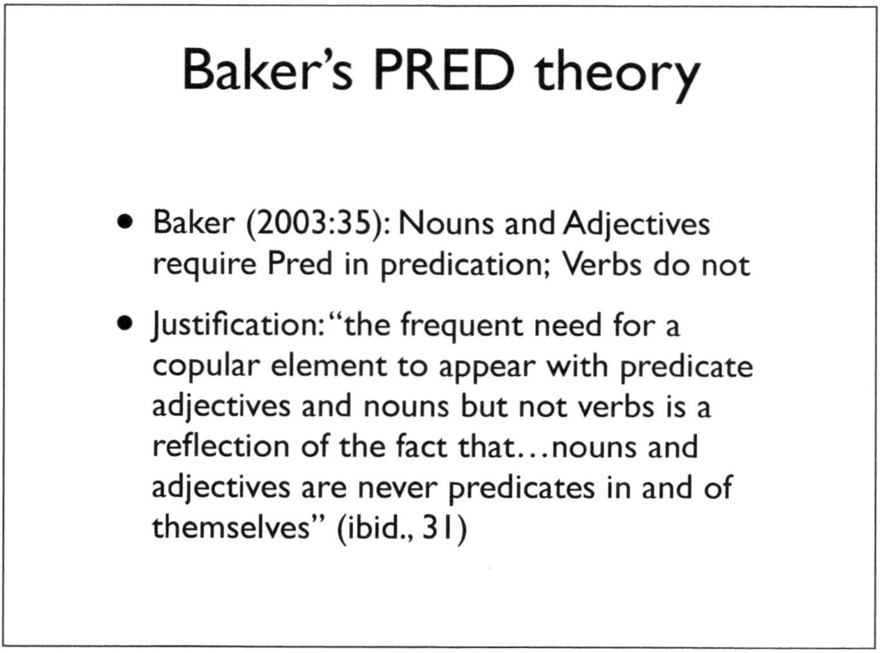

Baker's PRED theory

- Baker (2003:35): Nouns and Adjectives require Pred in predication; Verbs do not

- Justification: "the frequent need for a copular element to appear with predicate adjectives and nouns but not verbs is a reflection of the fact that...nouns and adjectives are never predicates in and of themselves" (ibid., 31)

FIGURE 45

extra hypotheses to rescue this assumption of universal syntactic elements. These hypotheses are basically what I call methodological opportunism. Methodological opportunism, I forgot to say, that's when you pick whatever construction you want, that will either prove the existence of categories you already believe to exist, or disprove the existence of categories that you already believe don't exist. That's putting the cart before the horse, as we say in English. You shouldn't assume what categories exist in a language and then look for constructions that fit it. You should look at the constructions consistently from one language to the next and then see what the facts are.

A classic example of methodological opportunism is a theory about parts of speech by a generative linguist who does do a lot of cross-linguistic comparison—Mark Baker. He wrote a book about this. And by the way, this came out because several years ago I was invited to actually co-teach a course with Mark Baker. That was supposed to be a dialogue course, between two diametrically opposed views about grammar. It was very interesting. I like Mark a lot; we got along quite fine, and all, although I'm sure we didn't really understand each other. But as a result, of course I read his book fairly carefully because the course was about parts of speech. I've looked fairly carefully at his arguments and that's why I'm able to give you some details here. Part of the

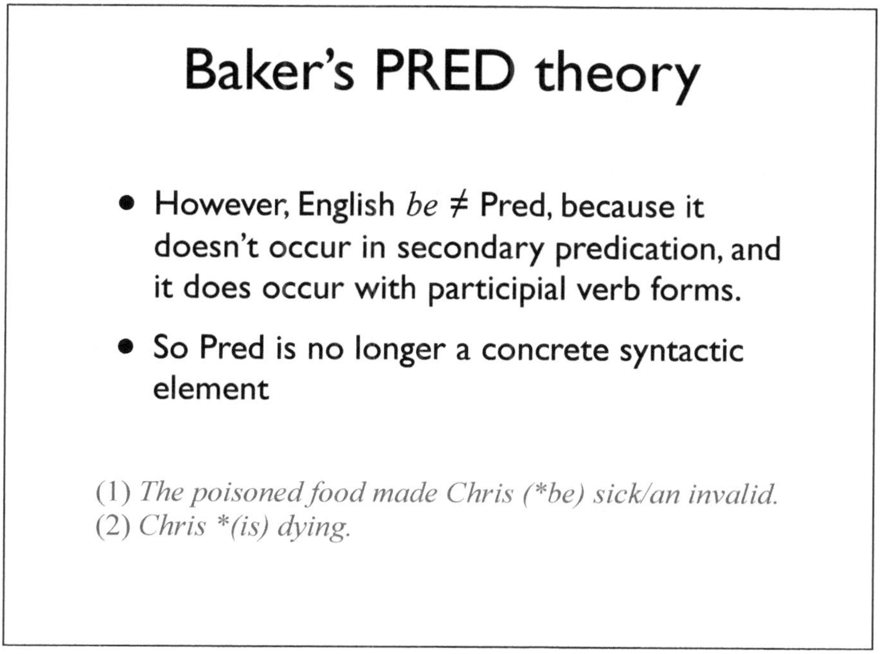

Baker's PRED theory

- However, English *be* ≠ Pred, because it doesn't occur in secondary predication, and it does occur with participial verb forms.

- So Pred is no longer a concrete syntactic element

(1) *The poisoned food made Chris (*be) sick/an invalid.*
(2) *Chris *(is) dying.*

FIGURE 46

analysis here is in a paper that I published. That was actually a kind of written-out version of my final presentation, my final lecture in this team course, this course that I taught with Mark Baker.

His theory—this is a theory about universal categories—so he's talking about nouns and adjectives across languages [Figure 45]. He says they require a category Pred in predication and verbs do not require that. His justification for this syntactic analysis is the frequent need for a copula element to appear with predicate adjectives and nouns but not verbs. He says that's a reflection of the fact that nouns and adjectives are never predicates in and of themselves. Well, of course this is very English-based, because in English nouns and adjectives require a copula verb: "She is a professor", "She is tall". And verbs don't: "She sings"—just the kind of examples I used at the beginning of this afternoon's lecture.

Ironically, however, Baker says that the English copula *be* is actually not an example of his syntactic category Pred in his theory [Figure 46]. The reason is because *be*, even though it's used to predicate nouns and adjectives, is not used in a couple of other important constructions. So in secondary predication, example (1), "the poisoned food made Chris sick", or "made Chris an invalid", you don't use the copula *be* there. For him that means that the copula *be* is not

Baker's PRED theory

- Edo *yé* = Pred, because it is required in secondary predication, and it occurs in floating quantifier position; it cannot be nominalized, undergo predicate cleft, or partake in serial verb constructions

(1) *ọ̀yá yá   ẹ́gógó wọ̀rọ̀
    it made bell   long
    'It made the bell long.'

(2) ozó (tòbọ́rè) yé (*tòborè) mòsèmòsè
    Ozo (by.self) Pred (by.self) beautiful
    'Ozo alone is beautiful.'

FIGURE 47

a Pred. And then the fact that if you say something like "Chris is dying", you have to have a copula with this participle construction, and he said that is also evidence—notice evidence, i.e. another construction that he looks at—that for him, means that English *be* is not Pred.

Of course the problem now—I think of it as a problem but in some respect it's an advantage—Pred is no longer a concrete syntactic element. So you can find it wherever you want to, because there is no concrete syntactic element in a language that it corresponds to: you can just pick what you want. So he did some work on an African language called Edo [Figure 47]. This language has a form, *ye*, which he claims does fall in the category Pred, because unlike the English form, it is required in secondary predication. It also occurs in another construction, that's what he calls a "floating quantifier" construction. And then this *ye* cannot occur in other constructions. So the examples below, which you can see in your handout package [Figure 47], illustrate the first two points. "It made the bell long", sentence (1), is bad because *ye* is not there. It's supposed to be there. The second sentence shows you that this thing that's translated as "by himself" or "by oneself" is what he calls a quantifier and you can put it before the Pred element *ye*. So for him, that's another piece of evidence that *ye* is his abstract category Pred.

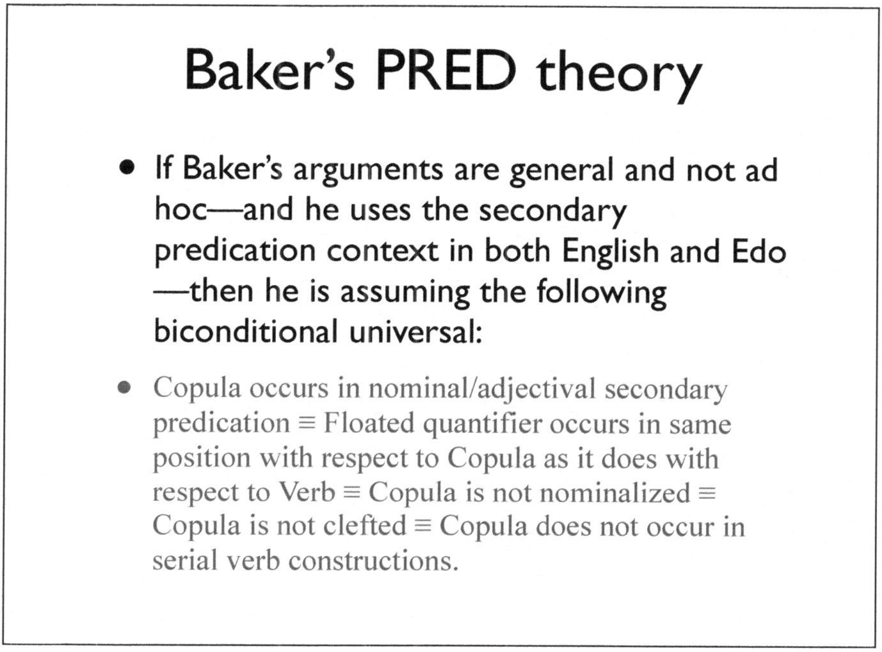

Baker's PRED theory

- If Baker's arguments are general and not ad hoc—and he uses the secondary predication context in both English and Edo —then he is assuming the following biconditional universal:

- Copula occurs in nominal/adjectival secondary predication ≡ Floated quantifier occurs in same position with respect to Copula as it does with respect to Verb ≡ Copula is not nominalized ≡ Copula is not clefted ≡ Copula does not occur in serial verb constructions.

FIGURE 48

Those of you who have read articles in syntax in the generative tradition or other traditions, this kind of argumentation should look familiar to you. You look at one language, and you see a few constructions, and the word works in a certain way, has a certain distribution, so you can come to a conclusion like, this word is Pred or this word is not Pred. Well, from a typologist's point of view, Baker's comparison of English and Edo actually is implying some kind of universal claim. After all for Baker, Pred is part of his universal model of syntax. So he's making a claim about all languages, not just English and Edo.

And what exactly is that claim? Well, basically you have to look at every construction that he refers to in his discussion of English and Edo and take all those into consideration, because if the occurrence of a particular construction in Edo is evidence for Pred in Edo, then that same construction ought to be evidence for Pred in any other language. Since he invoked, I think, five or six constructions, it's actually a very complicated statement about a biconditional universal [Figure 48]. He's making a claim that this Pred word has to occur in a whole bunch of constructions or not occur in a whole bunch of constructions across languages. So that's there, at the bottom of the slide.

Baker doesn't say this, obviously, but it's implicit in his discussion. So he goes to another African language which he has done some research on

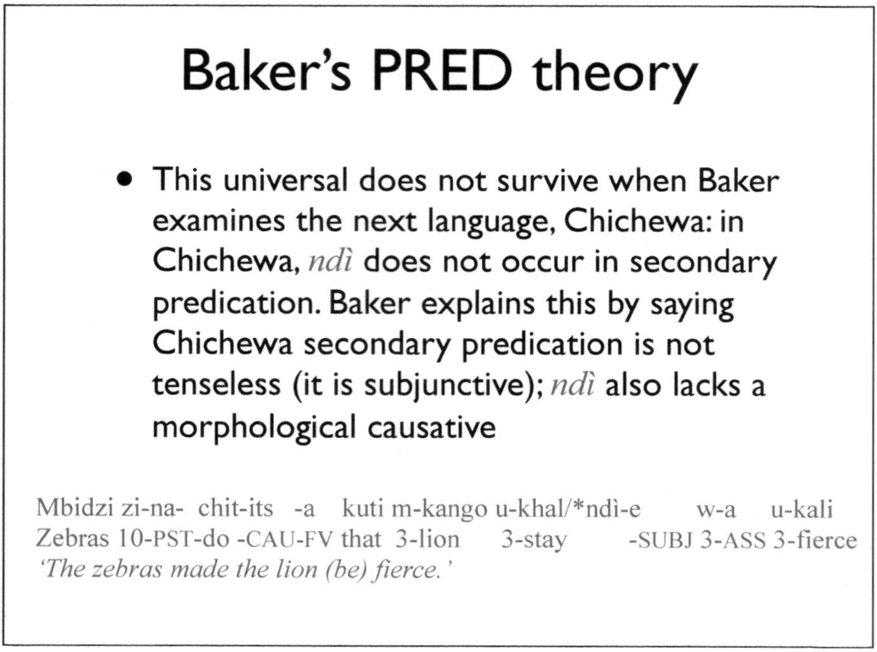

Baker's PRED theory

- This universal does not survive when Baker examines the next language, Chichewa: in Chichewa, *ndì* does not occur in secondary predication. Baker explains this by saying Chichewa secondary predication is not tenseless (it is subjunctive); *ndì* also lacks a morphological causative

Mbidzi zi-na- chit-its -a kuti m-kango u-khal/*ndì-e   w-a   u-kali
Zebras 10-PST-do -CAU-FV that 3-lion 3-stay   -SUBJ 3-ASS 3-fierce
'The zebras made the lion (be) fierce.'

FIGURE 49

called Chichewa [Figure 49]. And the claim that was made on that previous slide [Figure 48]—the thing in blue, the long statement here—actually the next language he looks at, the statement doesn't work. So Chichewa has a form, this *ndi*, that does not occur in secondary predication. And remember, that was supposed to be a requirement for being Pred. But Baker thinks that this element in Chichewa is Pred. So now we have to come up with the next explanation in Chichewa, why that element is Pred even though it does not occur in secondary predication. He explains this by looking at two more constructions. So he says that in Chichewa the secondary predication is in a subjunctive form, and that's the reason why you don't find *ndi* there. He also says that *ndi* does not have a morphological causative form in the language. So that's another reason why it really is Pred. In other words, he's gone to another language, he finds that his assumptions for the first two languages don't fit, so then he brings in two more constructions in this other language in an attempt to explain why this element really is Pred. The sentence at the bottom ("The zebras made the lion (be) fierce") just illustrates this for the secondary predication; you have to have it in a subjunctive.

Ok, so basically what that means is now if you add a third language, Chichewa, then you have to reformulate this biconditional universal with the

Baker's PRED theory

- **So the facts of English, Edo and Chichewa assume the reformulated biconditional universal (revisions are in italics):**

- Copula occurs in *tenseless* nominal/adjectival secondary predication ≡ Floated quantifier occurs in same position with respect to Copula as it does with respect to Verb ≡ Copula is not nominalized ≡ Copula is not clefted ≡ Copula does not occur in serial verb constructions ≡ *Copula cannot form a morphological causative.*

FIGURE 50

two extra facts that he brought in for Chichewa [Figure 50]. Those things are in italics. This statement is the same as the previous one, two slides back, but for the elements that are in italics. This is a very cumbersome way of trying to construct language universals. That's because essentially what he's doing is: He starts with one language, decides what the facts are. He goes to the next language. It doesn't fit, so he looks for a couple of more constructions to make the facts fit his assumption. Then he goes to a third language. And the facts don't fit the assumptions of the extra constructions in the second language, so he has to evoke two more constructions. And this can go on and on. In the next language you've got to do the same thing. And he goes on with like five languages this way.

So what are the problems with this strategy? Basically what it means is if you are looking for a universal category that you already believe exists—so this is really a belief, not an empirically testable hypothesis—methodological opportunism, the ability to choose any construction you want, allows you to justify the category that you want, because as I said, languages are quite variable and they're very complex. You can almost always find a construction to lump together two categories you want to lump together, or split apart two categories you want to split apart. In other words, you can assume that there is a universal syntactic category, whether it is verb or Pred or whatever, or subject, no matter what the diversity of the actual facts are, within languages or across languages.

Now the approach that Baker has taken is to go one language at a time. So you start with English, then you move on to Edo and pick different constructions, then you move on to Chichewa, take other constructions and keep going one language at a time. Well, if you keep doing this, as you can see, from the example I gave you, you keep adding more and more constructions and you get a bigger and bigger statement that has to be true of all languages. And yet the reality is, it doesn't work very well. In fact, the important reality is that linguists who use this method of argumentation almost never test the implicit universals they claim in a large sample of languages.

So what would be a truly rigorous syntactic method? Basically what I've spent this afternoon telling you is that the standard way that most linguists— not just generative syntacticians, most linguists—argue for categories, word classes or other kind of syntactic categories—these building blocks—is flawed. It's not really respecting the empirical facts of language, the diversity of languages. So what would be a truly rigorous method? The reason I make this point in this way is because some syntacticians make a big deal about the fact or the belief that they are using a rigorous method of syntactic argumentation in order to support their analysis. So my point here is that actually the method they use is actually not rigorous at all. It's very sloppy.

The question you might ask is: Is there a rigorous way to do this that is not sloppy? And the answer is yes. The first point I make is *cross-linguistic validation of hypotheses*. Any hypothesis about constructions that we saw of the type that Baker used must be tested against a broad crosslinguistic sample. It doesn't have to be a huge sample. You don't have to go out and look at a hundred languages like some typologists do. It's actually more important that you make sure the languages are from different parts of the world geographically, and they are from different genetic groupings. Looking at just Western European languages and just East Asian languages is not going to be sufficient. The second thing is to *use the same constructions across languages for argumentation*. My whole point is that when you do syntactic argumentation, what you are really doing is you are asking what words or phrases can fill a particular role in a particular grammatical construction. Well, if that's how you operate, then to be rigorous, you need to look at the same role in the same construction across languages. That can guarantee that you are looking at the same thing across languages and therefore, you can actually find something that might be universal about languages.

The third thing you should do is *examine distributional patterns in detail*. Part of the problem with Aarts's analysis of *since* is that he, at least in the article, he only looked at *since* and *before* which work the same way. He didn't look into *while*, *back* and *down*, the other forms that I mentioned. If you look at more forms, then you'll discover some of this variation and you get a more accurate description of what's really going on in the language.

And then if you have a problem in your analysis, and you bring in another construction to try to understand what's going on, what you are doing is for one particular language. But if you are going to say this other construction explains what's going on, you know some problem in your analysis, then you have to look at that construction across other languages: *Any language-specific constructional interaction to account for a counterexample must be crosslinguistically validated.* The explanation isn't valid as a universal explanation if it only works for one language. That just means that it doesn't really work; it's not the real explanation. The explanation is just ad hoc. And I think that's a basic problem with Baker's analysis that we saw there.

And then here is the toughest thing. You need to *use cross-linguistically valid criteria to identify potentially universal patterns*. This is perhaps the most important criterion of all. The problem here is, so to speak, if you look at grammatical structure, as I emphasized again and again, there's a huge amount of diversity across languages. You will see this as we continue with my series of lectures. You can't really use formal grammatical structure for cross-linguistic comparison. That's what the statistical types call the dependent variable. You need to have something that you can use as the basis of comparison across languages that's different from formal structure. And the truth is, the only fully valid criterion is functional equivalence.

So if you are talking about, say, predication, what you are doing is you are comparing predication as a function, a way of packaging information in a clause, from one language to the next. What formal structure a language uses, that's what you are interested in learning about: which formal constructions do they use and how do they use it? So to compare constructions across languages, you look at constructions that perform the same function. And again that's why I'm a construction grammarian, because in construction grammar constructions are a combination of formal structures and their function, so you can compare constructions based on their function or meaning. Since I am running out of time, I just want to say there's some formal properties that you think you might be able to compare across languages, but they all require some degree of functional equivalence. I won't go into the details here.

Now what I've described so far is basically the typological method. Any textbook in typology, such as the one that I wrote, will tell you about this in the first chapter. So to conclude: How does this connect to Radical Construction Grammar? I've taken you to look at some examples of crosslinguistic comparison, and said that the only rigorous syntactic method is the typological method.

Well, constructions, which are pairings of form and meaning, are ideally suited for crosslinguistic comparison and crosslinguistic validation of linguistic hypotheses. So again that's why typologists are or should be construction grammarians. Distributional analysis is based on constructions. Linguists may call it other kinds of things, but the truth is, they are talking about constructions and roles in constructions. Therefore, typological universals, that is, genuine universals about language, are universals about constructions, functionally defined, and not about categories, formally defined. And that's the end of my story for today. Thank you.

Radical Construction Grammar: "Parts of Speech" in Chinese

I'm going to talk this morning on parts of speech in Chinese. This is essentially going into detail on one example of the problem that I described to you yesterday afternoon about how you define categories and word classes in languages, and what is the role of word classes in syntactic theory [Lecture 2]. The argument that I presented yesterday afternoon is that the role of word classes is in fact essentially unimportant in syntactic theory. So now I'm going to talk about this in a little more detail, for an example that should be closer to all of you, parts of speech in Chinese. As I said yesterday, I'll be focusing mainly on Cantonese, because I'll be discussing an article written by Stephen Matthews and Elaine Francis on the problem of parts of speech in Cantonese.

So the traditional theoretical position—and I should say this is the western grammatical tradition, I'm not sure how things were in the traditional approaches to grammar in China—but the kind of traditional position that's articulated in most introductory linguistics textbooks is the one that you see on the screen. I'll read it to you here. This is from an introduction to Government and Binding Theory, so this is somewhat old—it's an introduction to generative syntax from the 1990s, but the statement here is one of the clearest statements of the traditional position. I could have found similar statements in other introductory textbooks. So the quotation is: "Words belong to different syntactic categories, such as nouns, verbs, etc., and the syntactic category to which a word belongs determines its distribution (this is the distribution in the sense I talked about yesterday [Lecture 2]), that is, in what contexts it can occur" (Liliane Haegeman, *Introduction to Government and Binding Theory*, 1994, p.36).

Now this traditional position presupposes the building block model of syntax [Figure 51]. In the building block model, syntactic structures or constructions

© WILLIAM CROFT, REPRODUCED WITH KIND PERMISSION FROM THE AUTHOR BY KONINKLIJKE BRILL NV, LEIDEN, 2021 | DOI:10.1163/9789004363533_004

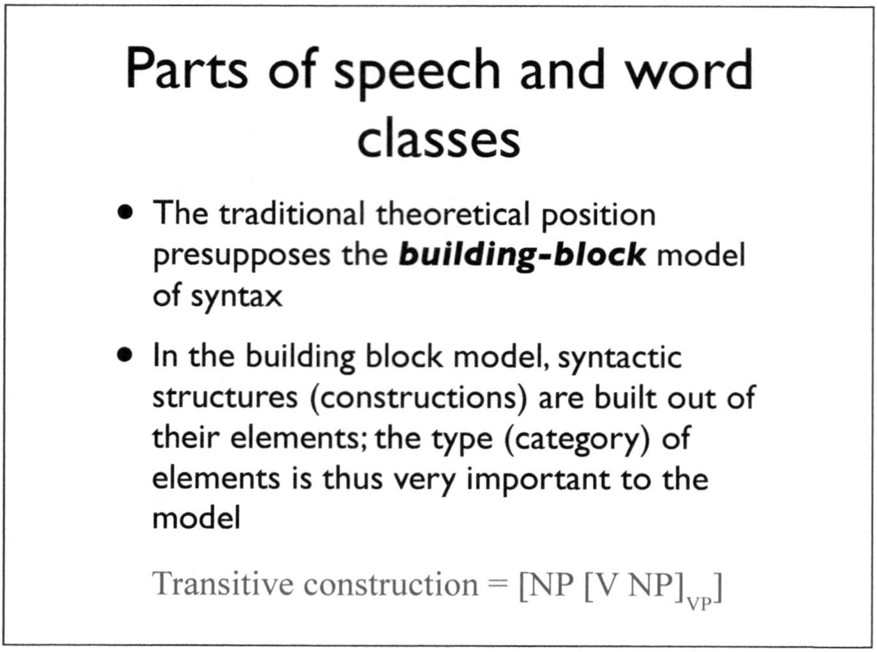

Parts of speech and word classes

- The traditional theoretical position presupposes the **building-block** model of syntax

- In the building block model, syntactic structures (constructions) are built out of their elements; the type (category) of elements is thus very important to the model

Transitive construction = [NP [V NP]$_{VP}$]

FIGURE 51

are built out of their elements. So the type or category of elements is thus very important to the model. So what defines the transitive construction, the same example I used yesterday [Lecture 2], are the different elements you see here and how they are combined. In the building block model of syntax that's very important, because the whole definition of a construction is what category of elements the construction built out of: a verb and two noun phrases in this case.

Now [the syntactic category] is also said to define distribution [Figure 52]. So in English, this word class view of parts of speech supports the traditional analysis into noun, adjective and verb. So you can see, for a noun, you see the combination *is* plus *a* in predication, so in this construction, it's a different construction than the one you find with adjectives where you just have the copula *be*, or with verbs where you have no copula, you just have an inflection here.

When we turn to Chinese, the answer is not so clear. I'm going to be using descriptions of Chinese written by mostly Western linguists, who write in English, since I don't speak or read Chinese. The examples I'm giving you are all from Western sources, such as Li and Thompson's textbook [Figure 53].

In the first example, we have "Zhangsan is a nurse". So you have a copula expression. But when you say, "he is fat", there's no copula. In "She sleeps on the

Variability in distribution

- In English, the word-class view supports the traditional analysis of parts of speech: Noun, Adjective, Verb

Noun: John is a nurse.

Adjective: He is fat.

Verb: She sleeps on the sofa.

FIGURE 52

Variability in distribution

- But when we turn to Chinese, then the answer is not so clear (Mandarin; Li and Thompson 1981:148, 143, 155)

??	Zhāngsān shi yi-ge hùshì
	Z. COP one-CLF nurse
	'Zhangsan is a nurse.'

??	tā pàng
	3SG fat
	'He is fat.'

??	tā shuì zài shāfa-shang
	3SG sleep at sofa-on
	'She/he sleeps on the couch.'

FIGURE 53

couch", there's also no copula, and of course there's no inflection either. So the first problem then, is, what are the parts of speech of Mandarin, given those facts that you just saw, which of course you are all familiar with. So a first answer would be a semantic answer. Mandarin has nouns, adjectives, and verbs, because we have object words, property concept words, and action words; that's the semantic basis of the traditional definition of parts of speech. A syntactic answer, which has frequently been offered, is that the categories are noun, verb and verb. The property concept words occur in the same construction as the action concept words, so we group them together into a single word class. A mixed answer, which is the one that's offered by Li and Thompson's grammar, is that there are three categories (sort of), but one is the subclass of the other; so we have noun and then what they called adjectival verb, and verb. You can see we have three different answers based on looking at the facts in the previous slide.

Now the term "adjectival verb" is similar to another term that is used for another category in Chinese, "co-verb". In a unpublished paper by James McCawley, he has a remark about the term co-verb, which I incline to agree with. He says, "I regard the use of the term 'co-verb' as an act of cowardice; it hints, but does not really say that the words in question are not verbs, while making it sound as if they sort of are verbs." So the first problem I have to deal with is: what are parts of speech? Can there be mixed parts of speech like "adjectival verb" that we just saw? So that's Problem Number 1.

Problem Number 2 is how do we determine what those parts of speech are? In another paper by McCawley that has been published, he discussed what he called universal adjectives and verbs, so he is trying to find criteria here that can be used across languages, both English and Chinese [Figure 54]. And, if you look at the criteria, I want to say a whole lot about them. You see there are a number of criteria here. But, the thing I want to point out is: in most of his criteria, he has some kind of hedging word. So it says:

> Adjectives *normally* can't combine with the direct object.
>   Adjectives take at most two arguments but *usually* take only one.
>   Adjectives combine with nouns as modifiers while verbs *usually* require some alteration.
>   Degree and comparative expressions combine *more directly* with adjectives than with verbs.
>   An adjective *generally* requires a copula when it is used predicatively while a verb doesn't.

So all of these terms are hedged, and of course that means we have to ask ourselves, well, if an adjective doesn't require a copula, but it generally does,

Problem #2: Criteria

- McCawley's (1992:232) universals of A[dj] and V[erb]

  ✦ Vs can combine directly with an object NP, but As *normally* can't

  ✦ Vs can take up to 3 arguments; As take at most 2 arguments and *usually* take only one

  ✦ As combine directly with Ns as modifiers, while Vs *usually* require some alteration

  ✦ Degree and comparative expressions combine *more directly* with As than with Vs

  ✦ An A *generally* requires a copula when it is used predicatively, while a V doesn't

FIGURE 54

Problem #2: Criteria

- Francis and Matthews' criteria for Vs in Cantonese (Francis and Matthews 2005:273-75)

  ✦ Vs do not require a copula in predication (cf. McCawley)

  ✦ Vs are directly negated (without a copula)

  ✦ Vs form polarity questions with the 'A-not-A' construction

  ✦ Vs allow *at least some form of* aspect marking

- Why these criteria? Which criteria should be used for parts of speech? Across all languages?

FIGURE 55

Problem #3: Circularity

- Francis and Matthews argue that possessing the syntactic feature [V] determines a word's ability to occur in the constructions they use as criteria for verbhood

❖ Compare the Haegeman quote above

- Invoking a word class doesn't explain anything. It simply restates the distributional facts in abbreviated form. [V] = 'occurs in the constructions used to define [V]'

FIGURE 56

should we call it an adjective or not? Now Francis and Matthews, in the paper I mentioned on the criteria for verbs in Cantonese, have another list [Figure 55]. It's not the same as McCawley's list. The first one is the same—"verbs do not require a copula in predication". Here they make a bald statement. They don't say "usually" or "generally". But even in the last criterion, they have "verbs allow *at least some form* of aspect marking". The main point I want to make here is that the criteria are not taken to be firm by the linguists who present them, and they differ from one linguist to another. So the question we can ask is, why these criteria? Which criteria should be used for parts of speech? And should they be used across all languages? So that's Problem Number 2.

Problem Number 3 is circularity [Figure 56]. This is basically the same kind of circularity I described yesterday afternoon [Lecture 2]. So Francis and Matthews argue that possessing the syntactic feature V for verb, determines a word's ability to occur in the constructions Francis and Matthews used to establish verbhood. It's the same point that was made by the quote by Liliane Haegeman, the generative linguist at the beginning: words belong to different categories, and the categories determine the context in which they occur, that is, the constructions they occur in. But the problem here is that invoking a word class label like "verb" doesn't explain anything. It simply restates the

Problem #4: Variation

- Francis and Matthews on variation between "property-denoting" [adjectival], stative and action-denoting verbs in Cantonese (Francis and Matthews 2005:276-83)

  ✦ Comparison with *gwo3* (property, state) vs. *do1 gwo3* (action)

  ✦ Intensification with *taai3* (property, state only)

  ✦ Intensification with *hou2* 'very': 'default' interpretation nearly obligatory (property), optional (state), prohibited (action)

  ✦ Aspectual *-zo* completive (action) vs. inchoative (property, state)

  ✦ Reduplication: attenuative A-A-*dei2* (property, state), delimitative A-A-*haa5* (state, action), extreme value A-B-B (property, action)

  ✦ Possibility of direct object NPs (state, action)

FIGURE 57

distribution of facts in an abbreviated form. So V, in Francis and Matthews's terms, simply means, "occurs the constructions used to define V". So you are not really saying anything new when you label a word V.

The fourth problem is variation [Figure 57]. Supposedly things like whether or not a word has a copula, or whether or not the word uses some kind of aspect particle, are supposed to be criteria for establishing whether a word is a verb or an adjective. But in fact, if you start looking more carefully, as Francis and Matthews do—and I think that's very good—they discovered that in fact there is a lot of variation. So if we take different kinds of words—property concept words, stative words, and action words—in Cantonese, they discovered that, in fact, there are a lot of differences in how they behave. So you can't just say they all act alike. Even if you called them all V, that wouldn't tell you very much about how the language works. If you are trying to learn the language, they wouldn't allow you to be able to speak the language properly. Just because they're all V means you can't tell, for all these constructions listed on the slide, whether the word fits or not.

So the problem is, how do we know which constructions to choose to define parts of speech, and which constructions can define subclasses? Obviously, they don't consider all the constructions [in Figure 57] to define different

Solving Problem #3 (Circularity)

- Word classes, or parts of speech, are really defined in terms of certain **constructions**. We should stop pretending otherwise.

- For example, a "word class" such as Cantonese [V] is simply a shorthand for a construction or set of constructions used to define that word class. It is not something independent of the constructions used.

FIGURE 58

classes, like adjective, verb and state. They consider them to define just subclasses at best. And particularly, the question for Cantonese and for Mandarin is, why are property words a subclass of verbs instead of a separate part of speech which we can call adjectives? That's the position taken by Francis and Matthews, that they are just verbs.

So now I'm going to take a Radical Construction Grammar perspective on this problem. I'm going to start with the problem of circularity [Figure 58]. That was Problem Number 3. So all of the sort of good points are here in purple. The first bullet point is that word classes or parts of speech are really defined in terms of certain constructions. And most important, we should stop pretending otherwise. So if you talk about word classes, or if one talks about word classes—I don't want to accuse any of you personally—if you talk about word classes in general, then you are really talking about certain constructions. And I think that we should basically be honest and say, now we are not talking about adjectives; we are talking about a non-copular predication construction. And then we want to ask, what words can occur in that construction, in Mandarin or Cantonese, or English? And the other bullet points, as I said before, is that the category V that Francis and Matthews proposes is simply a

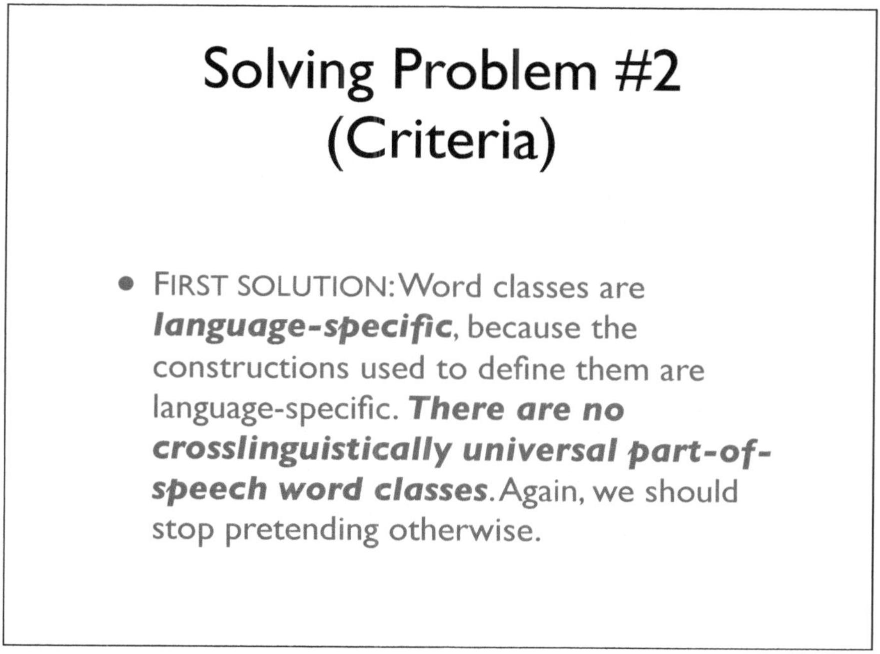

Solving Problem #2 (Criteria)

- FIRST SOLUTION: Word classes are **language-specific**, because the constructions used to define them are language-specific. **There are no crosslinguistically universal part-of-speech word classes.** Again, we should stop pretending otherwise.

FIGURE 59

shorthand for a construction or a set of constructions used to define that word class. It's not something independent of the constructions that were used.

So now let's back up to Problem Number 2: which criteria do you use [Figure 59]? Well, it's a fairly complicated solution. The first step is to recognize that word classes are language-specific, because the constructions used to define them are language-specific. There are no cross-linguistically universal part-of-speech word classes. So we should stop pretending otherwise. Now this is a point that's very difficult, I have found, for people to accept, because they really want to believe this. And in fact, Francis and Matthews, even though they acknowledge the position that I advocate in one passage here, they still really want to believe this. So they write in their article, "following Croft, we do not assume that 'verb' in Cantonese is the same category as 'verb' in Turkish or any other language, but rather we use the label 'verb' to indicate the syntactic categories whose members are prototypically used as semantic predicates in a particular language."

Well, that's actually a little different from what I say, because I don't consider verb to represent a syntactic category or word class. Yes, it has to involve predication, but it's not a word class. But the other problem is that, after making this statement, they say "we do not assume that 'verb' in Cantonese is the same category as 'verb' in Turkish or any other language". Then they go on and they say things which don't make sense unless you assume that "verb" does mean the same thing across languages. So it says, "in many languages, the lexical semantic feature [gradable] is associated with the syntactic category of adjectives ... This cannot be so for languages like Cantonese, for which most gradable property words are verbs." So again, that statement doesn't make sense, unless you can talk about verbs in Cantonese being similar to verbs or similar to adjectives in some other language.

Another quote: "One of our claims in section 2 was that the vast majority of property-denoting words in Cantonese are verbs. The idea that Chinese lacks adjectives (or has only a small class of non-verbal property words) is far from new." So again, this sentence only makes sense if you think of adjectives as something to compare from one language to the next. There's a better way of looking at this. So "verb" in Cantonese is defined by Cantonese grammatical constructions, and so it does not make sense outside of the Cantonese language. Instead of calling it a verb in Cantonese, let's call it a Cantonese Verb. And in English, instead of calling it a verb, let's call it an English Verb. That makes it very clear that these are language-specific word classes. And if you think of it that way, then it makes complete sense to say that English does not have Cantonese Verbs, and Cantonese does not have English Verbs. If you put it that way, then it's an obvious statement. And I think that's correct.

Ok, so what's the second way of addressing the problem [Figure 60]? The main problem was that we had linguists like McCawley or Francis and Matthews using different criteria to define adjectives, so how do we know who's right? What criteria should we use? Remember, this first solution was: we are really talking about constructions; we are not talking about word classes. So then the real question is, which constructions do we compare, from one language to the next, if we really want to find out about universals, what's universal about parts of speech, and not what's specific to Cantonese or to English. We can compare words—these things that are supposed to belong to word classes—cross-linguistically in terms of semantic translation equivalence. That's why I keep talking about object concept words, property concept words, action concept words. And we can compare constructions cross-linguistically in terms of semantic or pragmatic equivalence, so we can talk about predication constructions, modification or attributive constructions, and reference constructions for prototypical nouns. In particular, we want to compare a set of constructions that encodes a coherent paradigmatic set of functions. We don't want to just mix and match constructions; they all have to make some kind of coherent set. When you are talking about reference, modification, predication, that's a coherent set. And then we can posit and correctly show that there are

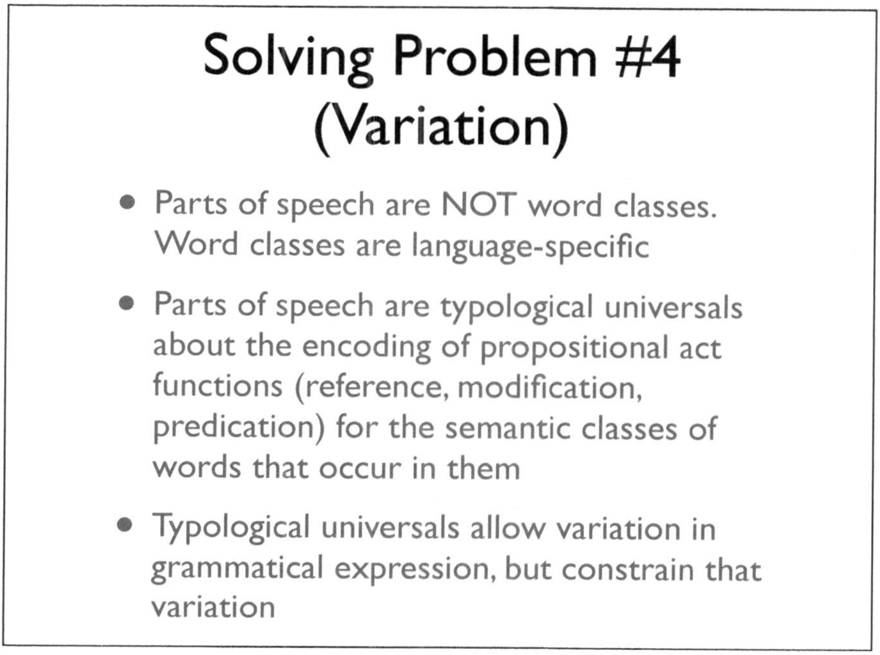

Solving Problem #4 (Variation)

- Parts of speech are NOT word classes. Word classes are language-specific

- Parts of speech are typological universals about the encoding of propositional act functions (reference, modification, predication) for the semantic classes of words that occur in them

- Typological universals allow variation in grammatical expression, but constrain that variation

FIGURE 60

language universals about the relationship between these three constructions. The other kinds of constructions that linguists have used to define adjectives as a word class just don't belong to this set.

That's what I said in this big quote (a similar quote, it's in a different article but it's a similar quote to what I gave you yesterday in discussing Bas Aarts [Lecture 2]): "The propositional act constructions are the constructions that figure prominently in discussions of parts of speech [we've already seen reference to predication constructions, in Mandarin and Cantonese] ... Since the universals are specific to the mapping between these constructions and lexical items [in this case, property concept words and action words], we have a principled reason to set aside the distributional facts about other constructions—the crucial missing ingredient from the standard form of syntactic argumentation". You see, the standard form of syntactic argumentation does not tell you what constructions to use, and which ones you shouldn't use. "For example, the transitive construction ... is excluded from consideration because the transitive construction is an argument structure construction: it encodes participant roles, not a propositional act." So if you realize that we are talking about constructions and not word classes, then it makes complete sense to just restrict your attention to certain constructions. You can't do everything at once. So you just pick certain constructions that you think form a set, a natural class of constructions, and then you describe what goes on there.

Ok, now what about variation? Just to repeat: parts of speech are not word classes; word classes are language-specific. Parts of speech: I am exploiting this term "parts of speech", because it doesn't have the phrase "word class" in it; this allows me to act like we can talk about parts of speech that are not word classes. It's not the traditional way of looking at it, but the whole point of my presentation here is that we have to go away from that traditional way of looking at it. So parts of speech are typological universals about the encoding of propositional act functions (reference, modification, predication) for the semantic classes of words that occur in them. And it varies. Typological universals allow variation in grammatical expression, but constrain that variation.

So an example would be copulas and "verbs". Let's take the example of a copula. We all talk about copulas. I gave you examples of a copula in English and a copula in Mandarin at the beginning of this morning's lecture. So I am using the same word "copula", the same grammatical term to describe something in two different languages. But I just told you that you can't define things cross-linguistically. Most categories are language-specific. So in what sense or how can we define "copula" so that it's a cross-linguistically valid concept? That's a very important thing. If you are going to compare languages, you have to have some criterion that is valid across all languages so that you can go to any language and say, does this language have a copula, for example. You can define it in a cross-linguistically valid way. We'll define a copula as *overt coding of predication*. Predication is a function. We can go to different languages and ask, what constructions does the language use for predication of different kinds of concepts, and then we can ask, does that construction have an extra morpheme in it, or not? And if it does, that word we'll call a copula. So you can use that definition for English, for Cantonese, for Mandarin, any language.

Now when you do that, you find that languages do not behave the same way. That is, it's not the case that every language uses a copula for the same set of words, the same semantic categories of words. As an example, here is another language from the Northwest coast of the North America, a native American language [Figure 61]. You remember from yesterday afternoon [Lecture 2] I gave you an example of a language called Straits Salish which was said not to have a noun/verb distinction. Well, typically what a linguist means when they say a language does not have a noun/verb distinction, what they mean is that there is no copula for any of the semantic classes you predicate. Makah is a language that is not closely related to Straits Salish (depending on who you

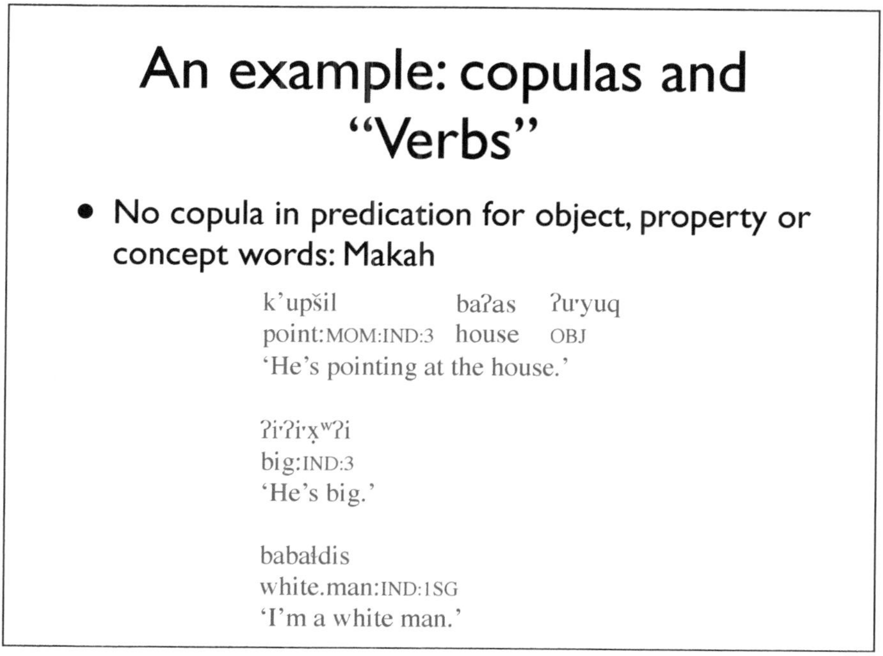

An example: copulas and "Verbs"

- No copula in predication for object, property or concept words: Makah

k'upšil   baʔas   ʔuʼyuq
point:MOM:IND:3   house   OBJ
'He's pointing at the house.'

ʔiʼʔiʼxʷʔi
big:IND:3
'He's big.'

babaɬdis
white.man:IND:1SG
'I'm a white man.'

FIGURE 61

believe). But the fact is, it's in the same linguistic area. And like Straits Salish, this language does not use a copula when you predicate object words, like "I am a white man"; it doesn't use a copula when you predicate a property word like "he is big", and of course it doesn't use a copula when you predicate an action like pointing.

So again what we have done is we've turned around the statement, people who say there is no noun/verb distinction in Makah, and we said that's not the right way to describe the facts of Makah. The right way to describe it is: there is a single predication construction without a copula that's used for object words, property words and action words. So I'm not denying the facts of Makah. I'm just saying this is the better way to describe those facts.

Now of course for Mandarin and Cantonese, looking at these examples from the first slide of my lecture again [Figure 62], we see that in Mandarin and Cantonese also, there is a copula for object predication ("is a nurse"), but there is no copula for property predication or action predication. So again, this is where you find that most linguists, if they tell you that in a language, adjectives are really verbs, what they almost always really mean is: there is a predication construction without a copula, and it is used for action words and property words. Again, I'm not denying those facts about a language; I am just saying

An example: copulas and "Verbs"

- Copula for object words only: Mandarin, Cantonese (but see below!)

> Zhāngsān shi yi-ge   hùshì
> Z.   COP one-CLF nurse
> 'Zhangsan is a nurse.'
>
> tā   pàng
> 3SG fat
> 'He is fat.'
>
> tā   shuì zài shāfa-shang
> 3SG sleep at sofa-on
> 'She/he sleeps on the couch.'

FIGURE 62

An example: copulas and "Verbs"

- Copula for object words and property words: English

> John is a nurse.
>
> He is fat.
>
> She sleeps on the sofa.

FIGURE 63

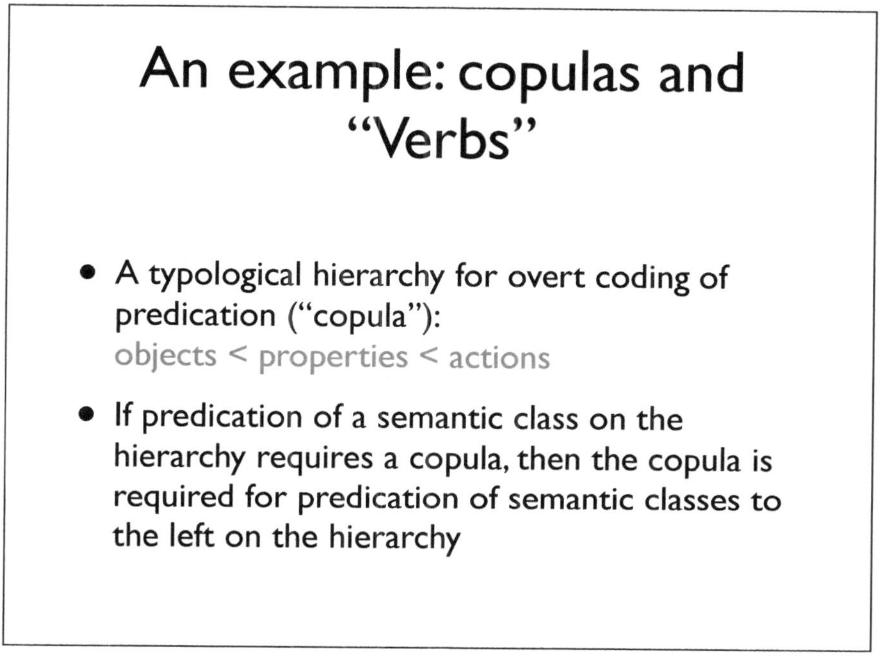

An example: copulas and "Verbs"

- A typological hierarchy for overt coding of predication ("copula"):
  objects < properties < actions

- If predication of a semantic class on the hierarchy requires a copula, then the copula is required for predication of semantic classes to the left on the hierarchy

FIGURE 64

that describing it in terms of parts of speech or word classes independent of constructions is the wrong way to look at it. When you say that, all you are doing is essentially telling somebody about this particular construction.

Now we go to a language like English, and here we have the same examples that I started with but now I am just focusing on the copula verb [Figure 63]. You have a copula for object words and a copula for property words, but not for action words.

Ok, so I've given you these examples, three example languages here, and you have seen they are all different, but they all have a general pattern in common. And that is described on the next slide [Figure 64]. And this is what they call a "typological hierarchy" for when you have an overt coding of predication or a copula. So in this case, basically, if you have any copula at all, you will find it on the predication of object words. If you have a copula for property words, you'll also have a copula for object words. And if you had some overt coding of predication of action words, you will expect to find an overt coding of predication on object words and property words as well. So in other words, there is a pattern here, and Makah, Mandarin and Cantonese, and English all conform to this pattern. What is universal is the pattern, the hierarchy I've just given you. That's what should be part of some kind of universal grammar, not any kind of set of word classes. The second bullet point is just the restatement of that hierarchy. So the hierarchy basically is a way of summarizing the possible kinds of languages we have, with respect to predication constructions with a copula and without a copula.

This particular fact is something that in linguistic typology, going back to the work of Greenberg from 1966, is called "typological markedness". The term "markedness" is used by many linguists for many different justifications. And often it is just used to mean that something is unusual or special. It's not a very useful description, but in typology it does have a very specific definition which you can always test. And the test here is when you have an overt coding, or when you have zero coding, of a particular conceptual function.

So structural coding, like a copula, can be formulated in general as follows: "If a language overtly codes a typologically unmarked value of a conceptual category, then it codes a typologically marked value of the conceptual category by at least as many morphemes." So here, the typologically unmarked value of the conceptual category, or least marked, value is actions for predication. That's the sense in which your prototypical predication is an action word. And then typologically more marked are properties, and typologically the most marked are objects. So what the statement says is, if you have—these are all conceptual categories—if you have some kind of ranking in terms of markedness, then the least marked ones are going to be more likely to have zero coding, and the most marked ones are most likely to have overt coding. And something in between will have overt coding or zero coding depending in part on its neighbors. It's a very important concept. It's very useful and it's actually the one that is most important for understanding parts of speech.

So, as I said, this shows that the typologically least marked predication is the predication of action, and the typologically most marked predication is the predication of objects, with properties in between. Languages like Cantonese and Mandarin are very useful because they have copulas only for object words, in contrast to a language like English. So the prototypical predication is the predication of actions. And that kind of makes sense; that's the intuition I think that's behind the traditional concept of parts of speech, at least in the Western grammatical tradition. There's a famous quotation from the American linguist Edward Sapir, who makes essentially the same point:

> There must be something to talk about and something must be said about this subject of discourse once it is selected. This distinction is of such fundamental importance that the vast majority of languages have emphasized it by creating some sort of formal barrier between the two terms of the proposition. The subject of discourse is a noun. As the most common subject of discourse is either a person or a thing, the noun

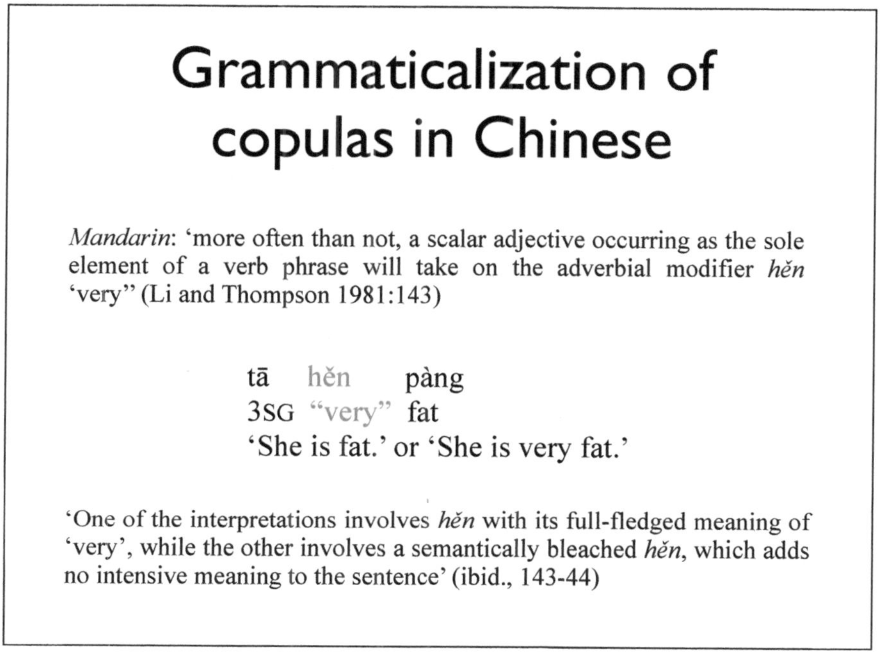

Grammaticalization of copulas in Chinese

Mandarin: 'more often than not, a scalar adjective occurring as the sole element of a verb phrase will take on the adverbial modifier *hěn* 'very'' (Li and Thompson 1981:143)

tā   hěn   pàng
3SG "very" fat
'She is fat.' or 'She is very fat.'

'One of the interpretations involves *hěn* with its full-fledged meaning of 'very', while the other involves a semantically bleached *hěn*, which adds no intensive meaning to the sentence' (ibid., 143-44)

FIGURE 65

clusters about concrete concepts of that order. As the thing predicated of a subject is generally an activity in the widest sense of the word, a passage from one moment of existence to another, the form which has been set aside for the business of predicating, in other words, the verb, clusters about concepts of activity. No language wholly fails to distinguish noun and verb, though in particular cases the nature of the distinction may be an elusive one.

SAPIR 1921: 119

As I said before, the chief reason many linguists argue that Chinese and other languages lack adjectives is because these languages do not use a copula for predicating property words. They often do not pay attention to other criteria. But again, what this tells us is something about predication constructions. It doesn't tell us anything about allegedly universal word classes such as "adjective" or "verb".

Of course there is an irony here that some of you probably have been thinking about already, since of course you are all native speakers of Mandarin or maybe some other Chinese variety: that in fact, both of these languages [Mandarin and Cantonese] are well on the way to grammaticalizing a copula

---

Grammaticalization of copulas in Chinese

Cantonese: 'a predicative adjective is usually preceded by a modifier such as *hóu*, which as an adjective means 'good'. *hóu* in this function may be regarded as merely an adjective marker, its meaning being much weaker than English 'very' (Matthews and Yip 1994:158)

Léih go jái   hóu   gōu
you CLF son "very" tall
'Your son is tall.'

'The same sentence without any intensifier…seems incomplete… although [it] is possible, it has a very restricted distribution…' (Francis and Matthews 2005:277)

FIGURE 66

for the predication of properties, just as in earlier stages of Chinese, there was grammaticalization of the copula that is used for predication of objects [Figure 65]. And a description of that historical process is found in another paper by Li and Thompson. So here is a quotation, it's actually from Li and Thompson's *Grammar of Mandarin*. It says "more often than not, a scalar adjective occurring as the sole element of a verb phrase will take on the adverbial modifier *hěn*", 'very'. So the expressions like the example in the middle of the slide could be translated as "she is very fat", but it can also be translated as simply "she is fat". They go on to say "one of the interpretations involves *hěn* with its full-fledged meaning of 'very', while the other involves a semantically bleached *hěn*, which adds no intensive meaning to the sentence". So that's a crucial thing: you have to look at the meanings of these expressions. And if you look and see that there are uses of this word which do not add intensive meaning, then the only function they are doing is basically helping you to predicate a property word. So this term, this expression, is actually already well on the way to being a copula for property concept predication.

Cantonese [Figure 66]: the same thing is true. However, I had to go back to *The Grammar of Cantonese*, written by Stephen Matthews and Virginia Yip, because in this grammar, they're a little more open about the role of this word

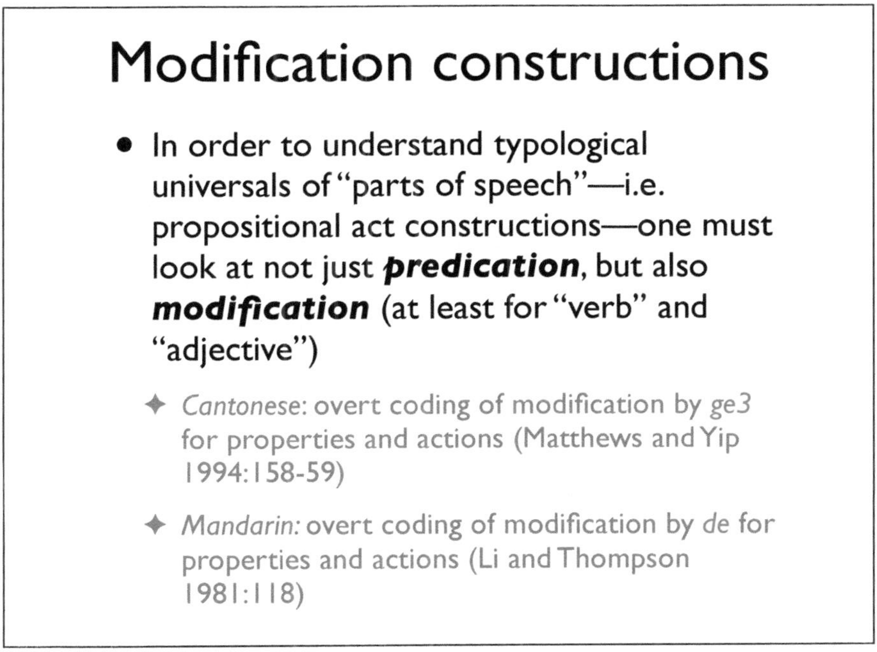

Modification constructions

- In order to understand typological universals of "parts of speech"—i.e. propositional act constructions—one must look at not just **predication**, but also **modification** (at least for "verb" and "adjective")

  + *Cantonese:* overt coding of modification by *ge3* for properties and actions (Matthews and Yip 1994:158-59)

  + *Mandarin:* overt coding of modification by *de* for properties and actions (Li and Thompson 1981:118)

FIGURE 67

that is essentially functioning the same way as the Mandarin word. It says "a predicative adjective is usually preceded by a modifier such as *hóu*, which as an adjective means 'good'. *Hóu* in this function may be regarded as merely an adjective marker, its meaning being much weaker than English 'very'." So it seems to be essentially the same facts as you find in Mandarin. Now Francis and Matthews, who have committed themselves to saying that property concepts are verbs in Cantonese, are now saying something slightly different, but they acknowledge that, as they say, "the same sentence without any intensifier ... seems incomplete ... although [it] is possible, it has a very restricted distribution ..." So it sounds like most of the time, for a Cantonese speaker, you cannot predicate a property without adding this word.

Now as I said, most linguists who take a word class view of parts of speech tend to look at only the predication construction. So when they make statements about a language not having adjectives, or a language not even having nouns, they are mainly talking about the predication construction. But you can't really do that. You have to look at all the propositional act constructions. In particular, you have to look at the modification construction [Figure 67]. If you do this for Cantonese and Mandarin, you find an unusual fact, or a seemingly unusual fact, which is that in Cantonese you have overt coding

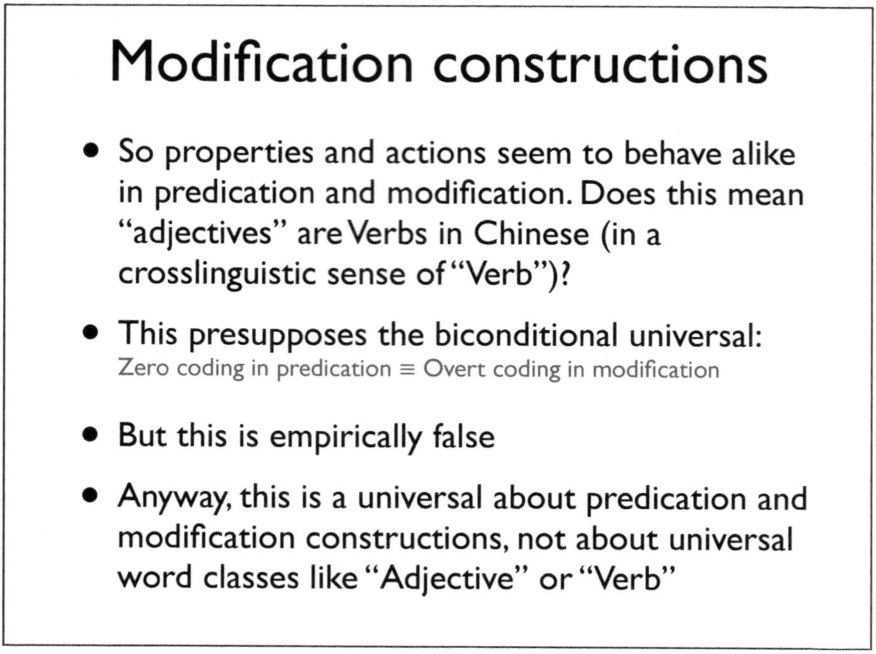

Modification constructions

- So properties and actions seem to behave alike in predication and modification. Does this mean "adjectives" are Verbs in Chinese (in a crosslinguistic sense of "Verb")?

- This presupposes the biconditional universal:
  Zero coding in predication ≡ Overt coding in modification

- But this is empirically false

- Anyway, this is a universal about predication and modification constructions, not about universal word classes like "Adjective" or "Verb"

FIGURE 68

of modification by this morpheme for both properties and actions. So you would expect that in structural coding, properties are going to be typologically unmarked as modifiers, compared to actions. Well, typologically unmarked only means that you have at least as many morphemes in that category for the unmarked value. You can always have the same amount of morphemes, either none, or in this case, in Mandarin and Cantonese, some overt coding. So it doesn't violate the general principle that the least coding is found cross-linguistically with the prototypical semantic class. It's just that sometimes the languages use the same amount of coding. So properties and actions seem to behave alike in both predication and modification.

If we ignore the grammaticalization of these 'very' words as copulas, it looks like, in predication, property words and action words look alike, and in modification, property words and action words look alike. So does this mean that adjectives are verbs in Chinese in some crosslinguistic sense [Figure 68]? Well, you have the rest of the slide in front of you, so you've already seen the answer. First, to do this, that presupposes a biconditional universal, because what we are seeing here, if you are looking at just Cantonese and Mandarin, what we have done is we are looking at two constructions instead of one. We're looking at predication constructions, and we're looking at modification constructions.

And we see that these words, these semantic classes of words behave the same way.

So are we going to make it a universal statement about that? Well, remember, as I said, there are no crosslinguistic word classes. Word classes are language-specific. So to understand this in a crosslinguistic sense, we have to translate that statement. And the translation has to be that if you have zero coding in predication, for any particular semantic word type, you are also going to have overt coding in modification. Those are the facts in Cantonese and Mandarin. That's what we call in typology a biconditional universal: one type of construction occurs if and only if you also have the other type of construction in the language. But this is empirically false, that is, there are other languages that don't work that way. So you can't say that what I've told you about or what we've been told about Mandarin and Cantonese is actually true of languages in general. It's just a fact about Mandarin and Cantonese.

And anyway, as I said, this is a universal about predication and modification constructions, not about allegedly universal word classes like "adjective" and "verb". So even if the statement was true, the one that's in blue, here, it's a statement about two kinds of constructions, predication and modification, it's not a statement about word classes. As I said, it happens to be false. But that's the whole point of typology: you look at a lot of languages to find out whether a statement like that is true or false. There are other statements that are less strong, less constraining, that are true about parts of speech.

Ok, now there's another thing besides structural coding that you have to look at, and that's what's called, or what I call, "behavioral potential" [Figure 69]. It goes back to Greenberg's work again. This one: when I teach typology to my students back in New Mexico, and before that at the University of Manchester, and before that at the University of Michigan, this was a concept that students always had great trouble with. So if you are not familiar with this concept from reading typology, you might have some difficulties grasping it too, because it's one of these theoretical concepts that's just hard to grasp. Some of you have probably taught introductory linguistic classes and you probably know that the concept of a phoneme is something that a student who has never done linguistics has great difficulty with, whereas for all of us, we are trained as linguists, this concept of phoneme seems normal. So it takes a while. Hopefully I can explain this to you a little bit now so that you can understand the examples I give on the next couple of slides.

So the idea is, again, we are comparing marked values and unmarked values of a conceptual category. And then you have constructions that express what I'll call the behavioral potential, the ability to express grammatical distinctions. What you sometimes find—actually more than sometimes—you often find is

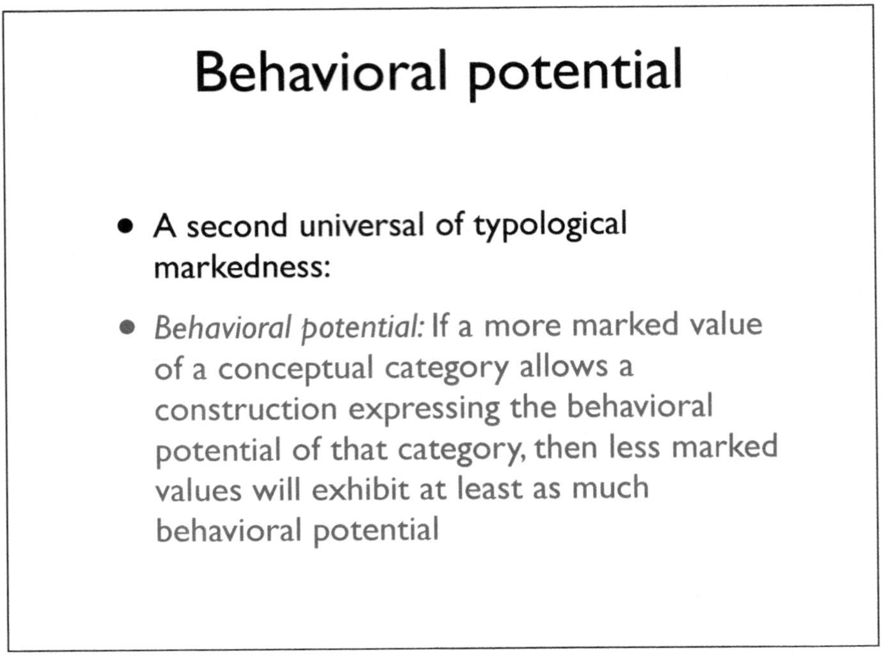

Behavioral potential

- A second universal of typological markedness:

- *Behavioral potential:* If a more marked value of a conceptual category allows a construction expressing the behavioral potential of that category, then less marked values will exhibit at least as much behavioral potential

---

FIGURE 69

that the unmarked value can express more grammatical distinctions than the marked value. So there's another asymmetry in the pattern here. And of course sometimes the marked value and the unmarked value express the same distinctions. So there is nothing wrong there. The crucial fact is: the asymmetry is always in one direction. Just as we saw the unmarked value would be zero coded and the marked value would be overtly coded, you can also find that the unmarked value has grammatical distinctions that the marked value lacks. You don't find the opposite.

Now when you are looking at parts of speech, you have to know what kind of grammatical distinctions you are looking for [Figure 70]. And it so happens that—for reasons that would take me another full lecture to explain and I am not prepared to do so—you have to look at different grammatical distinctions depending on whether you are looking at referring expression constructions, modification constructions, or predication constructions. And in fact, again, if you look at traditional discussions of parts of speech, these categories look very familiar, because one of the things that linguists ask themselves, if a word is a noun, is whether it inflects for number, gender, and case, and if it is a verb, whether it inflects for tense, aspect and mood, whether it agrees with the subject, or the object or other arguments of the predicate.

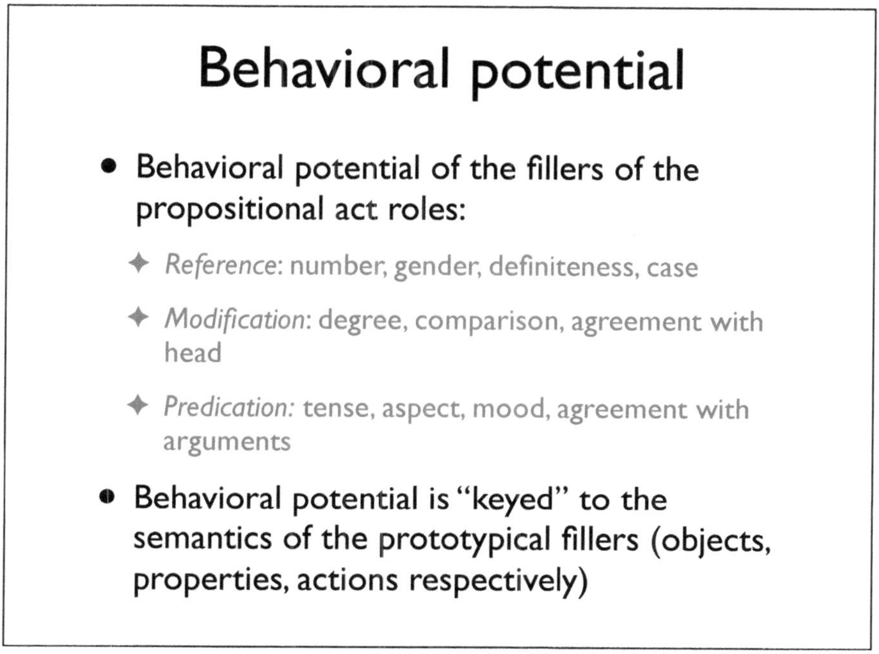

Behavioral potential

- **Behavioral potential of the fillers of the propositional act roles:**
  - ✦ *Reference*: number, gender, definiteness, case
  - ✦ *Modification*: degree, comparison, agreement with head
  - ✦ *Predication:* tense, aspect, mood, agreement with arguments
- **Behavioral potential is "keyed" to the semantics of the prototypical fillers (objects, properties, actions respectively)**

FIGURE 70

These categories are commonly used and, again, our main point here is that we are talking about constructions, so we are talking about grammatical distinctions found in predication constructions or modification constructions, or referring constructions. Now the only thing I'm going to say here is that these various grammatical distinctions reflect some conceptual or semantic distinctions. And those semantic distinctions are the ones that are usually relevant for the prototypical members of the category. So for actions what is highly relevant is their time reference, their temporal structure (that's aspect), modality, and it's also highly relevant that actions have participants. So those are the kinds of inflections you expect to find with predication.

Ok, now one factor that is important when you are trying to define an adjective word class, and even when you are trying to look at the typological markedness of properties as modifiers, is the occurrence of these words with comparative and other degree expressions like *very* or some kinds of intensifier, or a downtoner, because these categories express the semantic feature of gradability. Francis and Matthews argue that gradability is not a syntactic word class feature, it is a semantic feature. Well, that's fine but that's actually not relevant because the typological-universal theory of parts of speech is not about word classes, it is about semantic classes of words and the way they are

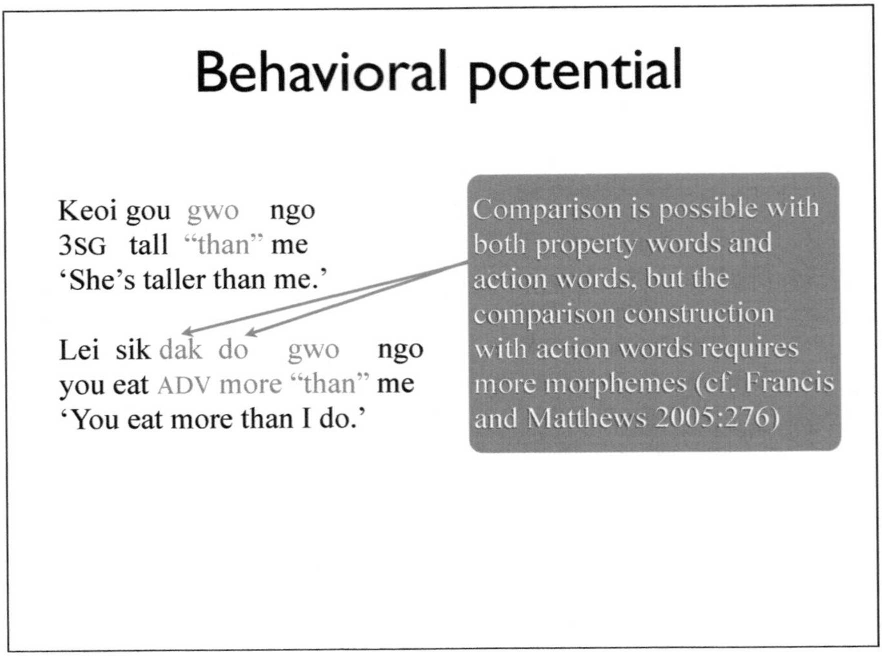

FIGURE 71

expressed in different kinds of constructions, propositional act constructions in particular.

And even so, there are some idiosyncrasies in comparison and degree constructions at least in Cantonese; I don't know what the facts are in Mandarin. So we have two examples here that are taken from Francis and Matthews' work [Figure 71]. And they point out that, yes, you can use comparison with property words and action words, but the comparative construction with action words requires more morphemes. So you see that here: more morphemes here (in the second example); and just the one morpheme with a property word (first example).

With an intensifier like *too* [Figure 72], Francis and Matthews say the intensification construction licenses gradable verbs but not non-gradable verbs—property concepts like *smart* (first example)—whereas you can't use it with a word like *walk* (second example).

Ok, so they describe that as non-gradable, but the problem is, if *walk* is not gradable, then why is the English translation semantically coherent and grammatically acceptable? So in English we can say "her sister walks too much". Well, we all understand that, we who are native speakers of English or have learned this expression in English, so in other words, there is a way to construe *walk* as gradable, and then use a gradable intensifier expression like "too

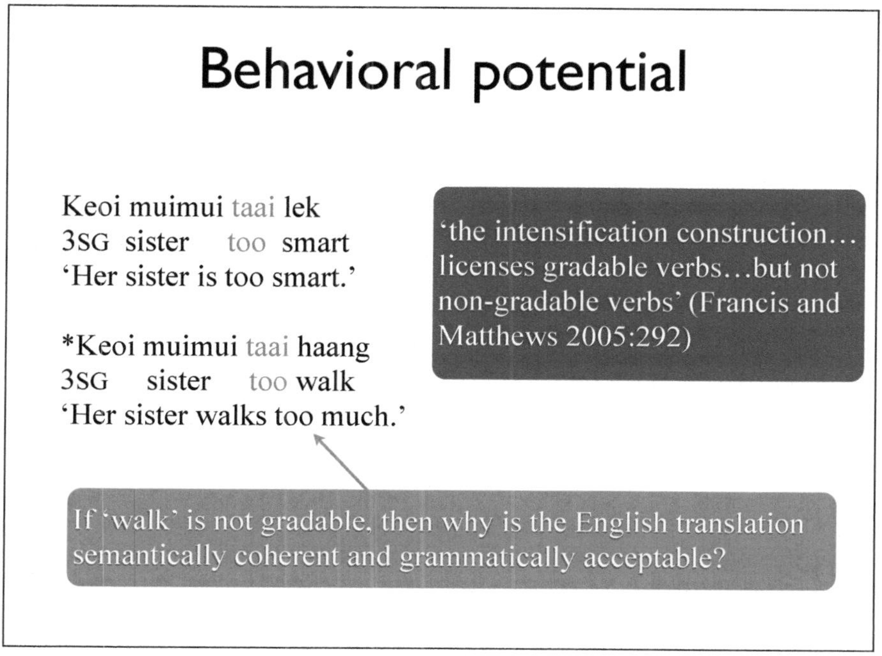

Behavioral potential

Keoi muimui taai lek
3SG sister   too smart
'Her sister is too smart.'

'the intensification construction…
licenses gradable verbs…but not
non-gradable verbs' (Francis and
Matthews 2005:292)

*Keoi muimui taai haang
3SG   sister   too walk
'Her sister walks too much.'

If 'walk' is not gradable, then why is the English translation
semantically coherent and grammatically acceptable?

FIGURE 72

much" to describe it. And just like in Cantonese, the intensifier expression for this kind of word in English has more morphemes than the one you would use for simple property words. You would say, you know, "her sister is too smart". So actually Cantonese and English are quite similar in this respect. It is just that in the Cantonese case, the expression here is unacceptable, whereas in the English case, you can use a expression with additional morphemes.

Another fact about Cantonese that is discussed by Francis and Matthews has to do with the perfective particle in Cantonese [Figure 73]. They point out that, if you use this perfective particle with property words, you get a construal as a process: "You seem to have put on weight" (in other words, "you seem to be becoming fat"). You don't get this change in meaning when it's used with action words, as in "he just left". So they say, "however, in our view, the fact that coercion [that is, a semantic shift process] is subject to language-specific constraints has no bearing on the syntactic category status of these predicates. Coercion applies to a semantically-defined subclass of verbs whose syntactic category is unaffected by the coercion operation."

Well, there are some problems with their reasoning. The first is that what they are calling a syntactic category has been defined by other constructions, not by the behavior with the aspect particle. So if you declare that construction to be irrelevant because you didn't use it to define the class in the first place,

Behavioral potential and construal (coercion)

Keoi aam-aam zau-ZO
3SG just-just leave-PF
'He just left.'

Lei houei fei-ZO gam
you seem fat-PF thus
'You seem to have put on weight.'

Use of the perfective -zo
with property words leads to
an inchoative (process)
construal, a change of
meaning not found when -zo
is used with action words

> However, in our view, the fact that coercion is subject to language-specific constraints has no bearing on the syntactic category status of these predicates. Coercion applies to a semantically-defined subclass of verbs whose syntactic category is unaffected by the coercion operation. (Francis and Matthews 2005:293, fn 12)

FIGURE 73

that's circular. That doesn't mean anything. Moreover, it doesn't explain an important fact here, which is: first, why aspect and intensification as inflectional categories are associated with prototypical verbs on one hand and prototypical adjectives on the other. And even more, it does not account for the fact that the direction of the semantic process of coercion, the semantic shift, conforms to the following language universal. I mentioned this in response to a question that someone asked me yesterday afternoon, so here is the actual presentation of the language universal:

> If there is a semantic shift in zero coding of an occurrence of a word ... in a part-of-speech construction, even if it is sporadic and irregular, it is always towards the semantic class prototypically associated with the propositional act function.
>
> CROFT 2001:73

So in other words, a property concept is stative; an action word is a process. Action words are prototypical for predication. So if you take a property word, you can use it in a predication construction, in this case with the aspect particle, then the meaning shift will always be towards the prototype, in this case from a state, the stative property, to the process of becoming that property. And

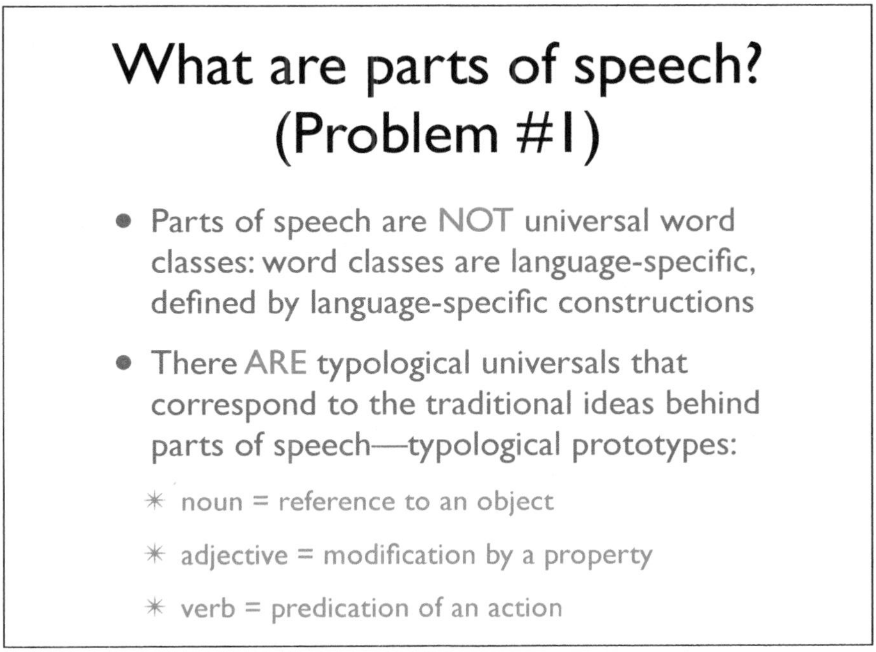

What are parts of speech? (Problem #1)

- Parts of speech are NOT universal word classes: word classes are language-specific, defined by language-specific constructions

- There ARE typological universals that correspond to the traditional ideas behind parts of speech—typological prototypes:

  * noun = reference to an object

  * adjective = modification by a property

  * verb = predication of an action

FIGURE 74

again, you find this across languages. If you can just take a word of a semantic type and stick it in a construction that, so to speak, has another semantic type as its prototype, the semantic shift would be always towards that prototype. So that kind of shows you that there's some psychological and conceptual cognitive reality to that prototype. It is affecting the way speakers behave when they use their language.

Ok, so now we can start to address the first question, that is, what are parts of speech [Figure 74]? As I said, parts of speech are not universal word classes. Word classes are language-specific, and they are defined by language-specific constructions. But there are typological universals that correspond to the traditional ideas behind parts of speech. These are typological prototypes: a prototypical noun is reference to an object, a prototypical adjective is modification by a property, and a prototypical verb is predication of an action. That's where the universals lie.

What are these universals? They are not universals about language-specific word classes. They are universals that determine or constrain how language expresses those combinations of propositional act and semantic class. They limit variation in structural coding and behavioral potential of these semantic classes of words. These typological prototypes are conceptual. This is a problem I've often encountered with people who are trying to understand what I

What are parts of speech? (Problem #1)

- The typological prototypes limit variation in *structural coding* and *behavioral potential* of semantic classes of words that occur in the propositional act constructions (reference, modification, predication)

- The typological prototypes are *conceptual*: semantic classes of words that occur in constructions with certain pragmatic functions

FIGURE 75

am saying with respect to parts of speech: they think that I'm saying that there is a word class prototype. And I'm not saying there is a word class prototype. I'm saying there is a functional prototype, a conceptual prototype about semantic classes of words and certain pragmatic constructions, for predication, modification and reference.

And as I said in the first bullet point, these prototypes do tell you something about how you express these combinations in actual linguistic constructions [Figure 75]. It doesn't force every language to be alike. It only limits the variation. But it still allows a lot of variation. And that is a theme that I'll be coming back to. It's a theme that Melissa Bowerman has been discussing in her own presentations, which is that a lot of variation is allowed grammatically. Exactly how you interpret the role of that variation in terms of speaker's cognition of the semantic categories that those grammatical constructions encode is an interesting question, which both Melissa Bowerman and I will be discussing in later lectures.

But the point is that a lot of variation is still allowed. There do appear to be some limits on that variation, certainly in the area of how do you predicate concepts, how do you refer to concepts, how do you use concepts to modify other concepts. And those constraints represent what is universal. And that's another very important point about the typological perspective on linguistic

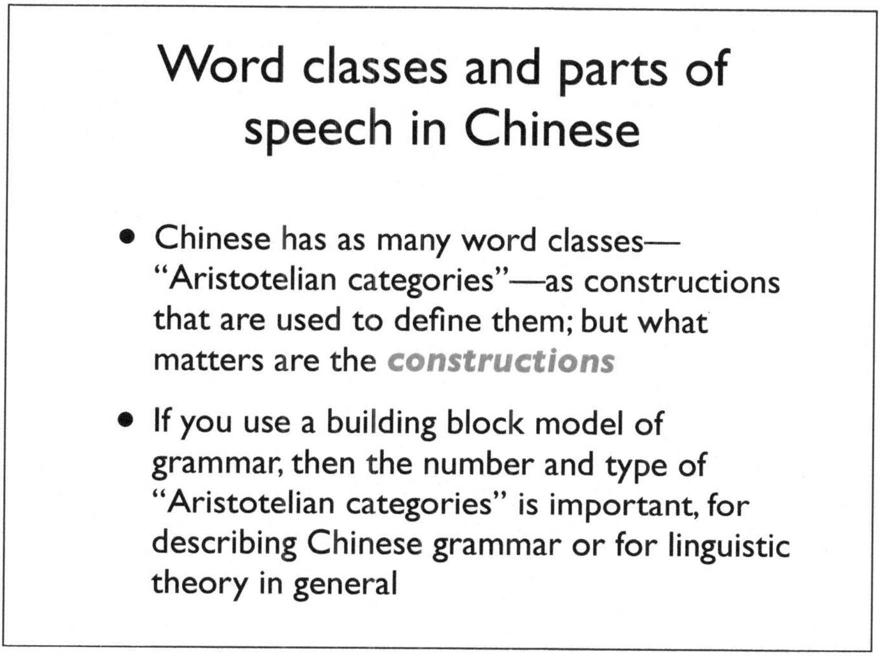

Word classes and parts of speech in Chinese

- Chinese has as many word classes— "Aristotelian categories"—as constructions that are used to define them; but what matters are the *constructions*

- If you use a building block model of grammar, then the number and type of "Aristotelian categories" is important, for describing Chinese grammar or for linguistic theory in general

FIGURE 76

analysis. It's that I talk about language universals, but almost never do I mean something that every language has, or something that every language doesn't have. Almost always when a typologist talks about language universals, they talk about some kind of limits on variation, on either what's possible or what's probable or likely to find in a language. This is a very difficult concept again for people who are not typologists to conceive, is that you can talk about universals that are not of the form "all languages are alike". That's the fundamental insight behind Greenberg's seminal work on universals back in the 1960s. And sometimes I think it is a concept that still is not understood by many people in linguistics.

So what do we say about word classes in Chinese, or any other language for that matter [Figure 76]? Well, basically, if you want to talk about word classes in Chinese, in some sense as far as I'm concerned, you can do whatever you want. Some people call them "Aristotelian categories", categories that have sharp boundaries: either a word is or isn't in the category. Chinese has as many word classes as constructions that are used to define them; but what matters are the constructions. So if you want to say, Mandarin has Mandarin Verbs, what is most important is to tell the reader—your fellow linguists, your students—what constructions of Mandarin you are using to define the word class. Learners of Chinese, also the same thing. What matters are those

Word classes and parts of speech in Chinese

- **But it is** insufficient and even unnecessary **for describing the representation of grammatical knowledge, or for linguistic theory in general**

A model of what a speaker actually knows about the grammar of her language has to specify which syntactic properties each formative [word or morpheme] has, that is, which constructions each formative occurs in (or not)...Once you have that, you don't need Aristotelian categories. Any Aristotelian categories you posit, either on the basis of the usual constructions invoked or on the basis of any other construction you choose, are merely epiphenomenal. (Croft 2007:420)

FIGURE 77

constructions. So you are basically either describing how Chinese speakers use them or teaching people learning Chinese when do you use these constructions, which words can you use in those constructions. Those are the facts about the language that you want to know if you are learning the language, and which you'd want to describe if you're describing people who are native speakers.

But the real problem, I think, is always this building block model of grammar, because if you take a building block model of grammar, so that you define the predication construction in Chinese as subject plus verb, plus something else, complements, then it's very important that you have a way of talking about verbs. That's why it's important. As I said, I'm trying to figure out, trying to understand why these linguists have a hard time accepting the concepts that I'm advocating here, even though when you look at the empirical facts of language, they all point in the same direction: you can't talk about large word classes. But if you are committed to the building block model, you kind of have to. And as I said before, what we really should do is abandon the building block model.

Why? Why should we abandon the building block model? Because the building block model is insufficient and it's even unnecessary for describing the representation of grammatical knowledge, or for linguistic theory in general [Figure 77]. So here is another quotation, from the paper where I criticized Aarts. It says:

> A model of what a speaker actually knows about the grammar of her language has to specify which syntactic properties each formative [that is, each word or morpheme] has, that is, which constructions each formative occurs in (or not) ... Once you have that, you don't need Aristotelian categories [i.e. you don't need word classes]. Any Aristotelian categories you posit, either on the basis of the usual constructions invoked or on the basis of any other construction you choose, are merely epiphenomenal.
>
> CROFT 2007:420

Again, think about it in the sense of somebody who wants to learn Chinese. So say I want to learn Chinese, it's not going to help me for you to tell me that Chinese has verbs and no adjectives. It wouldn't even help me if you told me that Chinese has adjectives and verbs. What would help me is if you told me Chinese has different kinds of constructions to express comparison, intensification, modification, predication, what kinds of words occur in those constructions; and what happens to those words when you combine them, say, with aspect particles, what kind of change in meaning happens when you do that. If you do that, then I will have learned at least that part of grammar in Chinese, and be able to speak it. But you have not said anything to me about word classes. You don't need to.

Mandarin and Cantonese conform to the universals for typological prototypes of parts of speech as much as any other language. I hope I have given you some examples of that here. If you are able to come to the lectures that are being held on Tuesday and Wednesday, on Tuesday I will give you some diagrams that I hope will make it even clearer that Mandarin, Cantonese, English, other languages conform to these universals [Lecture 7].

In other words, if you think again about speakers and cognition: Mandarin and Cantonese speakers have the same functional prototypes as speakers of other languages. So this cognitive combination of predications of actions, referring to objects, modification of properties, seems to be something that's a typological universal that's true of and underlies the grammars of all languages (to the extent that they really are correct generalizations). And so that says something about human cognition in terms of packaging information in discourse, even if it is the case that the range of use of particular language-specific constructions varies from those in other languages, and varies within Chinese itself. And that's all I have to say for this morning. Thank you very much.

The Internal Structure of Constructions

Thank you very much. I want to say a couple of words before I start here. As all of you who have attended my lectures have seen, I'm mainly talking about syntactic structure. And as I said on the first day, the theme of these first five lectures is that syntax is simpler than you think. So I've spent a lot of time talking about syntax.

I'll talk a little bit about semantics in the second half of my lectures. But I do want to say that I think that this is actually something that is fairly important for cognitive linguists to pay attention to. I mean I hope you all will be happy to hear that syntax is simpler. But, as a cognitive linguist, one must be able to defend that position to other syntacticians who use theories that are much more complicated. And you need to find arguments to justify why that's the case, why syntax should be simpler.

Now it's my belief that the strongest arguments in support of this simpler view of syntax comes from cross-linguistic diversity, from the structural diversity of languages around the world. That's really the single strongest argument, I think, to show that we can't try to develop a theory of syntax that's very complicated, because as soon as we make it complicated, then we keep coming across languages in the world where the theoretical machinery doesn't work. That's why I think we need to look at a simpler approach that can accommodate linguistic variation. So what I'm going to talk about today is similar in that respect, in that we are going to look at particular aspects of constructions and say that we don't need something that most linguists usually assume.

So here is a diagram [Figure 78] that I had on the first day of the lectures [Lecture 1]. This is the internal structure of a construction. This is what we called the "exploded diagram". There are actually similar diagrams in Langacker's 1987 classic book. So this here is actually a part of the construction, an intransitive verb construction. And all these lines here indicate relations that a construction grammarian has to assume. So any particular element or a part of a construction has a role in that larger construction. There are also syntactic

 All original audio-recordings and other supplementary material, such as any hand-outs and powerpoint presentations for the lecture series, have been made available online and are referenced via unique DOI numbers on the website www.figshare.com. They may be accessed via a QR code for the print version of this book. In the e-book, both the QR code and dynamic links are available, and can be accessed by a mouse-click.

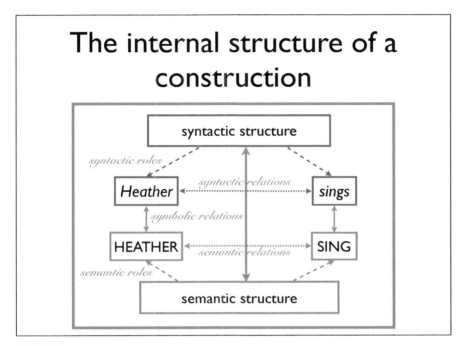

The internal structure of a construction

FIGURE 78

relations here, or at least there are proposed to be syntactic relations here, that hold between two different elements of a construction. Then of course on the semantic side, you have a semantic structure with the construction, so there are semantic roles in that semantic structure. And there are semantic relations between the components of your semantic representation. And lastly but also very important is that you have symbolic relations. So you still have the construction as a whole and its meaning as a whole and that's a symbolic link. But then you have the individual elements in the construction and they often symbolize some particular semantic component in the semantic structure. So you have a fairly complex structure here even when you are just looking at an example that has only two words, "Heather sings".

Now we are going to look at this more closely [Figure 79]. As a reminder for those of you who saw this on the first day [Lecture 1], about this terminology of "roles" and "relations": in our example of "Heather sings", the role is a part-whole relation, where a syntactic relation is a relation between parts. I'll say a little bit more; this is again reviewing what I talked about on the first day in the morning.

There are two kinds of syntactic relations we can talk about. One I'm going to call "coded dependencies" [Figure 80]. This is where the syntactic relation

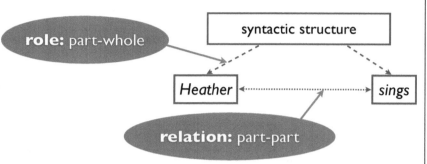

FIGURE 79

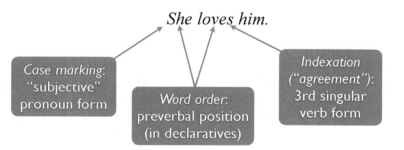

FIGURE 80

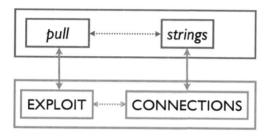

More on syntactic relations

- Two types of "syntactic relations":

- **_collocational dependencies_**: a conventionally specified relationship between two (substantive) linguistic elements

FIGURE 81

is explicitly coded by some grammatical device, like case marking, indexation, word order and so on. So we had this example from the first day, "She loves him"; I used this information as one way of talking about syntactic relations.

The second type of syntactic relation, which is illustrated by these idiomatically combining expressions like "pull strings" that I also talked about on the first day of lecture: these are called "collocational dependencies" [Figure 81]. There's a conventionally specified relationship between two specific or substantive linguistic elements. So as Nunberg, Sag, and Wasow argued, the combination of "pull strings" has the meaning of exploit personal connections, but only when *pull* is combined with *strings*. *Pull* only means "exploit" in that context, and *strings* only means "connections" in that context. So you have a relationship between *pull* and *strings*, and this is true as long as you have a certain relationship between these two words, and it does not necessarily have to involve a particular syntactic structure.

The first point I want to make—I'm not going to talk about this in detail, because this paper by Nunberg, Sag and Wasow actually discussed this in great detail—this is the statement that actually this relationship between *pull* and *strings*, this collocational relationship, is ultimately semantic [Figure 82]. So *pull* has a role in the construction. That's what this "Pred" stands for, for "predicate". *Strings* has a role in this construction. Their meanings occur only when

Collocational dependencies are semantic

- 'By convention...*strings* [in *pull strings*] can be used metaphorically to refer to personal connection when it is the object of *pull*, and *pull* can be used metaphorically to refer to exploitation or exertion when its object is *strings*' (Nunberg et al. 1994:496)

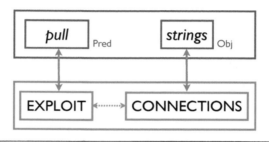

FIGURE 82

these two things occur in the same construction and in the relevant roles. Then it has the meaning of "exploiting connections". There is a semantic relationship here of course [between EXPLOIT and CONNECTIONS], because this is the whole meaning that has to be conveyed. But you'll notice there is now no dotted line here between *pull* and *strings*; that's to indicate that there is no syntactic relationship here. We have only the roles: *pull* is in the predicate role, and *strings* is in the direct object role. This is an important point because if we accept Nunberg, Sag, and Wasow's argument, what we are saying is that collocational dependencies, where they exist in a language, don't tell us about syntactic relations. They tell us about semantic relations: a semantic relationship that holds only when you have those two words in the right combination.

So does construction grammar need syntactic relations [Figure 83]? You saw that thing disappear. If we don't have syntactic relations, and that's what I am going to argue this afternoon, then the syntactic structure of a construction or the structure of the construction as a whole looks like this diagram. You see everything else is there: syntactic roles, the whole semantic structure, is the same as before. And you've got these symbolic links, and those will turn out to be very important. But you don't have any direct relationship between *Heather* and *sings*.

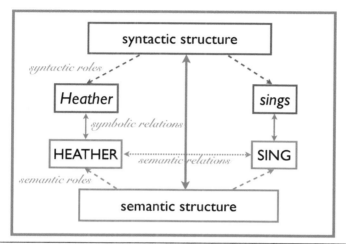

Does construction grammar need syntactic relations?

FIGURE 83

So what kind of arguments could we present to say that we don't really need syntactic relations in our syntactic structures of constructions? The first argument I'm going to give is a logical one, which is to think about the role of syntax in what language is used for, namely communicating meanings. Now in this particular case, how do you understand an utterance? Step one is: the hearer has to recognize the utterance as an instance of a particular construction [Figure 84]. So if you are a believer in construction grammar, then part of the knowledge of the language of English is that there are intransitive constructions. And then there are the various linguistic properties of "Heather sings" and the functional context.

Hopefully the hearer will recognize that it is an instance of the intransitive construction. Once the hearer has done that, then it's part of their knowledge of the language. So they can pull up the semantic structure of the intransitive construction [Figure 85] and the semantic structure includes not just some sort of overall general meaning but also the semantic components of that complex meaning. And at this point we just have the symbolic relation between the construction as a whole and its meaning as a whole.

Well, once the hearer identifies the construction, at least the syntactic structure, you can also identify the syntactic roles [Figure 86]. So once you know

1. The hearer recognizes the utterance "Heather sings" as an instance of a particular construction (the intransitive declarative construction)

> syntactic structure

INTRANSITIVE

FIGURE 84

2. The hearer accesses the semantic structure of the construction in her memory, via the symbolic link of the construction as a whole

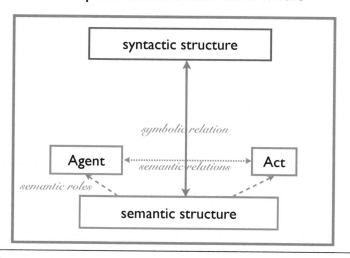

FIGURE 85

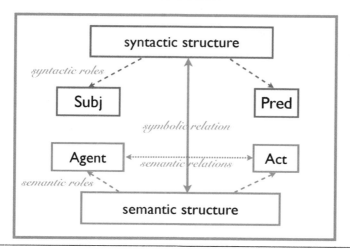

FIGURE 86

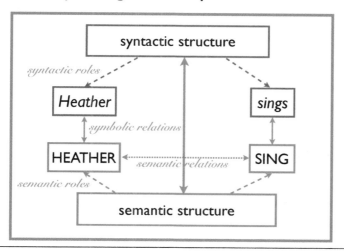

FIGURE 87

that you've got an intransitive construction, then you know that construction consists of a subject and an intransitive predicate.

Then the hearer can utilize the symbolic relation that identifies which syntactic role symbolizes what, which semantic component. So you have *Heather* and *sings*. And so then you can identify that the subject of this construction is *Heather*; the predicate of the construction is *sings* [Figure 87]. And the speaker therefore understood the utterance. They got the semantic structure and they managed to fill in the right fillers of the roles in the semantic structure.

Now the sequence I just gave you is not necessarily exactly how they've done it. Much language processing, like other cognitive processing, is not sequential. So in fact, it doesn't really matter what the order is. What does matter is that we can accomplish the whole process without having to have any kind of syntactic relations. So that in itself is an interesting point. It's that you don't have to have syntactic relations in order to use syntactic structure in how people understand utterances.

But the question is: do we have any stronger reasons to say, not only we don't have to have it, but actually it's not a good idea to propose syntactic relations? Well, the argument I just gave you depends on construction grammar. It is not going to work for other kinds of syntactic models. So this kind of analysis I've just given you is possible only with constructions which can be recognized holistically, so that there's some way in which you can recognize an intransitive construction as a whole. That means you can't do this in a building block model, because the building block model doesn't have constructions as wholes.

It's also possible only with constructional semantics, because the semantic structure gives you the semantic relations that hold together the syntactic elements of the construction. And, of course, constructional semantics means this is not a componential model of grammar. Componential models: this argument would not work for them either. And finally, it's possible only with the symbolic relations that hold between syntactic elements and semantic components of the construction. That's how we know that *Heather* is the subject, and *sings* is the predicate. And again, you only have symbolic relations between form and meaning in a constructional model, not in a componential model. So the kind of argument I just gave you about being able to comprehend utterances without syntactic relations presupposes that you are looking at construction grammar. That argument will not work if you are using the building block model or the componential model.

Now can this be done any other way? In the time when I was presenting my ideas and lectures before I published *Radical Construction Grammar*, of course I got a number of questions from various linguists saying, when I made this particular proposal, can this be done any other way? Can we have a model that

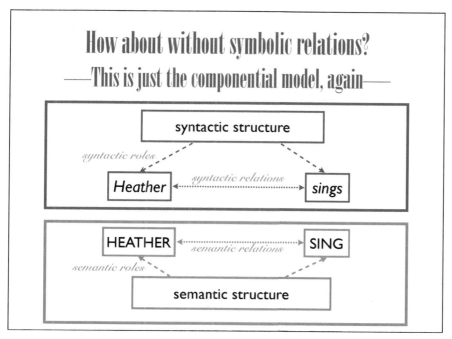

How about without symbolic relations?
——This is just the componential model, again——

syntactic structure

syntactic roles

Heather ◄·········· *syntactic relations* ··········► sings

HEATHER ◄·········· *semantic relations* ··········► SING

semantic roles

semantic structure

FIGURE 88

works, where instead of removing syntactic relations, we remove something else instead from that constructional model?

So how about if we try doing it without symbolic relations, so without the green symbolic links that pair together form and meaning in a construction [Figure 88]? Well, that's really just the componential model again. So we keep these components separate, syntactic structure and semantic structure. Can we do this with the componential model? What does it mean to say "do it with the componential model and not use symbolic relations"? Well, the componential model still requires linking rules or realization/interface rules to align linguistic form with meaning. But this cannot be done one construction at a time. You have to have general linking rules to link general syntactic structures with particular semantic interpretations. And most theories of componential grammar that have linking rules have some kind of principles that are basically iconic, that tell you that there's some kind of straightforward one-to-one mapping between syntactic elements, syntactic structure and the semantics. If you have non-iconic mapping, then you are almost certainly going to have to have construction-specific linking rules. And if you've done that, then you have to accept the existence of constructions and then we are back to construction grammar, which is where we started from.

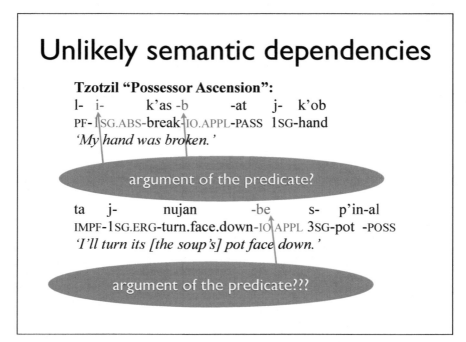

FIGURE 89

So the next few examples, which are a subset of the examples that I have in *Radical Construction Grammar*, are examples where it doesn't seem so obvious to have an iconic mapping, some kind of general mapping principle. So if you look at the first example, this is a construction that is traditionally called "Possessor Ascension" [Figure 89]. The translation is "My hand is broken". Semantically, the hand is my body part, so I am the possessor of the hand. If you look at the original language, though, you will see in Tzotzil that first person singular *i-* is actually the [passive] subject of "break", or the absolutive argument. It's an argument of the verb. It's not the possessor of the noun. Actually it's also a possessor of the noun (that's the *j-*) but in particular it's an argument of the verb. And then there's a particular suffix on the verb (-*b*) that essentially tells you that this argument of the verb is actually a possessor.

Ok, so the question you can ask yourself is, alright, we have a different way of expressing the relationship between form and meaning in Tzotzil than we have in the English translation. What does that mean? It's an argument of the predicate in a syntactic sense, grammatically. It isn't an argument to the predicate in a semantic sense. Well, some linguists have said, yes, if my hand is broken, then I, the body of the person whose hand it is, is also affected by the

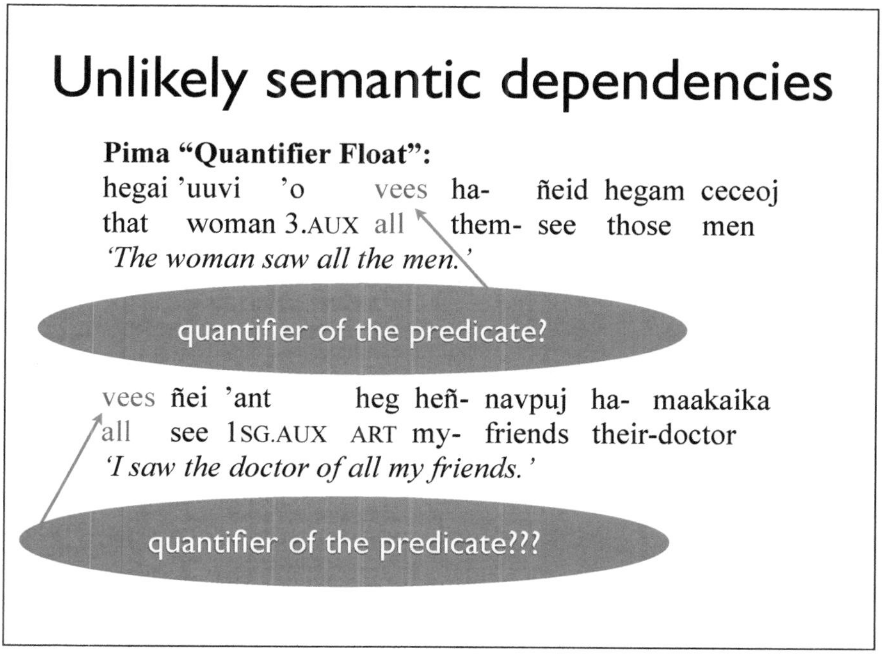

Unlikely semantic dependencies

Pima "Quantifier Float":

hegai	'uuvi	'o	vees	ha-	ñeid	hegam	ceceoj
that	woman	3.AUX	all	them-	see	those	men

'The woman saw all the men.'

quantifier of the predicate?

vees	ñei	'ant	heg	heñ-	navpuj	ha-	maakaika
all	see	1SG.AUX	ART	my-	friends	their-doctor

'I saw the doctor of all my friends.'

quantifier of the predicate???

FIGURE 90

action. So they have some notion of this representing the affectedness of the person whose hand is broken.

Well, that works fine in that first example, but then when we look at the second example, "I'll turn its [the soup's] pot face down", you are taking a pot that used to have soup in it, so the possessor is the soup, it is the soup that was in the pot, you are turning it face down. So is this really an argument of the predicate? The soup is not even there any more. So turning the pot face down doesn't really affect the soup, because the soup is already eaten. So it is implausible to say in this case that it's actually got a direct semantic relationship. And I would say that we shouldn't necessarily try to come up with some kind of semantic argument. It is not going to work very well.

And another example is a phenomenon in another Native American language [Figure 90]. This again has a traditional name based on transformational grammar, "quantifier float". So in this first example, "The woman saw all the men", *all* is not modifying "the men". It is actually an adverb, so to speak, in the clause as a whole. Now sometimes, you could say that's plausible here. It does kind of quantify the predicate, because if you see all the men, it's like a collective action of active perception. When you look at the second example

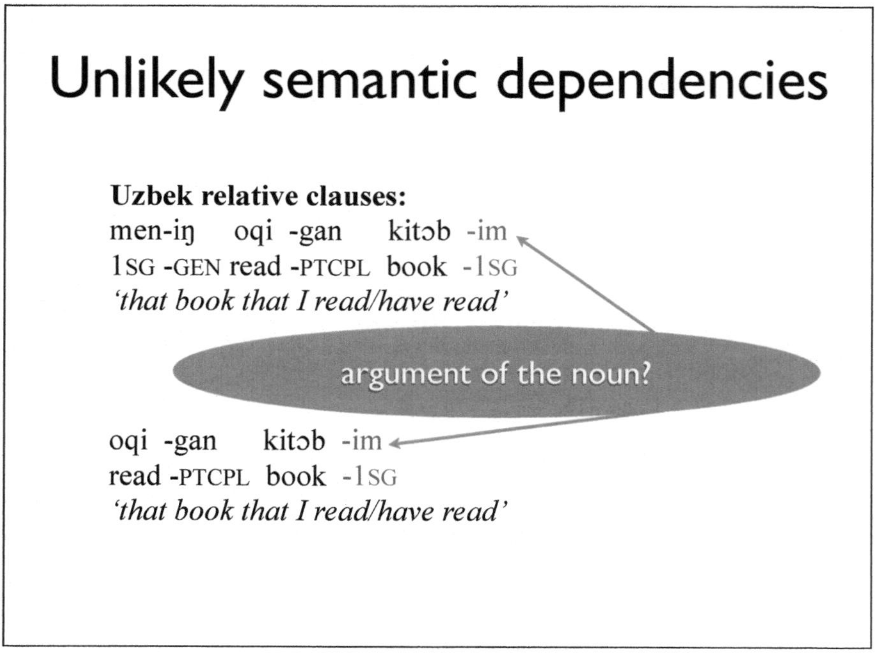

Unlikely semantic dependencies

Uzbek relative clauses:
men-iŋ   oqi -gan   kitɔb -im
1SG -GEN read -PTCPL book -1SG
'that book that I read/have read'

argument of the noun?

oqi -gan   kitɔb -im
read -PTCPL book -1SG
'that book that I read/have read'

FIGURE 91

though, "I saw the doctor of all my friends", in this language, you can use *all* as a modifier of the predicate *see*. But, clearly, you are not seeing all your friends; you are just seeing the doctor. So it doesn't really have the same interpretation. It's much less plausible to describe this as a modifier of a predicate.

Another example, Uzbek relative clauses, "that book that I read" or "that book that I've read" [Figure 91]. "I", this subject of the reading, functions as the possessor of the book; "the book" is the head noun; *reading* modifies *book*. Here's an example where you don't even have the expression of the person as an argument of *read*. So again, there's no sense in which this is an argument of the noun. I do not possess the book, it's just simply a book that I've read.

So, a general analysis, that has a mapping of syntactic arguments and a predicate onto a semantic predicate and its semantic arguments, is not going to work in these cases. But in a constructional account, it's pretty straightforward [Figure 92]. You have to represent the construction as a whole, so that would include the possessive construction as well. And then, you have a semantic representation which includes the arguments of the action, the participants in this action—"turning the pot down". And then you can have a possessor; that little dotted line is supposed to represent that the possessor is the possessor of the patient or the second argument of the semantic predicate. And then

Unlikely semantic dependencies

Tzotzil "Possessor Ascension":
ta   j-   nujan   -be   s-   p'in-al
IMPF-1SG-turn.face.down-APPL 3SG-pot -POSS
'I'll turn its [the soup's] pot face down.'

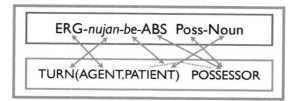

FIGURE 92

you have all these symbolic links that tell you who did what to whom and who possesses what. And that's all very straightforward in a constructional model because you have the possibility of including these symbolic links between elements. And you also have the possibility of representing the syntactic structure as an entirety: a single whole construction.

There are more examples that show you the same thing, where it is implausible to consider the subject as the argument of the predicate. And if you go to a language like Moose Cree, you will see that you have something where *Mary* is the subject of the predicate *hard* [Figure 93]. But you can't even translate it into English very easily. It looks like "Mary is hard to you make me believe (she) is sick." And again, *Mary* is obviously the person who is sick, but in this particular construction, you can't construe it really as being an argument of the predicate *hard*. So it is more implausible in that case. You get this clause collapsing thing.

In Quechua, another native American language in South America, you can say something like "I want to make a house in Huaraz" [Figure 94]. And what you see is you have "want" and then you have "making a house" as a complement of "want" just like in English. But "in Huaraz" is actually in the main clause. Now the argument that was made in the paper which presented these

Proposition vs. Subject-Predicate

English "Tough Movement":
Tina is hard to find.

Subject is argument of the predicate? Copula??

Moose Cree "Tough Movement":
ālimēlihtākosiw mēri [kihči-totawiyan   [kihči-tāpwēhtamān
she.is.hard   Mary [SUB-you.make.me [SUB-I.believe
[ē-   āhkosit]]]
SUB-she.is.sick
[lit.] 'Mary is hard to you make me believe (she) is sick.'

Subject is argument of the predicate???

FIGURE 93

Clause Collapsing

Ancash Quechua:
noqa Huaraz-chaw muna-a [wayi -ta   rura -y -ta]
I   Huaraz-in   want -1 house-ACC make-INF-ACC
'I want to make a house in Huaraz.'

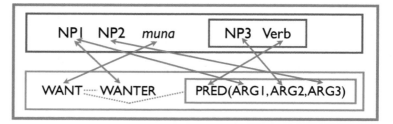

- This constructional analysis, like many others here,
  violates locality as this is traditionally understood

FIGURE 94

data is that you have a phenomenon which has been called "clause collapsing". You have a main clause and a subordinate clause, but you're starting to see these two kind of squished together and mixed together. And so what happens is, an argument of the subordinate clause verb "making a house" is now presented up here in this clause. Again, you can treat this all as a construction. As long as you can represent the whole thing as a construction in this form, and represent the symbolic links between the elements and the components, then you can get it all to work out fine.

Now all of these examples I've given you, I actually found them mostly in the generative syntactic literature, because they violate a principle which they call "locality", because they all involve some kind of dependency relation between something in a subordinate clause, or in a subordinate phrase and a higher clause or a phrase. But if you have a constructional model, you can include structures that are both at the main clause level and include properties, elements of the subordinate phrase, and then construct the symbolic mappings. And there is no problem with doing that.

So I should say I brought up these examples of non-iconic mappings. Now a lot of cognitive linguists think, well, we ought to make syntax as iconic as possible. But actually I'm suggesting here that may not be the right way to go. There are some messy relationships between form and meaning that you find in different languages. And again, it's where looking at the diversity of languages helps because you may not see this in English or Chinese, or some other better known languages. But I don't want to deny that syntactic structures are iconically motivated most of the time. The trouble is that they are not iconically motivated often enough to basically assume that constructions do not exist. So in some particular cases at least, construction-specific form-meaning mappings are required. But this defeats the purpose of the componential model. That's why these kinds of examples have been brought up in the generative syntactic literature: because they are problems they need to address, because generative syntax is a componential model. Such a model aims to avoid such mappings by using general linking principles which must be iconic in some sense—some kind of straightforward mapping.

So in other words, the componential model, if you start trying to apply it seriously to examples in lots of different languages, you are going to find that in fact, it's very hard to actually make it work without resorting to construction-specific mappings between form and meaning. And as soon as you've done that, it's kind of like you "let the cat out of the bag". If you are going to allow that, then you may as well go to a constructional model for all the reasons that I presented in the first lecture where many different linguists from Wierzbicka to Ellen Prince to Ray Jackendoff even, as well as Lakoff, Langacker, Fillmore, have argued that you need to use some kind of construction specific mappings

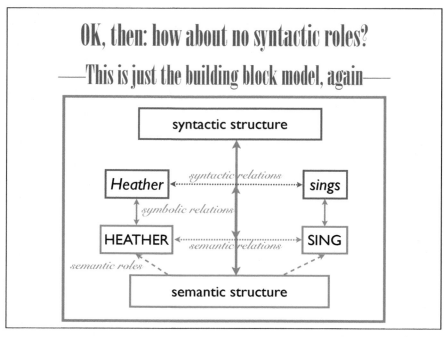

FIGURE 95

between form and meaning. That's really what I think is the important conclusion that draw from that. So that suggests that the componential model as such isn't going to succeed as a way of dealing with the empirical problems we find looking at languages in a way that the constructional model could deal with them, and in particular a constructional model without syntactic relations.

Well, there is another alternative [Figure 95]. We can try to get rid of syntactic roles, so, in other words, the relationship between particular constructional elements and the whole. What does that looks like? Well it's basically just the building block model again; we don't have constructions as a whole. In a building block model, constructions are defined simply in terms of their parts and how those parts are put together. So the parts are *Heather* and *sings*, and how the parts are put together is a syntactic relation. So this proposal is to say, ok, so I wanted to get rid of syntactic relations. Well, that's all fine and nice, but is that anything special? Couldn't we just get rid of syntactic roles instead? But notice that if we do that, now what we have to do is to have a mapping between syntactic relations and semantic relations. So we have the same problem like iconicity. All the examples I gave in the first part of this lecture are still a problem as well.

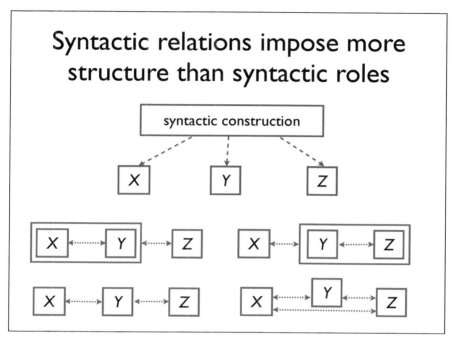

FIGURE 96

So can we do without syntactic roles? As I said, it's essentially the building block model. If we do without syntactic roles, then we must have a symbolic link between syntactic relations and semantic relations. This will also require strong iconicity which we've already seen doesn't work. But there are actually other problems with using just syntactic relations. Now I have to remind you that at the beginning of this lecture, I said there are certain kinds of relationships between linguistic elements that aren't syntactic: these collocational relations, they are ultimately semantic. Remember, we are talking about syntactic structures. So we can't cheat and use semantic relations. Just like when we looked at parts of speech in Cantonese, we can't cheat and say, well, just because Cantonese has property words, then it must have also adjectives.

Now, if you look at the representation of a syntactic structure that has three elements [Figure 96]: if you just have roles and no relations, it is pretty straightforward. You have the first element, the second element and the third element. They all play roles in the construction as a whole. If you don't have constructions, if you just have a building block model, then you have to make some choices about how you put these three elements together. Do you put X and Y together, and then add Z to it? Do you put Y and Z together, and add X to it? Or do you put X and Z together, and then add Y to it? Or do you just have X and

Fixed order of elements

Kilivila:

eseki	luleta	yena	guyau
he.give	his.sister	fish	chief
Verb	*NP1*	*NP2*	*NP3*

'The chief gave his sister the fish.'

- Fixed order gives no evidence of constituency

- Invoking semantic relations is "cheating"

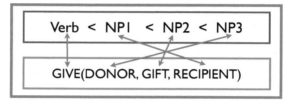

FIGURE 97

then Y and then Z? So you can't really decide, you have to have some independent reason to say we have these different kinds of syntactic structures.

As I said, my whole point is, syntax is simpler than you think. We should not
have to have this extra structure. And if you have a language—Kilivila is an
Oceanic language [Figure 97]—with a ditransitive verb like *give*, you simply
put the noun phrases in a particular order and that order tells you who gave
what to whom. So, "the chief gave his sister the fish", you can see that there.
Well, again, you don't really want to know what structure is there. There's fixed
order, so there's no idea that these two [NP1 and NP2] go together or these two
[NP2 and NP3] go together. They are just all three in a row. As I said, invoking semantic relations is cheating. So you can't say that, because the *chief* is
the agent, then it's a separate constituent from the other two. But in a constructional model, that's not a problem: because you have the construction as
a whole, remember, you have roles in a construction; so it doesn't matter how
you represent those roles. And then you just have symbolic links telling you
who gave what to whom.

Another problem you find with syntactic relations is: what if the syntactic
relation interrupts another syntactic, or supposedly syntactic, relation? So in
Macedonian and some other languages, you have a clitic for the definite article:
"the four hundred people" [Figure 98]. But it has to occur in second position,

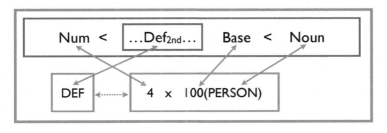

Second position

Macedonian:
četiri =te   stotini   lug'e
four   =the hundred people
'the four hundred people'

● Second position article breaks up constituents

Num < ...Def$_{2nd}$...   Base < Noun

DEF ◁┈┈┈▷ 4 × 100(PERSON)

FIGURE 98

and it can even interrupt the phrase "four hundred". Semantically, "four hundred" is a unit; it tells you the quantity. So it breaks up the constituents, and therefore it's a problem for syntactic relations. But again, it's not a problem for a constructional model, because you can just simply specify: this thing occurs in second position, this construction is inserted in second position. And then you have the mappings of all the individual elements.

Another kind of problem you get is what I called "nested relational coded dependencies" [Figure 99]. In a language like Russian, if you want to express the relationship between *hope* and *victory*, you have to use two elements, you have to use a case suffix on *victory* and you have to use a preposition *for*. You put the two together, and that tells you that victory is what you are hoping for. So a question that comes up is whether this preposition *na* codes the syntactic relation or is it an element itself which then has to be related to other elements. Is it functioning in some kind of signaling fashion as coding the relation or is it itself an element? And then we have to ask whether it holds another relation. The tendency or the trend in recent generative syntactic models is to treat both these elements, the *for* and the accusative marking, as separate elements that then have to be placed into a syntactic relation of the sort that you see with the simple tree here.

Nested relational coded dependencies

Russian:

nadejat'sja na   pobed -u
hope   for victory -ACC
'hope for victory'

- Does *na* code relation or is it an element? *-u?*

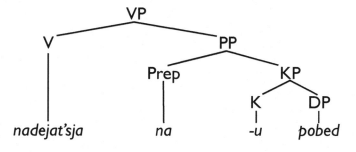

FIGURE 99

Nested relational coded dependencies

Russian:

nadejat'sja na   pobed -u
hope   for victory -ACC
'hope for victory'

- Does *na* code relation or is it an element? *-u?*

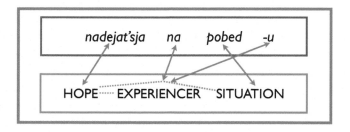

FIGURE 100

Absence of one unit in a relation

Spanish:

prefier -o es -a modern -a
prefer -1SG that -FSG modern -FSG
'(I) prefer the modern (house)'

- The "agreement" syntactic relation cannot relate to any syntactic element (the controller is absent)

- One can't assume that "agreement" is really the element being related; its occurrence varies, and it may even be completely absent

---

FIGURE 101

Another way to look at it though, from a constructional point of view, is that you don't really have to worry about answering that question [Figure 100]. You can simply look at it in terms of: here is *hope*, and here is the experiencer of the hope, which is not expressed in the example here, and then the situation that you hope for. And this *na* and *-u* together jointly express the fact that the situation, this expression *pobed* actually expresses the hope that you are hoping for.

But the real problem with syntactic relations is that if it is a syntactic relation, it has to be a relation between two syntactic elements. But a lot of the time, one of those syntactic elements isn't even there. In this sentence of Spanish, you have, "I prefer the modern (house)" [Figure 101]. So, "I" is expressed (supposedly) by the suffix. The suffix is supposed to indicate a syntactic relation between the predicate and a subject. But there is no subject. Likewise, this feminine singular suffix on "that" and "modern" is supposed to indicate a syntactic relation between these two modifiers and the head noun, but the head noun is not there either. So they can't really be expressing a syntactic relation.

Some people suggest that in certain languages, this is the syntactic element. This [the suffix *-o*] actually indicates the head noun, and this actually indicates the subject in a grammatical sense. The problem is when you look across languages, you see a lot of variation in when you get this "agreement marker" and

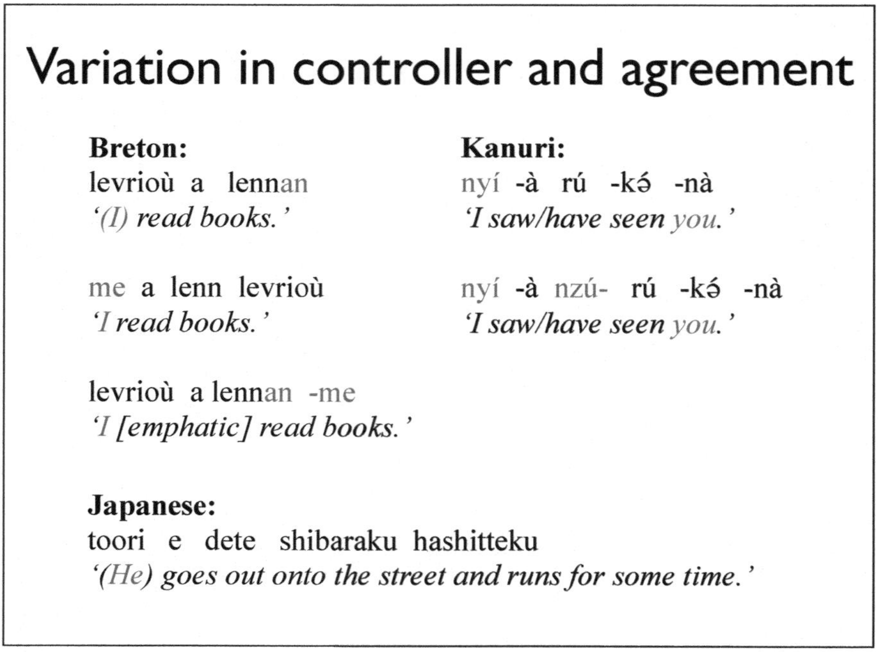

Variation in controller and agreement

Breton:
levrioù a lennan
'(I) read books.'

me a lenn levrioù
'I read books.'

levrioù a lennan -me
'I [emphatic] read books.'

Kanuri:
nyí -à rú -kə́ -nà
'I saw/have seen you.'

nyí -à nzú- rú -kə́ -nà
'I saw/have seen you.'

Japanese:
toori e dete shibaraku hashitteku
'(He) goes out onto the street and runs for some time.'

FIGURE 102

when you don't. So in Breton, a Celtic language, you have a suffix here (*-an*) which looks like the typical inflection of "I read books" [Figure 102]. So there is no phrase "I". Then if you actually do have the phrase "I" (*me*), then you do not have the suffix. So some people have suggested that in Breton this thing (*-an*) is really like an independent subject phrase, even though it's a suffix to the verb. But then there are other constructions in the same language where you have the independent word and you have the inflection on the verb. So in this language, sometimes *-an* looks like an independent inflection, and sometimes it looks like it's just an agreement marker indicating a relationship between one word and another. And in an African language, Kanuri, for the object pronoun, there is a pronoun here (*nyí*), but you don't have any marking on the verb. But that is actually optional. You can actually have a marking on the verb (*nzú-*) as well as the independent pronoun for "you". So again, you can't say that this thing is or is not representing some kind of syntactic relationship. In a language like Japanese, there is simply nothing there. And of course, Mandarin is similar. You don't have to have the subject or the object, but there is nothing on the verb that indicates who the subject or the object is. That has to be determined from the extralinguistic context.

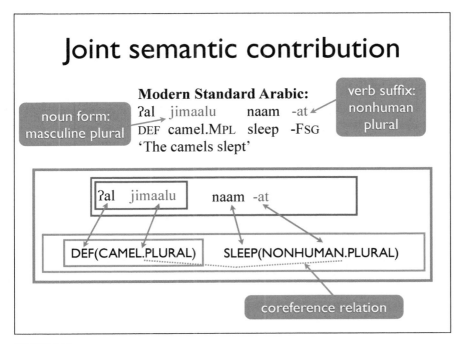

FIGURE 103

Now, one of the problems of analyzing these things is that there is this assumption in syntactic analysis—and this has nothing to do in particular with generative grammar or any other particular theory; it goes back to traditional Western analyses of grammar—that if you have a morpheme in the sentence, then it has to be either just an agreement marker signaling some kind of syntactic relation or it has to be a syntactic element in its own right, a pronoun, that actually stands for the person who is the subject, or object, or possessor, or whatever. But the real problem here is: there's a theoretical assumption that there is one and only one referring expression in a clause, and that one, whether it's the pronoun or the suffix, is the real participant, and then any other morpheme in the clause has to be agreement. So this is another one of these hidden assumptions about syntactic analysis which gets in the way, and I think we should just discard it. In fact, most typologists do that at least implicitly, because the term that is widely used by people who do crosslinguistic analysis is "indexation", because the term "agreement", the definition of that term is that it must agree with something. Well, what if that something is not there, it can't be agreeing. So the term indexing means it is actually indexing or pointing out the referent.

It gets worse than that. In some languages, such as Modern Standard Arabic, you have a combination [Figure 103]. So here, with "the camel" it's masculine plural. That indicates it's plural. And then when you have an ending which is otherwise used for feminine singular, if it's combined with a masculine plural subject, then this actually indicates that this is a non-human plural subject. So you have two grammatical facts, which jointly contribute the fact that the subject of this predicate is non-human and plural. And again, this kind of thing is straightforward to describe in constructional terms where you have the expressions and you have essentially the form of the word indicating that it's a camel and it's non-human, and then the dotted line indicating that the two concepts are essentially co-referential.

So these are arguments that suggest that if you take the building block approach, we are going to run into problems. I should say a little bit now perhaps about my own coming to this conclusion. These seem like fairly esoteric arguments, syntactic arguments. They still are, nevertheless, based on the facts about a lot of languages. You don't have to look too hard to find these problem cases. When I was first developing Radical Construction Grammar, I presented it at a summer school in Mainz, Germany, and I was preparing the lectures for that class. At that point, I still believed in syntactic relations. I thought that we had to have syntactic relations as part of the description of a construction. But I started coming across all these examples, you know, the Tzotzil possessor ascension and the Pima quantifier float and the Uzbek relative clauses and so on and so forth, and I was tying myself in knots trying to figure out, how can I analyze these in the way that I think is appropriate? How can I come up with some kind of iconic mapping when there is no semantic relationship that holds directly between these two elements, even though there looks like a syntactic relation that holds? How can I deal with cases like Kilivila where there is no a priori way to decide what the syntactic relations really are? And above all, what you do with this kind of indexation phenomenon?

It took me a while to finally realize that actually I was making trouble for myself by assuming that syntactic relations exist. And the best thing to do was to get rid of them. Of course, I had to hesitate and I had to ask myself, can I really get rid of them, and am I actually making syntactic structure too simple? That's when I came up with that argument about language processing that interpreting an utterance can be done in a constructional model without syntactic relations. So actually that's the last aspect of Radical Construction Grammar that fell into place for me. It really wasn't until I started thinking in terms of let's make syntax simpler, that we could actually come to this conclusion. But it's also because I had to look at a lot of languages. You can explain away a few problematic examples, if you're just looking at a small number of languages. But as soon as you start to look at a large number of languages, then the problem cases start multiplying. And then you start realizing that maybe this is not the right way to look at grammatical structure.

So what other consequences can we draw from this? Well, constructions still have part-whole relations, including these nested constructions that I showed you on the first day [Lecture 1]. So it's not just like there is no structure entirely. If you have a clause, let's just take a simple intransitive clause: you have a subject and a predicate. The subject itself can be a complex construction, a noun phrase with modifiers and an article and a head noun. So it kind of looks like a constituent structure. You've got your verb, you've got your subject, and then inside the subject, you've got the article and the modifiers and the head noun. It's not really constituency in the traditional sense. It's more in a sense of this part-whole relationship. And remember, of course, the part-whole relation is the only thing we have here in these constructions.

Now the other thing that's interesting is that—and I have not talked about this in much detail right now—is that morphosyntactic devices to identify semantic roles of syntactic elements, things like case marking and indexation: they aren't there all the time in languages. Sometimes they are there, and sometimes they are not present. Once again we can look across languages, and ask ourselves: under what circumstances do we find some kind of overt case marking? Under what circumstance does a noun or a noun phrase trigger agreement or indexation or not? And it turns out that there are regular patterns here. So, for instance, case marking appears for less prototypical referents in semantic roles. That is if you have, for instance, a direct object which is animate or definite, in many languages suddenly an overt case marking pops up to indicate that role. You expect the direct object to be inanimate. And if you have an animate referent, it's probably going to be the subject in a clause, in a transitive clause. So if you have something unexpected like an animate as the direct object, then you get it coded. Indexation tends to show up for more salient participants, so indexation is there to tell you which participants are the most salient ones in the actual event that is being expressed by the predicate.

So here's an example in some greater detail [Figure 104]. In Modern Eastern Armenian, you can have expressions that describe locations. You have predicates like *live*, which by their meaning, imply that there is some location involved. And you also have expressions like Erevan, the name of the capital of Armenia, which is a place name. So it's inherently a location by semantic type. So if you have a predicate that is locative, and you have an argument that represents a location, then you don't need to have any kind of case marking to say what the location is. It's obvious: the verb requires a location, the noun denotes a location. So you are in luck. You don't have to do anything special.

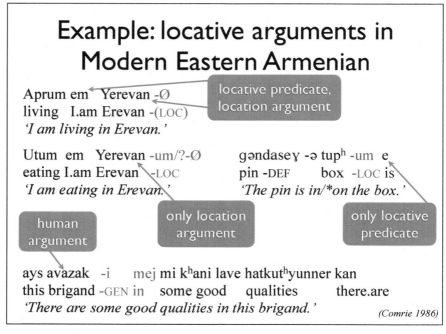

Example: locative arguments in Modern Eastern Armenian

Aprum em Yerevan -Ø
living I.am Erevan -(LOC)
'I am living in Erevan.'

> locative predicate, location argument

Utum em Yerevan -um/?-Ø
eating I.am Erevan -LOC
'I am eating in Erevan.'

gəndaseɣ -ə tupʰ -um e
pin -DEF   box -LOC is
*'The pin is in/*on the box.'*

> human argument

> only location argument

> only locative predicate

ays avazak -i   mej mi kʰani lave hatkutʰyunner kan
this brigand -GEN in some good   qualities   there.are
'There are some good qualities in this brigand.'

(Comrie 1986)

FIGURE 104

It gets a little more complicated when you don't have everything there. So if you say "I'm eating in Erevan", *eating* does not have a location as a prominent participant. On the other hand, *Erevan* is a place name, so it is reasonable for someone to infer that if you are talking about eating and you mention a place name, you are describing the location where the eating events took place. Actually, in Modern Eastern Armenian, as you can see, the zero coding is possible, but it's not as preferable as the locative coding. So it's like the locative coding has to be there because the verb is not a locative predicate. If you take "The pin is in the box", well again, you have a locative predicate. *Box* is not a normal location. However, a box is a container. So it's the kind of thing you expect to put something like a pin in. So, if you are talking about the canonical spatial relationship between a container and an object, then you can use the locative expression, but you don't need to say anything more than that. If you want to actually say "the pin is on the box", a non-canonical unexpected locative relation between an object and a container, then you have to actually use a more explicit postposition, *vəra* indicating that it is *on* and not *in*.

And then the last example—and this is actually found in many languages, not just in Modern Eastern Armenian—if you have a locative expression (here it's a metaphorical locative expression) and it governs a human argument (so "this brigand", in "there are some good qualities in this brigand"; *brigand* is some kind of thief or terrorist, whatever you want to call him), then you have to have a more complex expression. So you see that you have a postposition *in*, and you have a genitive case marking on the expression "this brigand". So basically, the less likely a locative semantic relation is involved, the more you are going to have to overtly express it in the sentence. The more likely you actually have a locative semantic relation, then the less likely you have to express it, because it's what you expect. And this is just one kind of elaborate version of a very widespread pattern of when you find case marking and when you don't find case marking.

Ok, so what happens if we have constructions without syntactic relations? Here is another puzzle that a functionalist linguist proposed. He was talking about English. Now remember I just said that you don't need marking if you know who did what to whom; it follows your expectations. Well, in a language like English, you do have to fix the order of subject and object. Even if it's a verb like *kill*, and the subject is what you'd expect—a human agent and the object is what you expect—some kind of animal. So Durie wrote:

> ... with respect to *the farmer killed a duckling* [this is a classic example from Edward Sapir's book on language], it is clear that ducklings don't kill farmers, and if English did have 'free' word order, there would be no need for a speaker to further disambiguate the sentence. Such further disambiguation would be redundant. As a disambiguating device, English svo word order displays functional over-generalization, or overkill: it is there even when you don't need it.

So Durie is claiming that you don't need to have fixed svo order in a sentence like "The farmer killed a duckling", because we all know that farmers kill ducklings and not the other way around. And of course there are other languages in the world, particularly in Australia where Durie worked, where you do have free word order and you don't have to worry about this. So, from the perspective of an Australian aboriginal language speaker, English is doing what looks like functional overkill: we're actually having to specify word order even when we don't have to.

But I would question that. I would say that actually it's not that we don't need to, because there is another thing we need. If we try to identify a transitive construction in a language like English, we don't have much to go on. There is no case marking of subject or object, agent or patient. There is hardly any indexation, just in English present tense third person singular only. So all you have is word order. And the crucial thing, remember, is if you want to understand a sentence, you have to recognize a construction as a whole. Well, a construction is a complex syntactic structure. There are lots of different constructions

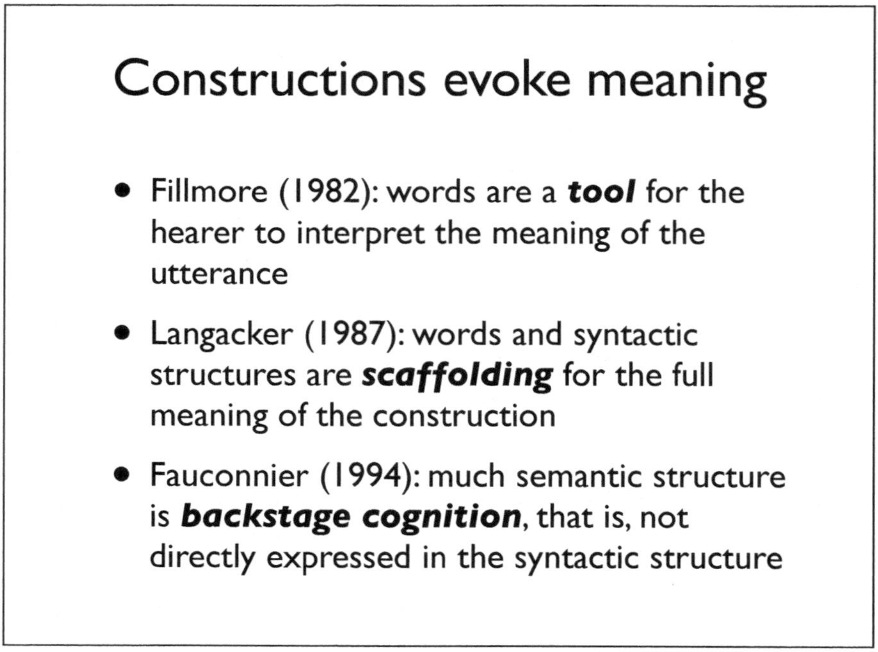

Constructions evoke meaning

- Fillmore (1982): words are a **tool** for the hearer to interpret the meaning of the utterance

- Langacker (1987): words and syntactic structures are **scaffolding** for the full meaning of the construction

- Fauconnier (1994): much semantic structure is **backstage cognition**, that is, not directly expressed in the syntactic structure

FIGURE 105

in any language. A speaker has to be able to recognize that we are looking at the right construction. So basically you want as many clues as possible. (All of you who are listening to me are probably wishing that you have more clues to follow all of my English constructions I'm using, since you are all not native speakers of English.) So in fact, having svo word order, that fixed order, even in a sentence like "The farmer killed a duckling", actually does have a functional value. It helps the listener recognize it as a transitive declarative clause. Once you've got the transitive declarative clause, then you can pull up the meaning, figure out who did what to whom and you've understood the sentence. So in fact, that extra functional overkill isn't really overkill. It is really essential for trying to identify the construction as a whole, because for most constructions you need to look at several different syntactic and morphological properties in order to say we're looking at one construction and not a different construction.

So constructions evoke meaning [Figure 105]. "Evoke" is actually a term that Fillmore uses in Frame Semantics. As you can see, this is a theme that goes through much work in Cognitive Linguistics. Fillmore says—this is paraphrasing him—"words are a tool for the hearer to interpret the meaning of the utterance" (Fillmore 1982). So the idea is that there is more to meaning than just what is expressed in a sentence, syntactically and morphologically. Langacker, in *Foundations of Cognitive Grammar*, says "words and syntactic

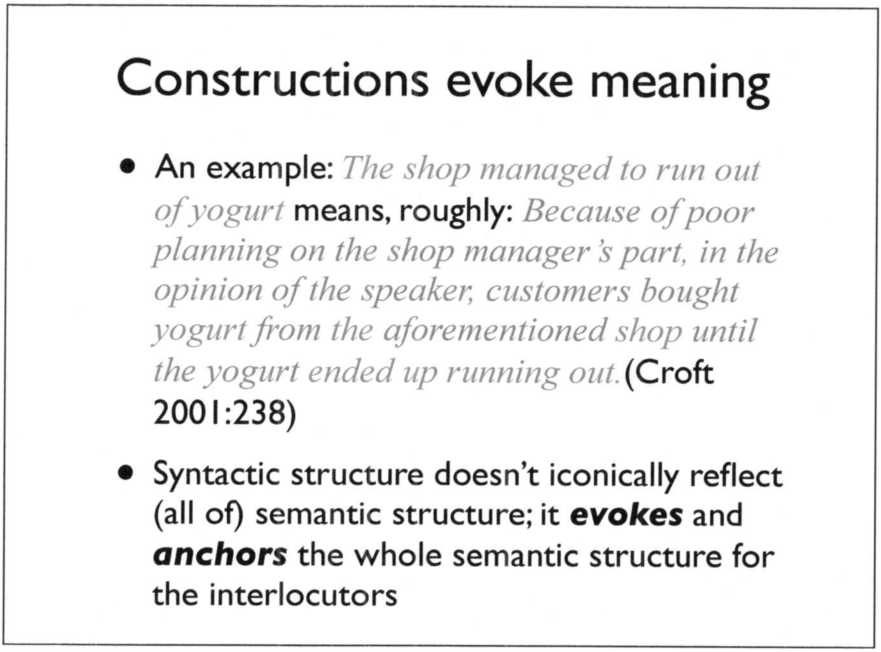

Constructions evoke meaning

- **An example:** *The shop managed to run out of yogurt* **means, roughly:** *Because of poor planning on the shop manager's part, in the opinion of the speaker, customers bought yogurt from the aforementioned shop until the yogurt ended up running out.* (Croft 2001:238)

- Syntactic structure doesn't iconically reflect (all of) semantic structure; it ***evokes*** and ***anchors*** the whole semantic structure for the interlocutors

FIGURE 106

constructions"—he uses what he calls the "scaffolding metaphor"—"words and syntactic structures are scaffolding for the full meaning of the construction" (Langacker 1987). So once you have the full meaning grasped, then the scaffolding can fall away, as he puts it. Fauconnier, in his work on Mental Spaces, coined a term which is probably familiar to most of you, "much semantic structure is backstage cognition", by which he means, again, there is semantic structure and semantic processing that is not explicitly or overtly coded in the syntax of the utterance; it's not directly expressed in the syntactic structure.

So, for example, take the sentence "The shop managed to run out of yogurt" (it always happened to me in England) [Figure 106]. What it means is something roughly like: because of poor planning on the shop manager's part, in the opinion of the speaker, customers bought yogurt from the aforementioned shop until the yogurt ended up running out. So only the words that are in red in that longer paraphrase are what is expressed in the original sentence "The shop managed to run out of yogurt." Nevertheless, the construction evokes the whole meaning that is expressed in that long paraphrase. So in other words, when we talk about iconicity in syntax, syntactic structure actually does not iconically reflect all of semantic structure; it evokes and anchors the whole semantic structure for the interlocutors. So what you express in an utterance

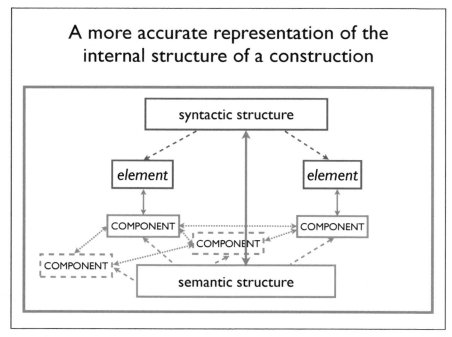

A more accurate representation of the
internal structure of a construction

FIGURE 107

picks out essentially the important bits that help the listener interpret what you are trying to convey as a whole. I'll be talking more about this idea in my second lecture tomorrow afternoon [Lecture 6].

So in other words, a more accurate representation of the internal structure of a construction is something that looks like this [Figure 107]. So now we have our simplified syntactic structure. All we have are syntactic elements and they play different roles in the structure. There's no relationship that holds here. But when we go on to the semantic side now, we have a much more complicated structure: We have the semantic components, and they are paired with particular elements and play roles in the overall meaning that is conveyed by the construction as a whole. But there are all these other elements that are evoked. These things function as scaffolding or tools in Langacker's and Fillmore's terms. These things represent the backstage cognition, the additional semantic structure that is evoked by the use of a sentence like this.

So in the end, what I have done here is not simply to make syntax look simpler, but (as many cognitive linguists have recognized) to make semantics look more complicated or make semantics look richer. I think this is the reason why so many cognitive linguists devote their attention to the study of semantic structure: because there are so many interesting and complicated things going

Conclusions

- No syntactic structure is needed apart from the construction as a whole and the syntactic elements that play roles in the construction

- The syntactic generalizations traditionally captured by syntactic relations are either not crosslinguistically valid, or are captured by symbolic links between form and meaning

- This "skeletal" syntactic structure is sufficient to evoke the much richer semantic structure whose communication is the functional goal of grammar

FIGURE 108

on that are wide open to be analyzed, since in western culture at least, linguists for so many decades focused their attention on grammatical structure and not on meaning. But to repeat the point that I made in the beginning, I think it is very important that we actually look at syntactic structure and make the arguments that syntactic structure is simpler than we traditionally thought at the same time that we we're also showing that semantic structure is more complex and richer than we previously assumed. So thank you very much.

So just to repeat [Figure 108]: we have this minimal syntactic structure, just the construction as a whole and the syntactic elements that play roles. The second bullet point is something I didn't mention before, and I should mention and emphasize that. Linguists have proposed syntactic relations in order to capture facts or generalizations about languages. Those generalizations still need to be captured even if we get rid of syntactic relations. Most of them, if they are valid at all, can be captured by the symbolic links between elements of the construction and their semantic components. And then that skeletal syntactic structure, as I emphasized, is sufficient to evoke the much richer semantic structure whose communication is the functional goal of grammar. So now I am really done. Thank you!

The Syntactic Space of Constructions

Ok, I will start by just having a quick review here of what constructions look like [Figure 109]. This is the second to last slide from my last lecture [Lecture 4]. So the first issue that we discussed, that I actually devoted two whole lectures to [Lecture 2–3], was the status of syntactic categories, and I argued that syntactic categories are actually roles in a construction. So these elements here are the categories, but the basic unit is the construction as a whole. The construction as a whole of course includes both the form in the blue boxes and the meaning and symbolic links that link the form to the meaning. We also talked

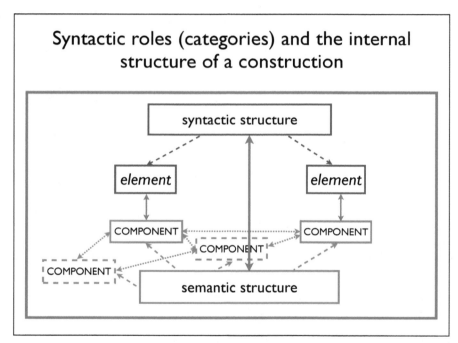

FIGURE 109

All original audio-recordings and other supplementary material, such as any hand-outs and powerpoint presentations for the lecture series, have been made available online and are referenced via unique DOI numbers on the website www.figshare.com. They may be accessed via a QR code for the print version of this book. In the e-book, both the QR code and dynamic links are available, and can be accessed by a mouse-click.

about how the meaning is actually a much more complex structure than the actual elements that you find in the linguistic form. The elements in the linguistic form evoke more a complex semantic structure.

Then yesterday afternoon [Lecture 4], I argued that in fact you should look at the syntactic structure here as only having this part-whole relationship. So you have the construction as a whole, and it has particular elements as parts. Of course these elements may themselves be constructions, complex constructions, and will have other elements as parts. But you don't have to have any relations between elements. So that simplifies the syntactic structure. This is basically it: the whole syntactic model can be summarized on a single slide. Part of the reason for that is because there is no set of building blocks. Remember, I criticized the building block model. So you don't have any universal categories. Of course, in any particular language you have categories that are defined by these constructional roles. But that's implicit in this diagram. It's all the possible things that can fill this role and this role and so on in every construction. There are also taxonomic relations among constructions: ways to capture generalizations about the structure or function of constructions. I will be talking about that in much more detail on Tuesday [Lectures 7–8] for those of you who can stay for the remainder of the lectures.

So that's the basic structure of constructions. And as I said, one important point that I made is that there aren't any universal building blocks; there are no universal syntactic categories that we should be constructing constructions out of. So you might ask: what about constructions themselves, these things up here? Is there a universal inventory of constructions that we can identify from one language to the next? And the answer I'm going to give is actually, no.

So, constructions are sometimes proposed to be universal discrete structural types that can be identified cross-linguistically. This is even said by some construction grammarians. A good example of this, the one that we'll explore in this talk, is the idea of a universal passive construction. However, as I will show you today, there is good reason to believe that there are no universal constructions in structural terms. Constructions of course can be compared by their function. In an earlier lecture Randy LaPolla asked me about this and I said that yes, if you want to look at the same construction across languages, it has to be a functionally equivalent construction. And then you can ask questions about how they differ in their structural form. But this doesn't mean that the possible constructions in the world's languages are just completely random. In fact, there is a syntactic space of structural possibilities and there are universal constraints on those. At least that's what we expect to find and we do find it in the case of voice constructions, which is the topic of today's lecture.

So we're going to go from universal constructions to a notion of a syntactic space and the kind of constructions I'm going to talk about here are voice constructions. Actually, I'm not going to talk about all types of constructions that linguists call "voice constructions". I will be restricting my attention to the contrast between what is called the active and passive constructions in the western European grammatical tradition and in western European languages. I will also be talking about a kind of construction that typologists have discussed. It's called the inverse construction. Some of you may be unfamiliar with it because it's not something that is talked about in most linguistics textbooks. As we'll see, the paradigm example of the inverse construction is found in a Native American language family, the Algonquian family.

Even typologists (who, as I said before, ought to know better) still have debates about whether a construction in a particular language is really a passive construction or really an inverse construction or really an ergative construction (we will see that later on). And these kinds of debates are basically the same kinds of debates that people have when they say, does this language really have adjectives or not? They are really, to me, pointless debates. We can't really answer that question and even if we did, it is not really an interesting question because the only way you can answer it is by doing what I called methodological opportunism, essentially picking out the facts that support your point and ignoring the facts that don't support your point.

So we are going to take a very different view of this. We first have to come up with a cross-linguistically valid definition of voice constructions. This is actually more difficult than you think. This is part of the problem: when people try to say this language has a passive, or doesn't have a passive, they don't really have a good set of crosslinguistically valid criteria to define a passive construction.

You can do it on a purely functional basis. Talmy Givón wrote an article many years ago in which he pointed out that if you use the functional basis for the passive, which would be something like the patient argument is more topical than the agent argument, then you are actually going to bring in a lot of other constructions that most people don't usually call voice constructions.

There's actually nothing wrong with that, and in fact there's something important about doing it that way, which I'll come to at the end of the lecture. But most people want to look at a narrower range of constructions than that. And there is a way to do this. It's what I called a "derived structural definition" in my typology textbook. You start from some kind of functionally defined basic voice construction. I will not tell you how I do it quite yet, but we are going to start by saying that there's a basic voice construction. The most reliable, though not completely reliable, criterion is that the basic voice construction is the one that occurs most frequently in a language. Once we've identified the basic voice construction—remember we are looking at this from Radical Construction Grammar, so that we have to find the constructions, and then we define the categories and roles based on that construction. So once we identify the basic voice construction, we will use the roles for participants in that construction and say, ok, this role is a subject role, this role is the object role, and then we'll also have an oblique for things that are neither subjects nor objects, that is, things that are coded in a different way.

So again, I'm using terms like subject and object and you might wonder, why am I using these terms? Well, I'm using them to mean a very specific thing that's different from what some other people use these terms for. It means a particular role in the basic voice construction of that language. And also the verb form you find is the verb form for the role in the basic voice construction that is filled by the predicate. So these definitions are all construction-specific. There's another way you can look at today's lecture: not just that I'm trying to make a general point about voice constructions and syntactic constructions in general, but that this will give you an example of how you would analyze a particular linguistic phenomenon in Radical Construction Grammar. So I've made all these general statements. I've made a lot of critical arguments about how not to do it. Here's a chance for you to see how I think you should analyze a construction.

Once we've identified the basic voice construction, then we can identify a non-basic voice construction. And at this point I don't really care about what you call it. Right now my interest is just to call them "basic" and "non-basic". Some people call them "active" or "direct", "passive", and "inverse". And I will use these names because that's what other people use; but do not assume at all that I think these are universal construction types. So the non-basic voice construction will be simply identified as another construction in the language that's structurally distinct. And then what we do is look at how it is structurally distinct from the basic voice construction. In particular we are going to look at how the verb is expressed. Is it in the same form as in the basic construction? And then how are the arguments, the participant roles expressed? Are they in same form as the basic voice construction or in a different form?

So for example, take English [Figure 110]. The basic voice is the one that English grammarians called the active voice. It's illustrated in a sentence like "Wolves followed us". So in this case we have two different roles, and following typological practice, I will give them labels, these letter labels, so P for patient, A for agent. I'll call them agent and patient but obviously their semantic definition will have to be broader than that. But we will focus on using the prototypical members. So by definition, the way that you express the patient in the basic voice we'll call the object. In English that means it comes after the verb

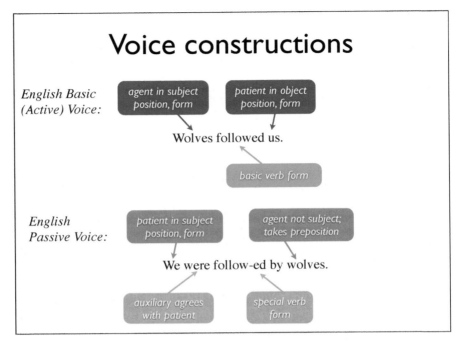

FIGURE 110

and the pronoun has to be in the correct object form. Again, by definition the basic verb form is the one that we find in the basic voice construction: simple verb form, inflected. The agent: again by definition we are going to call that the subject role, so the subject role is the one that is found in the basic voice construction for the agent. In English, it comes before the verb. If you have a pronoun there, it would be in the proper pronoun form for subjects.

English has another voice, which traditionally is called the passive voice. So this is a non-basic voice. It's actually very infrequent in language use in English. So that's good. That tells us it's non-basic. Now, we can ask ourselves, what does the verb look like? How is the agent expressed? How is the patient expressed? So now we see that the patient is expressed in the subject position and form. So the patient's behavior, the patient's structural properties are basically the same as the agent's structural properties there. The agent is not a subject. In fact, it doesn't look like an object either because it takes the preposition *by*. So it's an oblique. Again, we define an oblique as an argument role that does not look like the agent or patient roles in the basic voice construction. Now, the auxiliary also agrees with the patient. (I will use the term "agree" instead of "index". Sorry, I should be strict and use the term "index" all the time, but more people know the term "agreement", so I put "agree" in here [Figure 110].) So the auxiliary agrees with the patient. That's considered to be another indicator that the patient is like the subject and in fact, if we had an agreeing verb form here, it would agree with the agent. So again, in this respect it looks like the subject in the basic construction. And lastly, there's a special verb form, the passive participle verb form. So it's different from the basic verb form, and I'll just call it the special verb form.

Now when we look at the examples I'm going to give you on all the slides for today's talk, you'll see I'm going to identify the structural properties of the construction, comparing it to the basic voice construction in a language. I won't always give you an example of the basic voice construction simply for reasons of space and time. The properties will be color coded, the way it is coded on this the particular slide. So in English what we call the cool colors, green and blue, will be used to code properties of the construction that look like the basic voice construction. And in particular blue will be used for whatever the agent and patient phrases look like, and green will be used to describe the properties in the verb that looks like the basic voice construction. Conversely, we'll use what we call warm colors to describe the properties that don't look like the basic voice construction. So again, red will be used to describe properties of how the agent and patient are expressed in the non-basic voice when it doesn't look like the basic voice. And orange will be used to describe properties of the verb, including its agreement properties, if it doesn't look like the basic voice. And as you'll see, you're going to get a mixture of blue and green and red and orange properties in the various non-basic voice constructions.

Ok, I mentioned at the beginning of the lecture that there's this Western tradition that identifies the English passive voice, and some people have argued that there is a universal passive, not in the functional sense that Givón had of the patient that's more topical than the agent, but in a structural sense: there are certain structural properties of a construction, the form of a construction that you can use to identify a passive. Well, that kind of claim only works if there is a very sharp distinction like you see in English here between the basic voice construction and the non-basic voice construction in terms of their structural properties. So in this case (using English as a reference point) it looks like the English passive is totally different from the English active.

I also mentioned that typologists identify another construction which they were unwilling to call a passive, another non-basic voice construction. So they call this an inverse. No, I guess we're not there yet. There's another factor [Figure 111]. This is actually relevant to the inverse, which is that when we are looking at constructions—remember constructions are pairings of form and meaning. So the meaning of a voice construction is some kind of configuration of participants in an event and of course the event itself. So we have to define a

Voice constructions

- We also define a **conceptual space** to map the distribution of the basic and nonbasic voice constructions in a language:

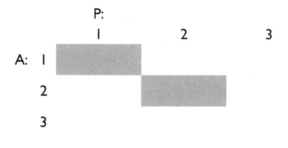

FIGURE 111

conceptual space to map the distribution of the basic and the non-basic voice constructions in a language. Now you have already seen a lot of conceptual spaces if you have been listening to Melissa Bowerman's talks at this lecture series. She's given many examples with things like *on*, and *in*, and *out*, and *off*, and *open*, and *break* and *cut*, where she had little pictures showing particular spatial relations and verbal actions, and then showing how languages use particular verb forms or proposition forms or whatever to express those different combinations of those scenes.

Well, I'm going to have to use something more abstract here. So this is supposed to represent scenes: A is the agent argument, P is the patient argument, the numbers refer to person, so first, second and third person. So we are going to start by defining the possible combinations in terms of who is acting on whom. So this box here [row 1, column 2] represents first person agent acting on second person patient. This box down here [R3C3], this blank, is third person agent acting on third person patient. These boxes [R1C1 and R2C2] are grayed out because they aren't relevant. They actually have to do with reflexives. So this is first person acting on first person—"I shaved myself"—or second person acting on second person—"Do you see yourself in the mirror?" So we're only interested in the boxes that are white here.

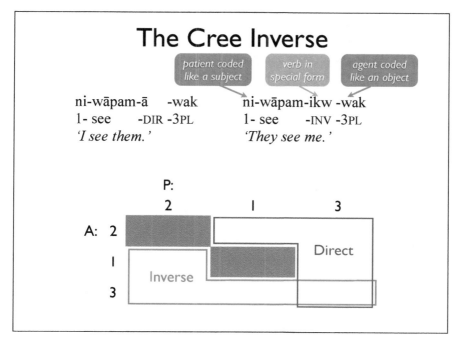

FIGURE 112

Ok, why is this particular combination of features—I am looking at grammatical person of agent and patient in the action—why is this relevant? It's because of constructions like this other construction called the inverse. So here I actually do give you the basic verb form in Cree: "I see them" [Figure 112]. You see that "I" is a prefix (*ni-*), "them" (third person plural) is the suffix (*-wak*), and then there is another suffix (*-ā*) on the verb form. So the basic verb form actually has a suffix on it.

Now if we contrast the inverse form on the right hand side, you see that the patient is coded like a subject, so that looks like the English passive; it's a prefix (*ni-*). The agent, however, is coded like an object in the basic voice construction (*-wak*), not like an oblique. This is why typologists balked at calling this a passive. The verb, however, is in a special form which again is like the English one. Obviously the labels that we give these special forms, that's what linguists give them; it's obviously not what the speakers do themselves. But the thing that really struck linguists who looked at constructions like Cree's is that you don't really have much of a choice whether you choose the basic form or the non-basic form in this language. In English, at least in theory though not in actual usage, you can use the active voice or the passive voice no matter whether the agent is first person, or third person, and the patient is second person, or first person, third person or whatever. But in Cree, you can only use the direct form, the basic form—there's actually a slightly different ranking here, of the second person and first person—if the second person is acting on first or third, first is acting on third, also third is acting on third. If it's the other way around, you have to use the inverse.

This is usually explained in terms of a hierarchy. So second person, the addressee, is sort of the top of the hierarchy, has the top rank; and the first person is in the middle rank, and the third person is in the lower rank. So if someone of a higher rank is acting on someone of a lower rank, first person acting on third person, we use the direct form. If someone of a lower rank is acting on someone of a higher rank, third person acting on first person, then you use the inverse form. So that's why you have this distribution in the boxes here. Again, I'm using the cool color blue to represent the basic voice form and the warm color red to indicate the usage of the inverse form. The only case where there's overlap is when there's third person acting on third person. Obviously, these [gray cells] are reflexives, so you don't have those combinations. But you can have one third person acting on another third person, and then you have both options. So there is some overlap. But most of time they are mutually exclusive and it depends on the grammatical person of the agent and patient arguments. So this fact struck people very much and that combined with the fact that the syntax here is a little different led linguists—both specialists in Algonquian languages and typologists that followed up—to call this an inverse construction, a non-basic voice construction that's different from the passive.

Ok, now, as a number of people have noted, including a paper by Scott DeLancey from thirty years ago, if you look at constructions that people would call passive, you get the same kind of restrictions about voice, and even if they are not categorical—you have to use the form or you can't use the form—you still get differences in usage, as you find if you looked at how people actually use the passive in English. So let's consider Lummi [Figure 113]. This is a Salishan language from the northwest coast of North America. So the agent is not a subject; it takes a preposition, so that's a red box: non-basic form. The basic form is on the left there, "You know the man", the verb agrees with the patient. That's what you expect again for a passive construction. So it looks just like the English passive. There is a special verb form which Salish linguists call a passive; so that's fine. A little oddly though, it still has a marker of transitivity, which you wouldn't expect because most people analyze the English passive as an intransitive verb form: a subject and no object. So even though here the agent is expressed with a preposition, it's got a transitive marker. So I've given that a green box—it does look like the basic form, it's identical to the basic form.

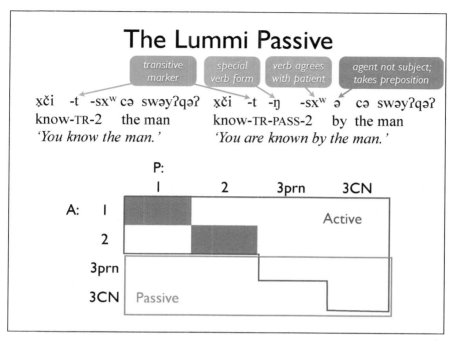

FIGURE 113

The other interesting fact about Lummi is that you also have a distributional pattern that is reminiscent of the pattern you found with the Cree inverse. And the thing you need to take note of here—so you've got first, second, third person pronoun, third person common noun, that's what the CN stands for—is that the active form is found in the upper right corner of this conceptual space; the passive form is found in the lower left corner of this conceptual space. So the upper right corner is where you have the highest ranked agent acting on the lowest ranked patient. The lower left corner is where you have the lowest ranked agent acting on the highest ranked patient, so the complete inverse situation.

And that, as we will see, is going to be the general pattern we are going to observe. So that's another reason why we selected this particular conceptual space. The basic verb form is going be associated with the upper right corner and the non-basic verb form is going to be associated with the lower left corner. What happens in between? Well, that's going to vary from language to language. In this particular language, the passive is a little more widely used than the inverse in Cree. So this is to show you that constructions that look more like the English passive voice construction, though not completely like it, also

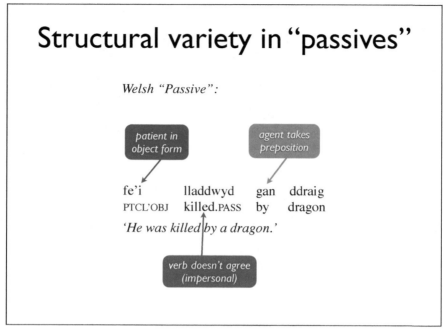

FIGURE 114

display this pattern in the conceptual space. And in a few examples I will show you more versions of the same thing.

But now what I'm going to do is to look at things that people have called passives in describing their structural variety. Welsh, a Celtic language spoken in Wales in Britain, has a construction that is sometimes called the passive [Figure 114]. It's translated there, "He was killed by a dragon". The agent takes a preposition; so, red. However, the patient remains in its object form. This is particularly with these pronominal objects. So that makes it still look like the basic construction. So now we have a kind of mixture of properties just like we saw in the Lummi example.

Now we're going to have to introduce another color, purple down there. The verb does not agree with either the agent or the patient. It's in an impersonal form as it's called in the Western grammatical tradition. So what you're going to find here—and we're going to find this in other languages—is, you are going to have to have things that look like the basic construction, and things that don't look like the basic construction—so the stuff I'll put in red and orange are opposed to the basic construction. And then you are going to have other structural properties that are neither like the basic construction but they are also not the opposite of the basic construction. So we are going to think of the properties that I describe with warm colors as being the opposite of what you found in the

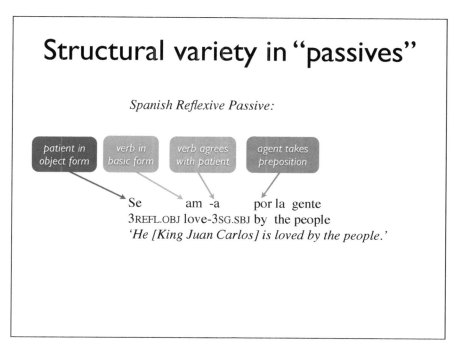

FIGURE 115

basic construction, the properties in the cool colors. And then purple, which is of course in between red and blue, is for properties that look like they share something about the basic construction and something about the non-basic construction.

Spanish [Figure 115]: Spanish has a construction with the reflexive pronoun that has come to have passive uses. Spanish speakers will sometimes object, because this is a sociolinguistically salient trait. This is actually a sentence I heard, so it does happen; but some Spanish speakers who are sensitive to what is proper Spanish will deny that such sentences exist or occur. The verb agrees with the patient. So that looks like a good non-basic property. The agent takes a preposition. What Spanish speakers object to is the presence of an agent phrase here; but as I said, it does occur. But the patient also occurs in the object form. And the reason of course is because this is a reflexive and in Spanish you express the reflexive by the reflexive argument having both the subject and the object encoding in terms of the basic voice construction. So we again have a mixture of traits. The verb of course is also in the basic form. There's no special passive form here. So we now have pretty much a mixture of traits.

And this is why some people don't think of this as a true passive. They call it a reflexive passive. Well, this is just like calling something an adjectival verb. It is kind of a cop-out as McCawley said. It's true that it's not like a passive—the

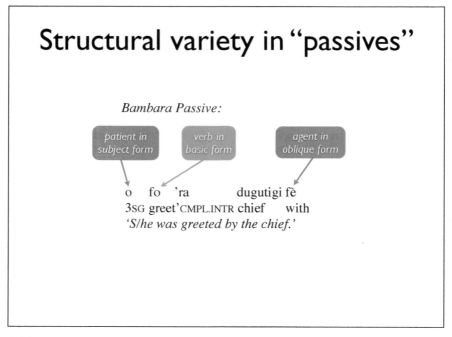

Structural variety in "passives"

Bambara Passive:

patient in subject form
verb in basic form
agent in oblique form

o   fo   'ra   dugutigi fè
3SG greet'CMPL.INTR chief   with
'S/he was greeted by the chief.'

FIGURE 116

properties are not all red and orange—but it's also not the basic voice form of the language.

Bambara, a language in West Africa [Figure 116]: the patient is in the subject form, the agent is in the oblique form, so this looks like a good non-basic [construction]—nice warm color properties. However, the verb is in the basic form. So it is a mixture of warm and cool properties.

Another Salish language, Upriver Halkomelem [Figure 117]: patient is in the subject position, so you can see in this language, the verb comes first. The subject in the basic verb form comes second. The agent comes in the object position—no preposition. So now it looks more like the inverse in Cree.

Now we get something that it's not usually talked about in studies of voice, but it's quite widespread in the world's languages. The verb agrees with the patient, but it uses special forms that are neither the subject agreement forms nor the object agreement forms. So the fact that the verb agrees with the patient looks like a non-basic fact, a property of the non-basic voice construction. But it uses a special form that you don't find in the basic construction, so we will call it purple because it's a little bit of both.

Here is another Native American language, actually spoken not far from where I live, in Arizona [Figure 118]. It is actually related to languages spoken in the pueblos in New Mexico. In this language, different linguists have called it

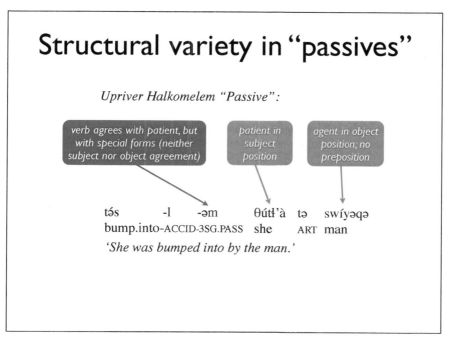

FIGURE 117

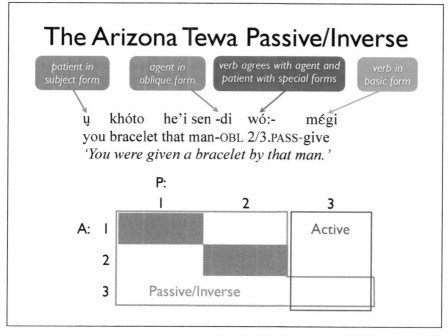

FIGURE 118

different things. So some call it a passive, some call it an inverse. Now from our perspective, that's kind of a pointless debate. The facts are: the patient is in the subject form, so that's what you'd expect for a non-basic voice. Agent is in the oblique form, which you'd also expect for a non-basic voice. The verb, however, is in the basic form. There is no special form, so that's like the basic voice. And then you have the special agreement pattern again.

So again, as I said, trying to call it passive or inverse is pointless. Trying to call it passive or inverse presupposes that there are universal passive constructions and universal inverse constructions. You should already have the idea at this point, if you've been following the lectures, that in fact there are a lot of different kinds of constructions that vary in many different properties, and mix and match properties that I've called basic and non-basic, and even properties that are neither basic nor non-basic, these purple properties. So calling this a passive or an inverse is not going to help us a whole lot because it doesn't tell us how this construction is different from Spanish, Welsh, or any of the other languages we've looked at. And in addition, Arizona Tewa has this restriction about the person of the agent and the person of the patient. Now you can see here, the passive construction is more extensive, but the important thing to remember is that the basic voice form is always found in the upper right. And if the non-basic voice form occurs, it describes the situation in the lower left.

Other things that have been called inverses: in Maasai, an African language, agent is in the subject case, patient is in the object case [Figure 119]. This actually looks like the basic voice form. The basic verb form is also like the basic voice. However, the verb does not agree with the agent, so that makes it look like a non-basic form. The verb does agree with the patient using special forms so now we have another mixed property.

The Yurok language, spoken in northwest California, has something that's called the passive [Figure 120]. It's used only when third person is acting on second person, so that's good: that's the inverse of the ranking in the hierarchy. Agent occurs in the subject form: that looks like the basic voice. Patient occurs in object form: also looks like basic voice. Subject-object-verb word order in this language. However, the verb agrees like a subject with the patient: not special forms, just like a basic voice agent; but it agrees with the patient instead. And you have a special verb form which is called the passive by the analyst. So we again have mixture of properties, a different kind of mixture.

Now I'm not going to give you examples here because in the language called Chukchi we actually have four different voice forms [Figure 121]. So one we will call basic form, and three non-basic forms. So the basic form is what they call the "bipersonal" forms. What that means is that the verb agrees with agent and patient. There are two different non-basic forms, one with the prefix *ine-* and another with the suffix *-tku*. These form unipersonal forms that are called

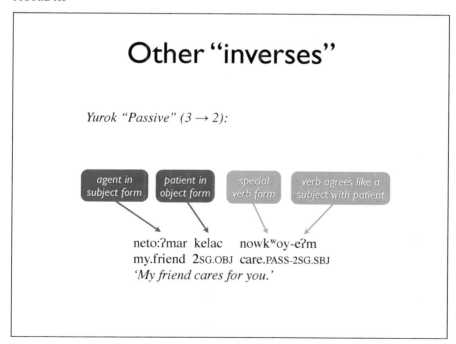

FIGURE 119

FIGURE 120

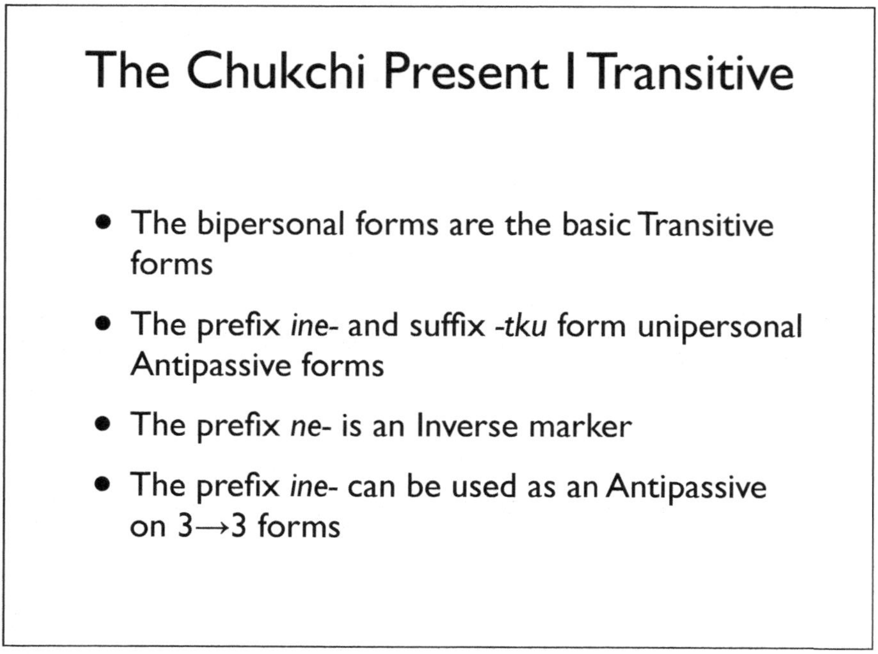

The Chukchi Present I Transitive

- The bipersonal forms are the basic Transitive forms
- The prefix *ine-* and suffix *-tku* form unipersonal Antipassive forms
- The prefix *ne-* is an Inverse marker
- The prefix *ine-* can be used as an Antipassive on 3→3 forms

FIGURE 121

"antipassive". What's important here is that the verb only agrees with one participant. Then there is a prefix that's analyzed as an inverse marker. This is the third non-basic voice form. And that prefix can be used as an antipassive if you've got third person acting on third person.

So what's interesting here is to look at the distribution of these forms in our little conceptual space [Figure 122]. So the bipersonal form is in the upper right. That's the basic form. This inverse form is in the lower left. And then what happens in the middle is much more complicated. The inverse form is used in some places, the bipersonal form is used in some places, and then you have these two other non-basic forms that are used in between. So I've got green and brown to indicate those possibilities.

Now the thing that's observed here is that—I'm going to make a couple of comments that will lead me towards the conclusion, those of you who heard me talk about parts of speech in Cantonese [Lecture 3]—bipersonal means this verb form agrees with both the subject and the object. The ability to agree with participants is an example of what in typological markedness theory we call behavioral potential, that is, the potential to agree or index arguments, both arguments. These things in the middle, they have the potential to agree with only one argument. This inverse form doesn't have any behavioral

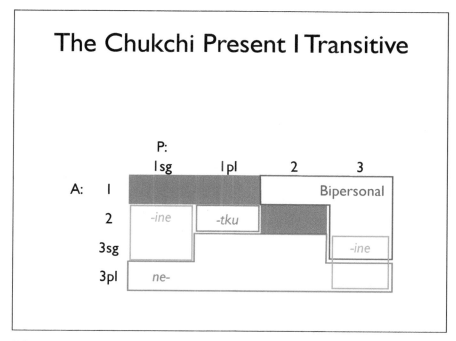

FIGURE 122

potential at all. It doesn't agree. The other thing to notice is structural coding. All of these non-basic forms have some kind of overt morpheme that expresses the non-basic verb form. The basic verb form doesn't have such a marking. So this combination here is what we are going to call a "typologically unmarked" combination, and the extreme cases, this combination, down in the lower left is a "typologically marked" combination. And that's, of course where I'm headed: that's the typological universal that underlies all the diversity of voice forms that we see here.

Ok, now there are languages where linguists have a hard time deciding what to call a non-basic form at all, and what the relationship is between that non-basic form and the basic or active form. A lot of these languages are in the Austronesian language family, spoken in Indonesia, the Philippines, and Oceania. Acehnese is spoken in Indonesia [Figure 123]. So you've got the patient in the subject form, so that looks non-basic. Agent is in an oblique form, so that looks non-basic. The verb agrees with the agent. That looks like a basic verb form, agreeing with the agent. And you have a basic verb form, so that looks like the basic voice.

Now in fact, with this language, there has been a debate about what the correct analysis is. So someone has argued that this is actually a passive voice

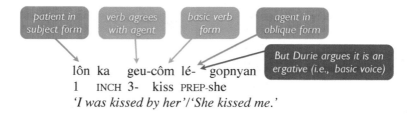

Active to non-active continuum

Acehnese:

patient in subject form	verb agrees with agent	basic verb form	agent in oblique form

But Durie argues it is an *ergative (i.e., basic voice)*

lôn ka   geu-côm lé-   gopnyan
1   INCH 3- kiss PREP-she
'I was kissed by her'/'She kissed me.'

- In Pukapukan, the Passive suffix to the verb form may be dropped, leading to an Ergative construction

FIGURE 123

form. But Mark Durie, who recently did field work on this language, argues that that oblique form has been reinterpreted as an ergative. So in other words, what we're looking at here is a basic voice form with a newly emerged agent form marked with this prefix. Since it's now interpreted as a prefix marking transitive subject, Durie calls it an ergative. That's the term that's normally used to describe a grammatical system with a special transitive subject marking. I'll talk more about those on Tuesday [Lecture 7].

Ok, so we have two alternative analyses. Why do we think they have these alternative analyses? Well, that's because linguists have reasons to believe that construction might be basic in terms of things like frequency. If you look at some of these Austronesian languages, you will find that a construction that has a mixture of traits like this actually becomes the more frequent form. So in another Austronesian language, Pukapukan, there's a passive [Figure 123]. It looks like Acehnese except that the verb form is not basic; the verb form has a passive suffix. But you can drop that passive suffix, and then what you've got is something that looks like a basic verb form if you assume that this transitive subject marking is ergative. Calling it an ergative basically means that linguists have decided that this is really the basic verb form, and so it's not an oblique any more. The agent is the basic form subject, by definition.

Active to non-active continuum

Kapampangan:

| special verb form | clitic agrees with agent with special form | clitic agrees with patient | agent in nonsubject form | patient in subject form |

pi>garal<an   ne (=na+ya)   ng   Nena ing Ingles
<GF>studied she.AGT.SBJ+it.SBJ NSBJ Nena SBJ English
'*Nena studied English.*'

- Actor Focus is taken as basic verb form, but it is also overtly coded; also, there is no 1,2<3 person hierarchy effect as with "Inverse" voice constructions

FIGURE 124

Here is a language from the Philippines, Kapampangan [Figure 124]. The patient is in the subject form. The agent is in the non-subject form. There's no sharp distinction between object and oblique in these languages, so linguists tend to call these non-subject forms. So it's kind of like the Cree inverse in structural terms again. But still it's non-basic so we code it with a warm color. There is a clitic, a pronoun clitic that agrees with the patient, so that looks like a non-basic form. There's a special verb form. But the clitic, this clitic is actually a combination that agrees with the agent, with a special form. So it's kind of a mirror image of what we have seen so far, languages where you have a patient with a special form. So the form that you see here is what traditionally is called by Philippine linguists the Goal Focus form. It contrasts with the Actor Focus form which is the basic form. That's what I use as the reference point for labeling all these properties of this construction. It's also overtly coded, so again, it's also like the Cree inverse. There happens not to be this hierarchy effect, so I haven't put that in there. So you can see it actually kind of looks like the inverse, though nobody really said this. The only difference is that it doesn't have that hierarchy of persons governing its use.

Now I have to say a little aside. Just like I said, after you start reading a bunch of grammars, and you see when people say that a language doesn't have

The Dyirbal Split Ergative

ŋinda   ŋayguna balgan
2SG.NOM 1SG:ACC   hit
'You're hitting me.'

bala yugu   baŋgul yara-ŋgu gunba-n   baŋgu bari-ŋgu
ART tree(ABS) ART   man-ERG cut   -PRS ART   axe-INST
'The man is cutting the tree with an axe.'

ŋaḏa   bayi yaṟa   balgan
1SG.NOM ART man(ABS) hit
'I hit the man.'

ŋayguna baŋgul yara-ŋgu balgan
1SG:ACC ART   man-ERG hit
'The/a man is hitting me.'

FIGURE 125

adjectives, what they really mean is that the predicating construction for prop-erty words is the same as the predicating construction for action words. When you read a lot of grammars of languages, and you see what linguists say when they call something an inverse construction, what they really mean is that there is a non-basic voice construction whose usage is governed by this per-son hierarchy. That's in practice what they're saying. But as we've seen, that's not the whole story. Constructions use the person hierarchy in different ways and the range of structural properties of these non-basic voice constructions is quite wide.

It turns out you can use this framework even to describe something which no one even talks about in terms of basic and non-basic voice [Figure 125]. There are a number of languages, particularly Australian languages, where you have a pattern which typologists call "split ergative". I won't explain what it means—I don't think that's the best term to describe it—but I will show you what the facts are. If you have a sentence like this, "You're hitting me", second person acting on first person, these first and second person pronouns have special object forms. They are called accusative. If you have a sentence like "The man is cutting the tree with an ax": here we've got third person acting on third per-son; "the man" gets an ergative form; "the tree" gets no marking—that's called

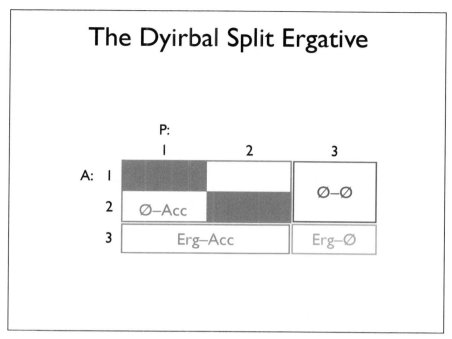

FIGURE 126

absolutive. If you say "I hit the man" which is first person acting on third person, the pronoun has the nominative form—there is no suffix—and "the man" has the absolutive form—there is no suffix either. If, however, you say "The man is hitting me"—so that's third person acting on first person—the pronoun is "me", has the object form (accusative). But the noun also has the ergative form. So basically first person and second person pronouns have special accusative forms. Third person pronouns and common nouns have special ergative forms, special agent forms.

So it looks like a complicated pattern, though it is a fairly simple rule I've just described, about when you use the accusative, when you use the ergative. What's the effect? That's on the next page of the slides [Figure 126]. The construction that is in the upper right corner has no extra coding. The construction in the lower left corner has the maximum extra coding: it has an ergative case marker on the agent and an accusative case marker on the patient. And then in between you have constructions where you have only one morpheme. Up here you have accusative because you've got a patient that's first and second person. Down here you get the ergative because you have an agent that's third person. So in other words, from the point of view of structural coding, the construction on the upper right has the least structural coding; the construction

The voice syntactic space

P CODING

| Sbj-like | Special | Direct Obj-like |

A CODING
Sbj-like

ACTIVE/DIRECT

Acehnese

Dyirbal

Maasai

Special   Seko Padang

Karo Batak
Kapampangan   Chukchi
Cebuano
Dir Obj-like   Cree prn   Yurok   Guarani

Arizona Tewa
Shilluk   Upriv. Halkomelem   Tangut
Cree obv
Pukapukan **Indonesian**

Pukapukan
Oblique   Bambara   Bella Coola
                                                            Russian
English   Spanish
                                              Welsh
                                                           Menomini
Prohibited **Lithuanian**   **Finnish**   **Maasai**

FIGURE 127

on the lower left has the most structural coding; and these two constructions in between have an intermediate level of structural coding. So once again we see this cline, this scale from the upper right down to lower left in terms of typological markedness, even though in this language it only in terms of the expression of the participants, the agent and patient coding; the verb doesn't change in any way.

So how can we analyze this complexity? Here is a colour coded version of what you've got on your slide [Figure 127]. The basic idea is we have—I will explain the color coding in a moment—we have a range of languages here. There are more languages on this than I've given you; if you look at Chapter 8 of *Radical Construction Grammar*, you'll see discussion of the missing languages. What I've done is I range them by looking at properties of the language. So if the patient looks more like a subject, the language goes over to the left. The patient that has special coding is in the middle. The patient that looks like a direct subject is over here. Agent coding which is more subject-like is up here, if it's more object-like it's down here.

So I said these languages kind of mix and match features that we think of as active and direct, so active and direct is in the upper right. That's where agent looks like subjects, patient looks like objects. That's by definition. And then we see how non-basic constructions in different languages deviate to a greater or lesser extent from this active or basic voice type. And some of them deviate a lot. Others are sort of not so deviant.

As I said I'm not the first person to make this observation. Although some typologists agonize over whether a language has a passive or an inverse, other typologists who have done crosslinguistic surveys of this particular construction don't agonize. They just admit the facts. Anna Siewierska (1985:1), in her typological study of passives says, "The analysis of the various constructions referred to in the literature as PASSIVE leads to the conclusion that there is not even one single property which all these constructions have in common". She went by constructions that were called passive in literature, but even if you are more rigorous about defining a non-basic voice construction, you still come to the same conclusion. Chad Thompson, in his survey of inverse constructions (1994:61)—he was trying to identify an inverse construction type as opposed to the passive and he basically admitted defeat—he said "I know of no structural features which can define inverse constructions and distinguish them from passives". Masayoshi Shibatani, discussing a paper on passive voice (1985:821)—he has worked a lot on the Philippine languages and these Austronesian languages. So he is aware of the issue and trying to define passive voice versus active voice. And he concluded the "passive forms a continuum with active sentences" or constructions as I would say.

So how can you define this syntactic space? When you look at the structural properties of constructions, the contrast between basic voice and non-basic voice in this case: we came up with things like case marking, indexation, word order, special forms of predicates. What we find is they can vary independently of each other. So that is not the cluster you can find in the English passive voice. All of the features that are the opposite of the basic voice features clustering in one construction, and then all the basic voice features in the basic construction: cross-linguistically that's unusual, or it's not universal anyway. You have things that come that are in between. So you have to come up with a way of describing the relationships between these constructions, these different kinds of non-basic voice constructions.

So why is this so? That is, this seems to be the way it is empirically. What is the reason for this? The main reason is that language change is gradual. And the fact of the matter is languages change what voice construction they have. A non-basic voice construction may increase in use, increase in frequency. It becomes reanalyzed as the basic voice construction. It changes its form, but it changes its form only gradually. So what does that mean? Only gradually, it means it drops one syntactic structural property at a time. And therefore if you can catch a language family in which new voice constructions are emerging,

Syntactic space

- *Language change is gradual*
- *Multiple paths of grammatical change:*
    - Indefinite subject transitive active > passive: Maasai, Turkana, Finnish (?)
    - active reflexive > middle > passive: Spanish, Upriver Halkomelem
    - goal focus > passive: Indonesian (?)
    - passive > ergative (active): Pukapukan, Dyirbal (?)
    - goal focus > passive > active: Shilluk, Karo Batak (?)
    - goal focus > ergative (active): Acehnese (?), Kapampangan (?)
    - passive > inverse: Bella Coola, Lummi, Arizona Tewa
    - passive > inverse > transitive: Yurok
    - inverse > transitive: Wardaman, Chinook, Ngandi, Nunggubuyu
    - third person agent > inverse > transitive: Seko Padang, Chukchi (?), Guaraní (?)

FIGURE 128

like the Salishan language family of the northwest coast of America or the Austronesian language family, you get a lot of diversity, a lot of intermediate voice types.

So we have multiple paths of grammatical change in there [Figure 128]. This is the color coding that corresponds to the examples that were on the syntactic space slide [Figure 127]. And you can see there, what those patterns are. We can look at these, we can plot these gradual processes in the syntactic space [Figure 129].

So you can see one kind of change; another, Goal Focus to passive; passive to ergative; Goal Focus to ergative; passive to inverse, and then this third person agent form becoming an inverse and then a transitive. They don't all go in the same direction but a lot of them follow similar paths in the syntactic space. So that gives you some comfort that the syntactic space does reflect gradience in structural properties.

So the point here is that when we look at the grammatical structure, there is a kind of continuum. And if you've been listening to Melissa Bowerman's lectures, you'll know that looking at the meanings of forms, in her case, verbs and prepositions also often form a continuum. Think of the "cutting" and "breaking" map. I will be showing you other maps of this kind on Tuesday [Lectures 7–8]. But it is true for syntax as well. Syntax also can be described in terms of a

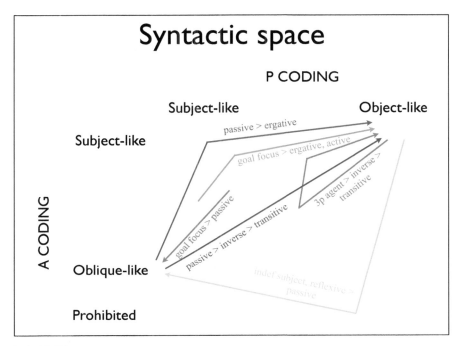

FIGURE 129

continuum. So instead of looking at the properties of spatial relations, certain kinds of properties like tearing and separation and integration and so on, we are going to look at structural properties of the form of a construction. And you can make a space defining the relationships between different constructions just like you can make a space defining relationships between different kinds of actions or spatial relations.

So we have a syntactic space. It's actually systematically related to that conceptual space. As I've been saying over and over again, basic voice constructions are always associated with a higher animacy agent acting on a lower animacy patient, and derived voice constructions, or non-basic voice constructions, with a lower animacy agent acting on a higher animacy patient. Animacy constraints are really a conventionalized version of salience or topicality constraints, so that's the sense in which Givón's functional definition of a passive, or more accurately a non-basic voice, is one where the patient more topical than the agent, at least in the prototypical sense. And this point has been made by Chad Thompson and Anne Cooreman, a couple of functional-typological linguists.

So if we map the conceptual space onto the syntactic space [Figure 130], the agent coding represents a continuum between the more salient agents which are going to look more subject-like and the less salient agents, being

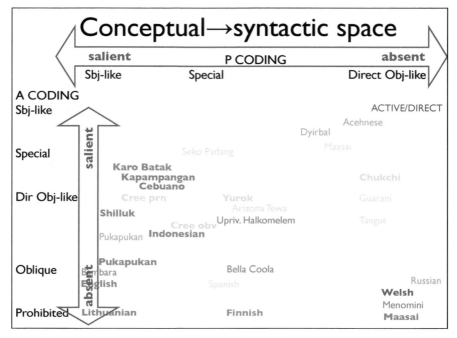

FIGURE 130

more oblique-like. And then absence: there are many languages where in the non-basic voice form you cannot express the agent at all. The same is true for the patient coding. So if the patient coding is more salient, then it is going to be more subject-like, and then as we go down to less subject-like, it is less salient and it can also be absent. This actually reflects another family of voice constructions, the ones that typologists call antipassive constructions, which I did not explore in the study. But those would push the space off in the direction of this right hand side of the slide to constructions where the patient is actually absent. It's lower in salience, and absent.

So my conclusions: syntactic properties form a syntactic space that should be analyzed in the same way as a conceptual space. I'm kind of anticipating here because I haven't shown you how to analyze conceptual space but basically it's the way that you've been shown by Melissa Bowerman. And I will talk about it more in the lectures on Tuesday [Lectures 7–8]. Constructions are made up of a combination of syntactic properties. No particular combination of syntactic properties represents a universal construction type. But the crosslinguistic distribution of syntactic properties correlates with dimensions of conceptual space. In particular, the voice construction that has the least structural coding and the most behavioral potential will indicate a more topical agent acting on a less topical patient. And the construction with the greater structural coding with the more limited behavioral potential will represent the inverse relation of a less topical agent acting on a more topical patient. So that's the kind of pattern we find in this particular domain.

This way of looking at syntactic constructions is actually fairly new to typologists. As I said, a lot of typologists are still trying to assume that you can identify universal construction types in formal terms. But this sort of study I've given you, which I think of as an example of how a Radical Construction Grammarian would analyze a particular linguistic construction, should (I hope) point the way to analyses that will respect the structural diversity of constructions in the world's languages. Thank you.

Grammar and the Verbalization of Experience

If you came to my opening lecture [Lecture 1] you might recall that I said that my lectures fall into basically two halves. The first five lectures: the theme was that syntax is simpler than you think. We focused on Radical Construction Grammar and the model of constructions and syntactic structures that I've advocated in Radical Construction Grammar. So I concentrated most of my attention on looking at linguistic form and showing that if you take a typological perspective on linguistic form, it actually tells you that linguistic syntactic structures are quite simple, in that all of the work happens in the semantic representation, and also in the mapping between form and meaning. So the themes of the rest of the second half—I put a long title on it, but basically, I'm going to be looking mostly at the mapping between form and meaning, what's the relationship between linguistic form and linguistic meaning. And you'll also see that in these lectures a lot of what I'm going to talk about has overlapped with a number of themes that Melissa Bowerman has presented in her lectures here, that she's already started discussing in her lectures and presumably will continue to do so.

The lecture I'm going to give this afternoon focuses on one aspect of constructions. You recall that in Radical Construction Grammar, constructions are the basic units of analysis [Lecture 2]. Syntactic categories are derivative because they are defined by the roles in constructions. And there are also no syntactic relations, there's only the syntactic roles that these parts of constructions have in the construction itself [Lecture 4]. So the question that comes out, that I was frequently asked when I first started presenting the concepts behind Radical Construction Grammar, is: if constructions are basic, and categories are derived—that is if we don't have a building block model, so that a construction is defined by its building blocks—how do you define constructions?

The first point I would like to make is that the building block models, although it looks like they don't have this problem, they really do have the same

All original audio-recordings and other supplementary material, such as any hand-outs and powerpoint presentations for the lecture series, have been made available online and are referenced via unique DOI numbers on the website www.figshare.com. They may be accessed via a QR code for the print version of this book. In the e-book, both the QR code and dynamic links are available, and can be accessed by a mouse-click.

© WILLIAM CROFT, REPRODUCED WITH KIND PERMISSION FROM THE AUTHOR BY KONINKLIJKE BRILL NV, LEIDEN, 2021 | DOI:10.1163/9789004363533_007

problem. Just as a reminder, building block models use distributional analysis in order to identify categories, the categories that form the building blocks. But distributional analysis is the distribution of these elements in roles in constructions. So, distributional analysis presupposes the ability to identify constructions too. So, you can always say to someone who advocates the building block model, how do YOU define constructions—the constructions to use for distributional analysis? And as I said in an earlier lecture, what this means is we all are in the same boat: we all need to find a way to define constructions.

Well, analysis of constructions from my point of view is basically an inductive categorization problem over tokens of constructions in language use. This answer here is basically connected to what is called the usage-based model. And the idea of the usage-based model—what it's really about—is the notion that our grammatical knowledge is both determined by and continues to be influenced by language use. So it's not as if in learning a language we either start with innate concepts, semantic or syntactic, but we start with what we hear around us. And we use that language in order to construct categories, or construct the kind of semantic categories that Melissa Bowerman described, and also to construct grammatical categories, that is, the types of constructions that we find. And then the usage-based model emphasizes the fact that the learning process is inductive. Now I will also be talking in later lectures about what the child or the adult brings to the language learning process and the language use process. And I think my story is going to be pretty similar to what Melissa Bowerman has been telling you. But one important aspect of this is that there is an important role for the inductive learning process.

So categories: we are talking about categories in general. Constructions belong in categories that we call passive, or active, or relative clause or whatever. So they possess a gestalt of properties with characterize them. A point I made in an earlier lecture is that a construction has a bunch of different properties which together jointly characterize that construction. There are discontinuities in this gestalt of constructional properties that can differentiate construction types. There are lots of different properties that distinguish active and passive voice in English for example. But you also can find all the usual categorization phenomena that cognitive psychologists describe: prototype structure, gradience, overlapping category membership, fuzzy boundaries and so on. So that's actually not surprising, that constructions are no different from other kinds of conceptual categories that people use.

Since constructions are pairings of form and meaning, semantics plays a central role. Constructions that are syntactically similar or identical will be semantically or pragmatically distinct. And the actual categories defined by syntactic roles of seemingly identical constructions will differ and that is often

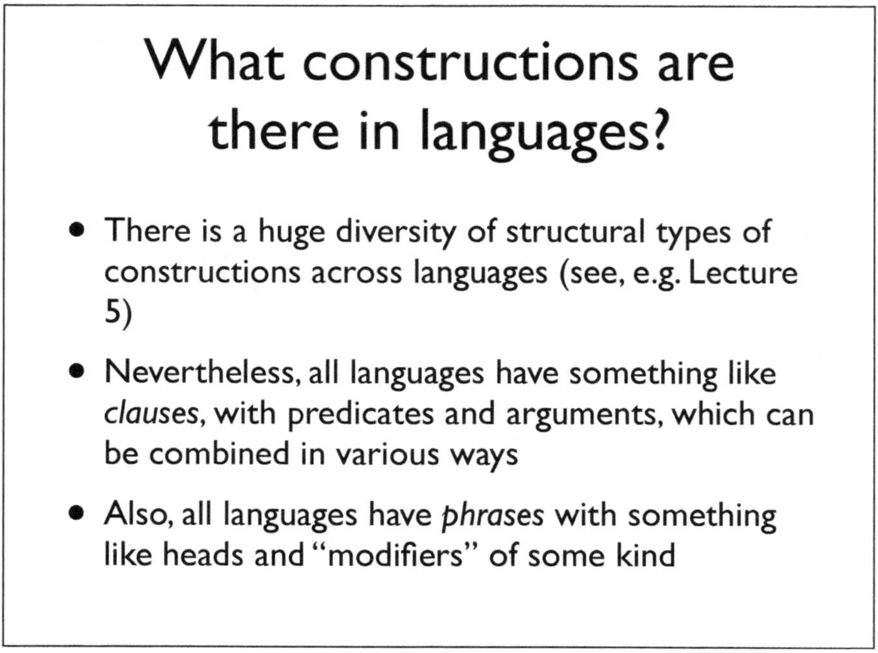

What constructions are there in languages?

- There is a huge diversity of structural types of constructions across languages (see, e.g. Lecture 5)

- Nevertheless, all languages have something like *clauses*, with predicates and arguments, which can be combined in various ways

- Also, all languages have *phrases* with something like heads and "modifiers" of some kind

---

FIGURE 131

on a semantic basis. In other words, if you look at two constructions that might look quite similar to each other, the categories that they define will usually be different.

Thinking of an example right off the top in my head, take the ditransitive construction, one that Adele Goldberg and many others have written about. Well, she identifies several subtypes. If you look at the verbs that fall in the subtypes, they are very different, in fact, they are mutually exclusive, and even the arguments that fill the subject and object and indirect object roles in the ditransitives of these different subtypes are different. And when you start looking more carefully, looking at what actually occurs, you'll see there are many more differences there. One of the things we know about human beings and also children learning languages: they're very sensitive to these probabilistic or frequency-based differences, and they can register those and make distinctions of the kind that we observe as linguists analyzing language.

So this tells us that we can distinguish constructions. But what kind of constructions are there? How do we count constructions or divide up our grammar into constructions [Figure 131]? Well, in my lecture this morning [Lecture 5], I said there is a huge diversity of structural types of constructions across languages, using the example of voice; but you find that in other domains as well. Nevertheless, I'm now going to make some big generalizations. As all of you know, my main area of research is typology. So I emphasize the structural diversity of languages, and I have emphasized that in all the lectures. But now I'm going to come back to some of the commonalities you find in languages.

So there's usually something that looks like clauses with predicates and arguments. Of course there are going to be particular constructions where it is difficult to say, is this a clause, or is this one clause? But on the whole, you can say that; and the kinds that are problematic represent some sort of possibly non-basic type. Also, languages have phrases with something like heads and some kinds of modifiers in terms of their function. So one of the things we want to ask ourselves is: ok, if we can talk about languages having various kinds of clausal constructions and various kinds of phrasal constructions, and while we're at it, complex sentence constructions—constructions that consist of combinations of clauses that are integrated to a greater or lesser extent— why is that?

Finally—and this is the point that Melissa Bowerman talked about in her lecture this morning—there are at least recurrent lexical and grammatical categories and constructions which are ubiquitous if not universal [Figure 132]. Melissa focused on the proposals originally made by Len Talmy, and he focused on things that were specifically inflectional categories. I'm going to broaden the view here, and that's why the bullet point says lexical and grammatical categories and constructions. So we look at things like number, case, gender, degree, definiteness, tense, aspect, modality, indexation or agreement: These are the kind of inflectional categories that Len Talmy asked the question: why does language seem to have these categories over and over again, and not other kinds of categories?

But I'm going to add to this mix, what are often expressed in terms of minor lexical categories, as they're sometimes called: numerals, quantifiers, adpositions, articles, demonstratives, auxiliaries, adverbs. So I'm going to also ask about these categories, not just the inflectional ones in the first point here. And lastly there are a lot of constructions around: relative clauses, possessives, anaphora, copular constructions, switch-reference, conditionals, a lot of other kinds of constructions which tend to recur in the sense that languages often have a construction that is dedicated to the purpose. Not always: there are even languages that don't have relative clauses and lots of languages that don't have a special purpose conditional construction. But a lot of languages do seem to treat these functions as things that we need to have a special construction for—a structurally distinct construction.

What constructions are there in languages?

- Finally, there are recurrent lexical and grammatical categories and constructions which are ubiquitous if not universal:

  ✦ number, case, gender, degree, definiteness, tense, aspect, modality, indexation (agreement), etc.

  ✦ numerals, quantifiers, adpositions, articles, demonstratives, auxiliaries, adverbs, etc.

  ✦ relative clauses, possessives, anaphora, copular constructions, switch-reference, conditionals, etc.

FIGURE 132

So, is there a functional motivation for these universal patterns? We don't want to take this as simply given, that we are going to have a list of constructions—the kind of template people who write grammatical descriptions of languages use. We'd like to see if there is some motivation for this. And the answer, I think, is found in the phenomenon which is called the "verbalization of experience". This is the term that Wallace Chafe used in his research that he did in the 1970s, that culminated in the project that led to the Pear Stories film, that some of you are familiar with; the film that was used essentially for trying to investigate the question of: how do people verbalize experiences? I'm going to be using a lot of examples, and I'm going to show you a study that I did using the narratives that Chafe collected on the Pear Stories. That'll be on Wednesday [Lecture 9]. I might even have time to show the film, if, depending on how long my lecture is that day, if you haven't seen it already.

So what is the verbalization of experience? This is actually not the way that most grammarians look at grammar. Most grammarians, not only generative grammarians, most grammarians of any stripe, tend to look at grammatical constructions and ask, how are they used, what kinds of functions do particular constructions have, either by their own introspective judgment or questioning native language consultants, or by looking at a corpus. So that's going from the form to the meaning. They even ask questions like what meanings do these forms acquire, what meanings do they lose over time? And I'm interested in that question, too.

But I want to look at it from the other way—and I think this is really important; it's going to be a theme in the rest of my lectures—to look at it from the point of view of: there is an experience that we want to express in language, like I'm doing right now, like you do when you're talking with your friends; how do I go about this? What is the nature of that experience that we start with? And how do we manage to frame it in language? I think looking at this perspective is the only way that we can answer questions like why do languages have clauses, why do languages have number inflection, why do languages have articles, and questions like these which most linguistic theories don't usually ask.

So I'm going to start by some comments. A lot of this is inspired if not directly taken from the two classic papers that Chafe published in 1977. When I go back and read them, I see that I was somewhat liberal in interpreting them. I don't know if Chafe would disagree with some of the things I have said. But I have also elaborated it in certain ways that go beyond those original papers. And I will talk a little bit about that, because Chafe has also written more on this topic since 1977.

But the basic idea I want to start with is that an experience that you want to convey is a *unique whole*. If you think of something you want to tell someone that you did yesterday or last night, that experience is a unique thing. It may be similar to something you did before, but that experience and its totality is unique. And also it's a total experience, that is, it's something you went through; it's not preprocessed, broken up into parts. On the other hand, when you actually verbalize it and tell your friend about it, the utterance consists of what I would call reusable parts, namely language. Whenever you produce an utterance, you are reusing words and constructions that you've used in prior utterances to describe some other experience, not the one you are describing right now. And of course you've also broken up the experience into the parts that correspond to the words and the constructions that you used in the utterance.

So how do you get from one to the other? They are qualitatively very different kinds of things. Chafe's model is disarmingly simple, but I think he addresses the question in the right way and basically the way I framed it in that last slide. So even if he might disagree with the answer that I'm basically going to follow, it's the right way to pose the question and if we have an alternative we have to think about it starting from the same point. So in his model of verbalization, he describes it in several processes. The different processes may not occur in sequence; I'm going to describe it as if it's in a sequence, but we all know about human cognitive processing that a lot of processing occurs in parallel, and a lot of processing is pre-chunked.

Chafe's model of verbalization

- A speaker takes the whole experience and breaks it into smaller chunks of the same holistic type - **subchunking**

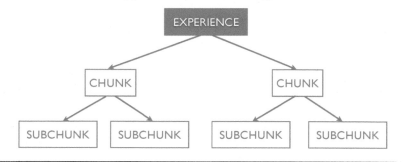

FIGURE 133

Chafe's model of verbalization

- Chafe later (1994) describes this process in terms of **consciousness**: a focusing of consciousness that moves around a semiactive periphery of consciousness

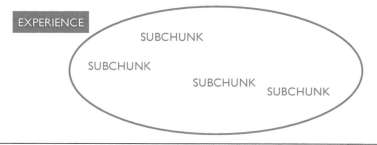

FIGURE 134

So the first thing according to Chafe, and the first thing in this metaphorical sense of order, is that the speaker has to take that whole experience, that unique whole, and then break it up into smaller chunks that are of the same type [Figure 133]. They are not analyzed, but they're just smaller chunks of that larger experience. And in one of those papers, he calls that "subchunking". So this is the original idea he had in the 1970s: you have an experience, that thing in the top, and then you break it up into the chunks, and then you can break it up into further subchunks that you will eventually verbalize in utterances.

In his later work though, he focuses very much in terms of this process, in terms of consciousness [Figures 134]. When you are looking at a whole experience, you are not trying to take the whole experience and slice it into pieces and then slice it into more pieces, and then take each piece and express it. What you are doing is that you have the whole experience in your consciousness as you want to describe it to someone else; you're moving around, identifying particular subchunks; then you move on to another subchunk and another subchunk and another subchunk. And all of this is occurring in what he calls the periphery of consciousness, which you can think of as the whole experience that we want to convey ultimately. So I'd like to think of it in this way; I think this is a more accurate description of how we actually cognize experiences.

For each of these subchunks then, however we come to them, the speaker then analyzes these chunks into parts of different types [Figure 135]. And the basic division he makes is the parts are going to be of two types: individuals that recur across chunks, so as your mind wanders around the experience there will be certain things that will be appearing in multiple chunks; and the remainder, which is the event that's left. So the thing that is distinctive or particular to that chunk, or is transitory, is the remainder. In his articles, he called this "propositionalizing", because this corresponds to the division between predicate and argument in logical representations, even if it is framed here in terms of his psychological model of verbalization.

So we start with the subchunk. We break it down into individuals. What's left is the events, and then presumably the individuals may recur in another subchunk in which another event takes place. So now what we have is a decomposition of the subchunk into parts of different types. And once again I should emphasize it's not like when you evoke this event. Those of you who know Fillmore's models of frame semantics should know that there are lots of different participants or frame elements as he calls them, and you don't actually evoke or express every one of them. And likewise the event has many different facets, and you don't express every facet of event in a sentence, in an utterance.

Chafe's model of verbalization

- A speaker then analyzes the chunk into parts of different type: individuals that recur across chunks, and the remainder, which is the event in the chunk - *propositionalizing*

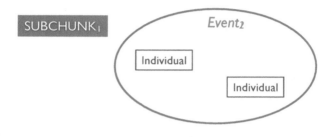

FIGURE 135

In Chafe's later work, he attributes propositionalizing into individuals and events to what he calls "universal properties of human experience". Well, I think it is not really that universal. They vary too much to leave this process out. We don't have to go to some exotic language. We can just look at the variation in the way speakers of the same language verbalize particular experiences.

And this is where I'll be looking at the Pear Stories for the first time. So consider this first example [Figure 136]. Here is an object. So we are going to back to the old business of parts of speech here, where we talked about object concepts, property concepts, action concepts, and reference, predication, and modification. Here, we have two different descriptions. This is actually taken from a paper of Chafe's, not from the Pear Stories. And you see the two different descriptions and in the two different descriptions you are talking about the same category, or the same object, namely, the bamboo grove. But in the first one, it is referred to, so it's a referring expression construed as an individual. In the second passage, "it was only a bamboo grove you know?", it's expressed as a predicate. Yes, it's a categorizing predicate, but it's a predicate. Those are the two different types that Chafe described in his act of propositionalizing. So it shows that it is not a universal automatic cognitive process how you actually divide a subchunk into individuals and events or predicates.

Variation in propositionalizing

- Object as individual or predicate (Chafe 1998:283)

  126 And I noticed someone go past.
  127 My back window there,
  128 by this bamboo grove.

  18 And no one ever walked by back there,
  19 it was only a bamboo grove you know?

FIGURE 136

Variation in propositionalizing

- Property as predicate or individual

  11,112 [.85] He's a little [.45] bewildered.

  18,83 [.4] It's-- a [.2] there's just this look on
  his . . his face of bewilderment.

FIGURE 137

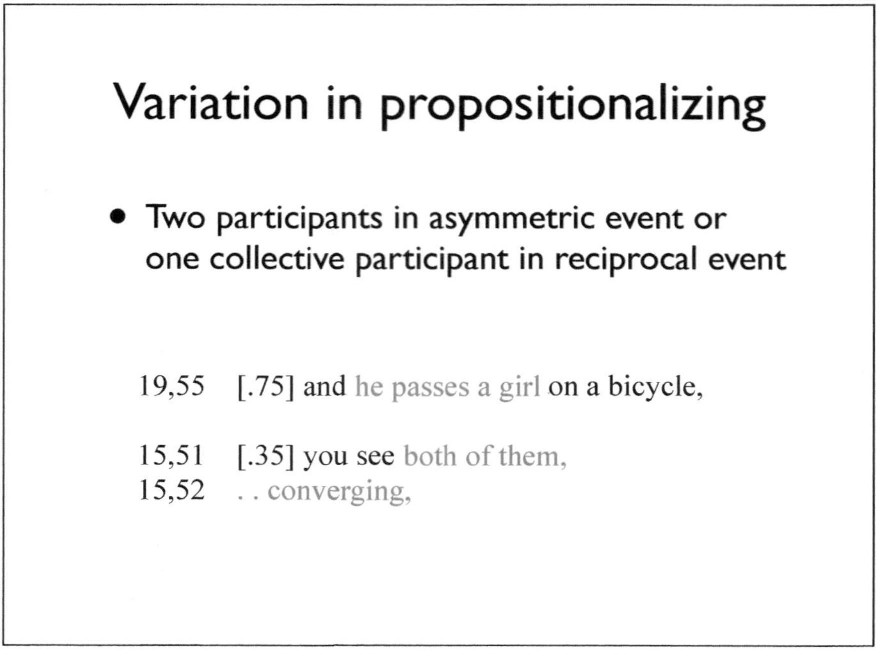

Variation in propositionalizing

- Two participants in asymmetric event or
  one collective participant in reciprocal event

19,55   [.75] and he passes a girl on a bicycle,

15,51   [.35] you see both of them,
15,52   . . converging,

FIGURE 138

Here is when you have property as a predicate or individual. So the first example, this is from the pear stories: "He is a little bewildered" [Figure 137]. So
you predicate this state of bewilderment. And a different speaker said "there's
just this look on his ... his face of bewilderment." So here it's expressed as a
referring expression.

Another kind of variation of propositionalizing has to do with the type of
event and the relationship with the participants in the event [Figure 138]. So it
is action that you can see as two different participants, so we subchunk it with
two individuals: "He passes a girl." *He* and *a girl* are the two individuals. Or you
propositionalize the subchunk as one participant or one basically group participant, both of them, and the action is converging. So again, we see that there is
a difference in how you break this subchunk down into individuals and events.

Another is what counts as the individual you are going to talk about, so,
object or part of object? These two speakers are describing the same scene in
the film [Figure 139]. In the first case, "He takes the pears, and he puts it on the
bicycle", we have the pears and the bicycle. If you know the film, it is actually
a basket of pears and the other speaker says "and then he decides to take the
whole bushel", instead of referring to the pears, "and then he puts it on his bicycle rack" instead of "put it on his bicycle" as the other speaker said. So again
the choice of individuals varies from one speaker to the next.

Variation in propositionalizing

- Object or part of object as individual

2,46   He takes the pears,
2,47   [.7] and he . . puts it on the bicycle,

8,23   and then he decides to take the whole bushel.
8,24   [.9] And he puts it on his [.35] b—icycle rack
           in front,

FIGURE 139

Variation in subchunking ⇒ variation in propositionalizing

- Different subchunkings of experience

1,15   [3.3 [.85] A-nd u-h [1.5]] and then he gets
           down out of the tree,

7,14   [2.25 [.6] tsk [.1] A--nd [.75]] he-- [.35]
           was going up and down the ladder,

FIGURE 140

Variation in subchunking ⇒ variation in propositionalizing

- Verbalization at different levels of granularity

1,62   [.45] I think he [.85] he picks up the b—asket
            of pears,
1,63   and he puts it on his bicycle,
1,64   . . on the front?
1,65   [.25] And he rides off.

3,14   [.55] And he rips off. . one of the [1.0]
            baskets of . . of pears that he has.

FIGURE 141

Sometimes the differences come because the subchunking was actually done differently. So, here are essentially two speakers trying to evoke a particular part of the film [Figure 140]. And the first one focuses on one movement action on the part of the pear picker: "He gets down out of the tree". And in the second one, he's now focusing on a multiple series of events: "He was going up and down the ladder". And of course he picks out the ladder instead of the tree.

You have verbalization at different levels of granularity [Figure 141]. So the first speaker subchunks this particular passage in the film, with three subchunks: "He picks up the basket of pears; he puts it on its bicycle; and he rides off." The other speaker subchunks it as a single subchunk: "and he rips off one of the baskets of ... of pears that he has."

So all of this is to show, to emphasize to you that we can't just assume that in propositionalizing, you are just following some universal cognitive predisposition. So it's kind of like what Melissa Bowerman was saying in many of her lectures: that there's no kind of cognitive primacy and automaticity in how this is done. We have to ask the question of how these speakers can do this. And we need to keep that process in here. I'm not going to answer the question here exactly, how and why they do it in different ways. The point is that it is a process that people can manipulate, do in different ways and of course that

Chafe's model of verbalization, *cont.*

- Finally, a speaker identifies those parts (entities) in terms of previously verbalized, similar parts of prior experiences - **categorizing**

- Chafe's later work retains this function

FIGURE 142

means children have to learn how to do it in these different ways. It doesn't come automatically.

Finally, the speaker identifies those parts that were subchunked out and propositionalized in terms of previously verbalized, similar parts of prior experiences—this process is of course categorizing [Figure 142]. So if you want to talk about a particular individual in your experience, you might decide to describe it as essentially the same category as previous experiences that you had of jars. So you use the term *jar* and you've now categorized that experience. And it's a bit too important to avoid categorization as a cognitive process, so Chafe's later work does retain that function, though he doesn't talk about it a lot.

So if we see this process, which is basically the model laid out in his 1977 papers, the speaker can verbalize this originally unique, whole experience as reusable parts. You take it from the whole experience. You've picked out subchunks. Within that subchunk you've picked out or broken it up into individuals and an event. And then you categorize those individuals and events, and those of course correspond to nouns, verbs, and adjectives, at least in the informal sense of that term. So now we know how the nouns, verbs and adjectives came to verbalize experience. Obviously it's a very general model. A lot of interesting questions—many, many interesting questions—remain. But this is the basic model that Chafe proposes.

And the model also accounts for the universal organization of utterances into clauses, or at least intonation units, which closely correlate to clauses, and to some extent phrases; the clause is basically a subchunk. But the model does not account for the function words and grammatical categories and constructions that I listed on an earlier slide, the one where I said we need to explain why these things exist and these things that are so widespread in human languages. Now I do have to say that Chafe has worked on this problem. It's incomplete in my opinion. I developed this model I'm going to present here independently of this, but then I was prompted by a referee of the paper that I published who was remarkably knowledgeable of all of the work of Wallace Chafe. I read a lot of his later papers, and it's a lot of great stuff of course. But I still think that there are some ways in which the model I propose is more complete.

So how are we going to elaborate this model? I'm saying there is nothing wrong essentially with the outline we've seen; it is just not everything we need. Basically, his model describes how the unique whole of experience is broken down and then the parts you've broken down are identified by categories. But at that point what you've got are general categories and a bunch of parts, it's like you took something apart and now you have all the parts lying around. You know what each part is. You know what category it belongs to. But if you want to go back to the original experience, you have to know not just what category each part is, but the particular instance you want to talk about. And you also want to be able to put those parts back together in the right way, so it represents the original experience that you had. So that's the process of reconstitution that I describe here.

So that is what I am going to give you a model of, and it's the thing that I think is missing from Chafe's earlier model, and it's also why we have all those grammatical categories and inflections and constructions. And then you can actually convey in a reconstituted, i.e. conceptualized form, that unique whole that you originally wanted to communicate to your addressee.

So here's the basic model [Figure 143]. The items on the left column are the processes that Chafe talked about: subchunking, you take that subchunk and propositionalize it, you relate it to prior experience by categorizing it. And then the processes on the right are the ones I'm going to add. Once you decide that something belongs to a general category, you have to somehow convey to the listener that you are actually talking about a unique specific instance of this general type. And that's the process I will call "particularizing"; and we have two subtypes which I'll come to. Then you also have to put these things back together again. So once you've broken an event down to individuals and

Elaborating Chafe's model of verbalization

Taking it apart...	...and putting it back together again
Subchunking/Focusing of consciousness	Cohering (Flow of consciousness)
Propositionalizing	Structuring
Relating it to prior experience...	...and re-establishing its unique specificity

Categorizing	Particularizing:
	    Selecting (Instance)
	    Situating (Grounding, Orientation)

FIGURE 143

the event, the subchunk, you have to put it back together in the right way. And lastly, with the subchunks, you have to put them back together again, in some kind of coherent discourse, or coherent complex constructions. That will then allow a listener to somehow to get an idea of the original unique entire experience that you want to communicate.

So now I'm going to go into some details. Let me say a little bit that I have already talked about before I go to the details. This is the point that sometimes has been misunderstood about how I have been using Chafe's model, which is that a speaker does not verbalize everything in the experience she wishes to convey. You remember the tool metaphor, the scaffolding metaphor and the backstage cognition I referred to a couple lectures back [Lecture 4]. It's all people saying the same thing, that is, what you verbalize has to evoke the whole experience. It doesn't have to actually systematically enumerate everything that actually happened. Instead the speaker selects chunks, individuals and events so as to evoke that original experience, and categorizes them so as to relate the conveyed experience to prior shared experiences. Because when I'm telling you about something, I need to somehow relate it to things that you and I can both share, communicate about, understand, and so that categorization will serve that purpose. Obviously when you categorize something in one way, as a jar, you then cut off other ways to categorize that object that might

Particularizing

	Individuals	Events
Selecting	*a hummingbird,* *two hummingbirds,* *a pair of* *hummingbirds*	*flew,* *was flying,* *is about to fly*
Situating	*the hummingbird* *in the nest,* *a/the hummingbird,* *Joey's hummingbird*	*will fly, might fly,* *flew yesterday,* *flew on Tuesday,* *Joey thinks it flew*

FIGURE 144

be useful, but for the purposes of your communication, you want to call it a jar for whatever reason. And then, nevertheless, as I said, the categories must be particularized, and the parts recombined to successfully convey the whole experience. So using selected subchunks of the experience and selected individuals and events there doesn't mean you are relieved of the responsibility of particularizing it, reassembling, reconstituting that skeleton you created in your utterance to get the whole experience evoked.

So let's look at particularizing [Figure 144]. As I said, categorizing relates an entity in experience to prior entities by subsuming them under a general category or type. So, for example, if you chose to describe a bird as a hummingbird, you've categorized this experience you had. But the experience you're verbalizing is an experience with a particular instantiation of the category. It's not that often that we talk about hummingbirds in general as a general category. We are talking about a particular hummingbird that I saw or whatever. So how does the speaker do it? Basically, there are some instances, some particular instances and you have to select that instance and you have to situate it in physical space and mental space, or time as we'll see for events.

So let me give you a few examples from English. Let's start looking at some of these. With an individual, what's selecting? Well, things like the indefinite article, picks out the hummingbird. In particular the indefinite article in English in most cases picks out a referent that the speaker can identify but the listener does not know. "Two hummingbirds", the numeral and the plural marking shows you that the instantiation you pick out is more than one individual, specifically how many individuals. Another way of construing that pair of individuals is as "a pair of hummingbirds". So expressions like "a pair of" also select this. When you select an instance, it may not be a singular instance; you may have to select a group of some sort or an indeterminate number, or an indeterminate amount.

Now another way to pick out an individual is to situate it in the world. So if you say "the hummingbird in the nest", that's situating it in physical space: you identify the particular instance by its location in space. This is a useful way of doing things because you don't have two objects in the same place at the same time. Articles like *a* vs. *the* also situate the individual, but in a mental space. So the use of "the hummingbird" situates it in the mental space of our shared knowledge of the identity of individuals. If I use "a hummingbird", it situates it in a different mental space, only my own knowledge of the identity of this individual. Another way to situate something is with reference to some other entity, like "Joey's hummingbird".

Now you can do the same thing with events, so particularizing cuts across individual and events, the two different types of things you broke up your sub-chunk into. So selecting something: a particular entity in the past tense typically refers to a bounded event. "Was flying" on the other hand picks out a middle phase of some kind of event that is described. So we are selecting here now a temporal part of the event as it unfolds over time. "Is about to fly", another kind of expression that also picks out something: a different phase, the phase that just precedes this event as described by this category—fly.

Situating: "will fly", and of course the past tense in "flew", those situate the event in time, past, future or present. "Might fly" situates the event in the mental space of evidence or uncertainty or possibility. I'm using the term "mental space" of course as in Fauconnier's original work, where he used this model of mental spaces to capture modal and other relations. "Flew yesterday"—*yesterday*, this temporal adverb, does express again this location in time. "On Tuesday", using a proper name for a time unit, also locates the event in time.

So you can see I'm taking a broader perspective than Talmy does in saying how do we explain things. We have to explain not just things like past tense inflection, but we need to explain deictic temporal adverbials and temporal adverbial phrases. "Joey thinks it flew", again here the classic example from Fauconnier's model is you have a mental space, the belief, and that belief is

Selecting

	Nouns/Arguments	Verbs/Predicates
Instance		
Unit	unit terms, classifiers	perfective, durative phrases
Group	group terms, collectives, classifiers	collective
Part	part terms, body parts, orientation terms	imperfective, phasals, causal derivations
Quantify	number, cardinal numerals, quantifiers	iterative, quantifiers, cognate objects
Distinguish	"same"/"other", ordinal numerals, set-member terms	repetitive, retaliative
Generic	articles	generic, habitual

FIGURE 145

anchored by a particular individual who has that belief. So again you are situating this event in the mental space of Joey's beliefs.

So this gives you some examples. These are the kind of functions that are performed as part of this verbalization process [Figure 145]. So these things—these expressions that you see on the screen—are examples that are recruited for part of this verbalization process. I won't go into this in detail. It would take too long; there're no particular examples here. I hope you will recognize many of these terms. But these are examples of the kinds of categories that are used to select objects in space and to select events in time. And I'll just mention the categories that are defined here in the left, the different row.

So this is the process of looking at instantiation, picking out a unit, picking out a group like a pair of hummingbirds, or picking out a part if you wanted to talk about the part of an object. Quantification like numerals and quantifiers: it's a function I'll call "distinguishing", it's the function performed by words like *same* and *other*, ordinal numerals. And then we can use articles to express a generic function. Languages do give you the possibility to talk about hummingbirds as a general category if you want to do so. So that is accomplished at least in some languages with articles; sometimes languages have a special generic article or particle. And then you have essentially the same parallel of kinds of constructions used for selecting events.

Situating in a physical space

Physical dimension	Space	Time
Deictic	demonstratives, deictic locatives, directionals	tense, nominal tense, deictic temporals
Topographic		
Relative	compass, topographic	time-cycle adverbs
Absolute	place names	event/time names
Geometric	adpositions, locative/ directional cases	adpositions (e.g. points vs. intervals)
Somatic	body part locatives	front/back metaphors

FIGURE 146

Now many linguists have noticed some of these parallels, so I certainly don't claim any originality here in that respect. What I'm arguing though is that once we identify these kinds of functions and we see that there are these constructions that occur for these functions, constructions in the broad sense, then we have to still ask ourselves why are these functions there, not just that they exist and there are parallels between nouns, verbs in these functions. And as I said, the answer has to do with this verbalization process, I believe.

Situating: we can look at the same thing [Figure 146]. This is a classification, that's something I've been using in my semantics classes for 25 years now, and have not published, about how to characterize spatial things. It's somewhat different from the way Steve Levinson and his colleagues have developed the typology of spatial conceptualizations. I won't go into it for now. The main point simply is that languages have a variety of means to situate entities, situate objects in space, situate events in time, sometimes you can even situate objects in time and events in space.

And languages also have the possibility of situating entities in a mental space: spaces of people's thoughts, beliefs, possibility, necessity and so on [Figure 147]. And again there are a number of constructions we find that are used here to perform those functions. These are the kind of recurrent constructions we see in the world's languages. So you can see where I am going with this,

Situating in a mental space

Mental Space	Nouns/Arguments	Verbs/Predicates
Deictic	definiteness (articles)	modality
Relationship	fictional context nouns	world-creating predicates
Source of space	possessor (of fictional context nouns)	persons (subjects of world-creating predicates)

FIGURE 147

as I have been saying, trying to answer the question why do languages have the constructions that they do. Basically it's to serve the purpose of verbalization. So the kind of constructions that we find in the world languages: hopefully we can explain that by looking at the nature of the verbalization process, either a model like the one I am presenting here today or some similar model.

I want to take a little time to talk about particularizing relational entities. Relational entities are things like possessed nouns, like body parts and kinship terminology, and property concepts and action concepts. Properties are always predicated of some entity, and actions always involve interactions among entities. That's what I just said: these relational entities inherently presuppose an associated participant, also called an argument in more logically oriented approaches to semantics. Now of course relational entities can be selected and situated to be particularized, that's what those previous slides were that I didn't go into, there are lots of ways to situate events in time, for instance. But another important way which you identify particular events is who participated. So if Janet kisses Jack, that is a different event from Mary kissing Mark, or for that matter from Janet kissing Mark. So these different kissing events can be differentiated by who is participating in them. That's what makes them different events.

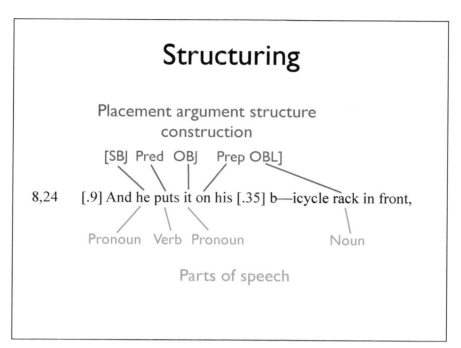

FIGURE 148

So I would like to suggest that the function of agreement—argument indexation—is to particularize relational entities. There's kind of a puzzle about what the role is that agreement plays in languages. As I already argued a couple lectures back [Lecture 4], its function is not to syntactically relate two words in a sentence. So what function does it have? I think it is partly to particularize relational entities. That's why when you find indexation or agreement, it's usually attached to the relational word, a relational noun like a kinship term, a modifier like a property word, or a main predicate as in subject and object indexation.

Structuring: this is how we put the events back together, put the subchunks back together. It's basically about who did what to whom. So you take these particularized entities—you've now identified the instances, we are not talking about general categories any more—the event, participants, and their properties, and then we reassemble them into that subchunk, something that will evoke that subchunk. So grammatically, structuring represents clause structure, including argument structure and modification within phrases, and the division into parts of speech. I'm just going to pick one example just to show you what it is [Figure 148]. At some level what I've said to you should be obvious. If you have a sentence like "he puts it on his bicycle rack in front"—we've

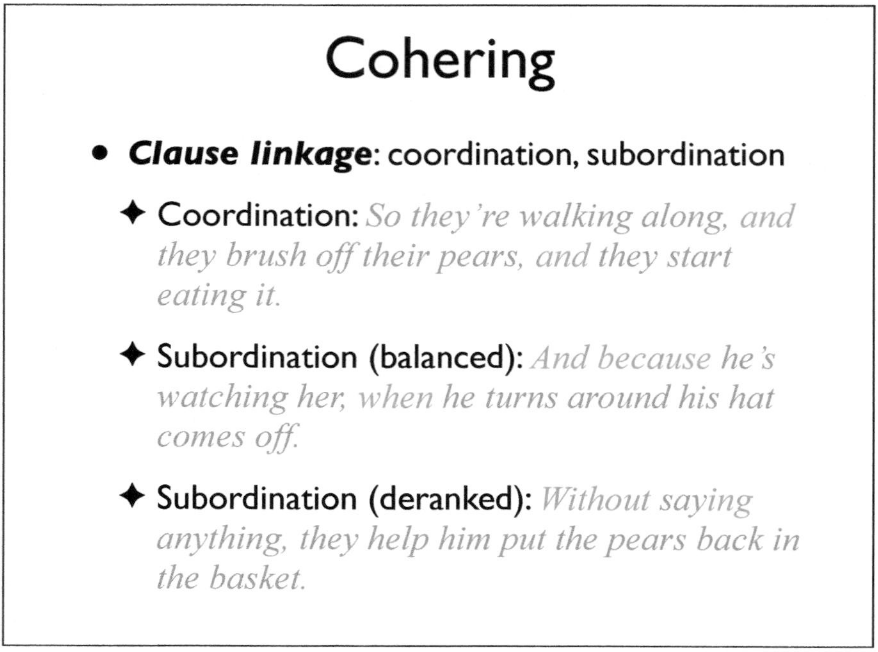

Cohering

- **Clause linkage**: coordination, subordination

  ✦ **Coordination:** *So they're walking along, and they brush off their pears, and they start eating it.*

  ✦ **Subordination (balanced):** *And because he's watching her, when he turns around his hat comes off.*

  ✦ **Subordination (deranked):** *Without saying anything, they help him put the pears back in the basket.*

FIGURE 149

seen this sentence already—there is what we call a placement argument structure construction, something that describes causing something to be located at a place. And so we have that argument structure construction, which then essentially reconstitutes the subchunk, the subchunk that was divided into *put, he, it,* and *bicycle rack.*

Likewise, we have parts of speech: pronouns, verbs, and nouns. Now I mean this in the sense of parts of speech that I've talked about in the previous lectures when I focused on the syntax [Lectures 2–3]. But here I did talk about these so-called propositional act constructions—predication, reference, modification—and of course these are all illustrations of those. That's also about how you package information in a clause. I could go on about this. This is an area where there's a lot of controversy about the proper analysis, both syntactic and semantic. I have enough slides here to give you a whole separate lecture on the best way to analyze structuring. But I'm not going to do it here because I want to finish this story. So you just have to take my word for it or look at the article this lecture is drawn from, which was published in the journal *Cognitive Linguistics* in 2007.

Instead I'm just going to go on now to cohering: how do you relate the subchunks you chose to verbalize in order to evoke the entire experience that you

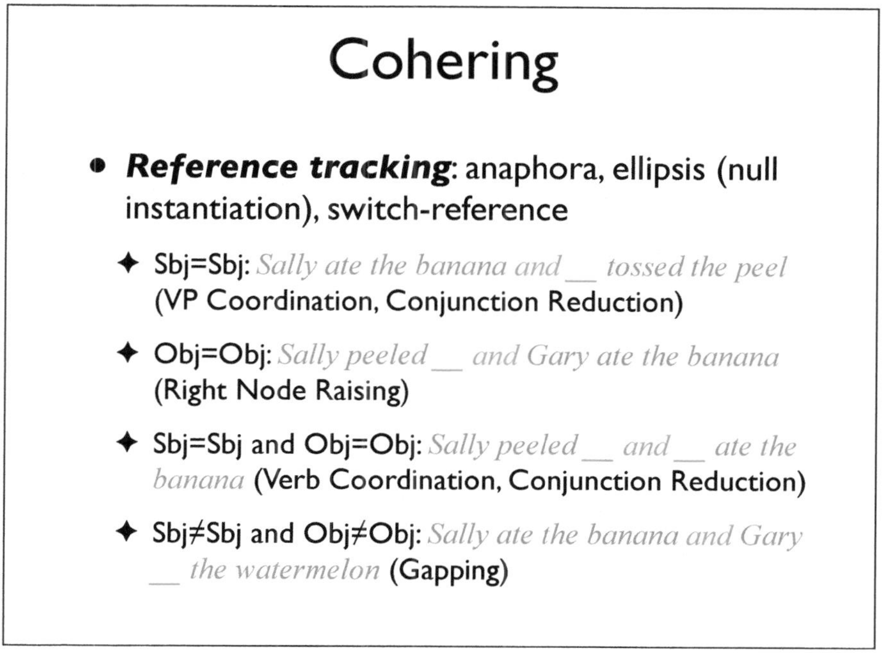

Cohering

- **_Reference tracking_**: anaphora, ellipsis (null instantiation), switch-reference

  ✦ **Sbj=Sbj**: _Sally ate the banana and __ tossed the peel_ (VP Coordination, Conjunction Reduction)

  ✦ **Obj=Obj**: _Sally peeled __ and Gary ate the banana_ (Right Node Raising)

  ✦ **Sbj=Sbj and Obj=Obj**: _Sally peeled __ and __ ate the banana_ (Verb Coordination, Conjunction Reduction)

  ✦ **Sbj≠Sbj and Obj≠Obj**: _Sally ate the banana and Gary __ the watermelon_ (Gapping)

FIGURE 150

started from? Cohering is two major families of constructions that have the cohering function. One is of course various kinds of *clause linkage constructions*, such as various types of coordination and subordination constructions [Figure 149]. So you can take an example like this. These are examples that I picked out of the Pear Stories; it's basically just for illustration here. So: "they're walking along, and they brush off their pears, and they start eating it." That's what they said. Subordination, there are two kinds. Certain typologists recognize what they called "balanced subordination" where you have what traditionally is called the "finite clause"; the subordinate clause is structurally very similar to the main clause: "And because he's watching her, when he turns around his hat comes off". "Deranked subordination" is when that subordinate clause is linguistically in a form that looks different from what you'd find in a simple main clause. So "without saying anything": it's introduced by a preposition *without*, and has the gerund form *saying*: "Without saying anything, they help him put the pears back in the basket."

The other cohering function that you find is many different kinds of systems of *reference tracking*, so anaphora, ellipsis or as Fillmore calls it in his construction grammar "null instantiation", and various kinds of switch-reference and other types of reference tracking devices [Figure 150]. Again I'm just going to illustrate it with some examples from English, since my point here is not to present a comprehensive typology, of course, but just to show you what kinds of constructions I'm talking about that are performing this function in the verbalization process.

So for instance, English exploits some kinds of ellipsis in order to tell you the coreference relations between two clauses that are coordinated. So if you want to have a construction in which you show that the subject participant in the two clauses is the same, you use the construction here: "Sally ate the banana and tossed the peel" (these are invented examples). Traditional generative grammar called this "VP coordination" or "conjunction reduction", names that reflect two different transformational analyses. If you want to show the two objects are the same, you can use a construction like "Sally peeled and Gary ate the banana". In generative grammar, that was called "right node raising". If you want to show that both subject and object are the same, you can say "Sally peeled and ate the banana", traditionally called in generative grammar "verb coordination" or "conjunction reduction". And lastly if you want to show that neither of them are alike, while the event type is the same, you have a construction that generative grammarians called "gapping": "Sally ate the banana and Gary the watermelon". So my point here is not to defend any particular analysis. It's just to show that you can characterize this range of constructions in English, and it's all telling you something about reference tracking between the two clauses that are conjoined.

Now Chafe discusses this as well, not using the term cohering. This is an example he had from speakers that verbalized a film that was essentially a pilot study for what became the pear film project [Figure 151]. And the way I've characterized it, you can look at the different kinds of coordination constructions and see the pattern of subchunking that this speaker used in verbalizing the scene from this film. So you first have different subjects between the two clauses. In the beginning, you have verb phrase coordination, "he picked up some hay and lifted it over the corral fence and into the corral". So prepositional phrase coordination, "over the corral fence and into the corral", shows the tight link between the events that Chafe labeled C6 and C7 and then a less direct link between that combination which he called C5 with event C4. Then you have a switch to a different subject, "all of the animals" instead of "he". So, "all of the animals went after and began eating the hay". That's the verb coordination construction that shows the link between those two subchunks, and then the fact that you have different subjects shows that those two clusters of subchunks are ultimately just connected by the cohesion of the sequence of sentences in the discourse.

So, all of that was simply to illustrate those constructions. I find that some linguists don't find this terribly exciting. Maybe you don't either. But the point

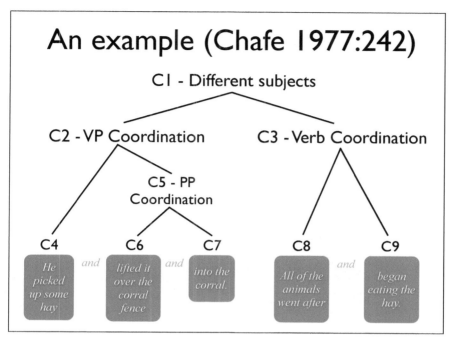

An example (Chafe 1977:242)

C1 - Different subjects

C2 - VP Coordination   C3 - Verb Coordination

C5 - PP Coordination

C4 — *He picked up some hay*   *and*   C6 — *lifted it over the corral fence*   *and*   C7 — *into the corral.*   C8 — *All of the animals went after*   *and*   C9 — *began eating the hay.*

FIGURE 151

that I think is important here is that we can't just assume that these constructions exist. We have to ask why they are there. And the answer to that question,
I have argued, comes from looking at the process of verbalization. And the
process of verbalization of course is more than just linguistic analysis. It's a
proposal about how human beings take an experience, somehow conceptually
analyze and structure it and reconstitute it in communication in utterances.

So what there is to say about the inventory of constructions? That's where I
started. What kinds of constructions are there in the world's languages? How
do we break it down? How many are there? Somebody asked me after a lecture, how many constructions are there in a language? That's a tough question
to answer, but the starting point is to look at the kinds of functions that you
expect to find in languages, and then come up with some framework that tells
you what functions you find, like this verbalization framework.

So the verbalization process motivates the types of constructions found
across languages [Figure 152]. Particularizing involves various adnominal and
adverbial constructions including what Talmy calls "satellite" constructions as
well as the various inflectional categories that we've talked about. Structuring
motivates clausal constructions, that is, the predicate-argument or argument
structure constructions, attributive constructions of different types; also information structure constructions—one of the things that I skipped over in those

The inventory of constructions

- The verbalization process motivates the types of constructions found across languages:

    * *Particularizing*: various adnominal and adverbial (including "satellite") constructions

    * *Structuring*: clausal (predicate-argument) and phrasal (attributive) constructions, including argument structure and information structure constructions

    * *Cohering*: many complex sentence constructions; reference tracking, including anaphora, null instantiation, switch-reference

FIGURE 152

many slides—had to do with the interaction between argument structure and information structure. And cohering motivates the existence of many complex sentence constructions, including phenomena that cross clauses, like reference tracking including anaphora, null instantiation and switch-reference.

Now I want to go back to the question that Melissa Bowerman talked about this morning, the question that Len Talmy asked, which is why are these things grammatical? Now, I'm taking a broader view of "grammatical" than Talmy did. I'm talking in terms of these minor lexical classes as well as the inflectional categories. Because those minor lexical classes recur across languages, just like the inflectional categories do as well.

The first point I want to make is that all of the processes of verbalization could be expressed lexically, using so-called content words: nouns, verbs and adjectives in the traditional sense. These are called periphrastic constructions in traditional grammar. But these reconstituting processes—the ones that I added to Chafe's original model (particularizing, structuring and cohering)— are highly likely to be grammaticalized. So it's the stuff on that right hand side of that table I presented back there [Figure 143] where you are likely to get grammaticalization to occur. You are less likely to get grammaticalization on the left hand column. That's where lexicalization takes place.

Why is this the case? Again we should always ask the question why, because that will bring us the kinds of functional models that will motivate why languages are structured the way they are. I think one of the reasons why is because, once you've already broken down an experience and you have categorized its parts, putting it back together again and particularizing it can be done in many fewer ways. There are lots and lots of different ways you can subchunk an experience, identify individuals and events and categorize them. But once you've done that, you've already imposed a lot of construals on the experience you are trying to communicate. Once you impose all these construals on the experience by categorizing things and breaking down the experience in certain ways, there's a relatively limited number of ways you can put it back together again and instantiate it.

Because the options are limited, then any particular option comes to be used more frequently. And as Melissa Bowerman mentioned and Joan Bybee, my colleague at New Mexico, has emphasized, frequency of use is a primary driving force in the grammaticalization process. And usage patterns, in addition to driving the grammaticalization process, also lead to particular combinations of multiple verbalization processes to be grammaticalized into single complex constructions. So take argument structure constructions: if you've already decided to categorize the event as a giving event or sending event, you have already committed yourself to a ditransitive construction as one of the few options for reassembling the event and its participants. So there are a lot of conventionalized combinations of the parts of the verbalization process that speakers employ in recurrent fashion. Yes, you can find a novel way to subchunk an experience or propositionalize it, and get up some interesting alternatives like the ones I showed you from the pear stories. But there are of course the same old ways of describing very commonly recurring experiences. And those get grammaticalized into constructions that seem to be doing more than one step of the verbalization process at once—a single construction doing multiple things in the verbalization process.

So this talk I am just finishing up here is very programmatic. I've given you a very broad outline of how I think one should go about answering the question, what constructions are there in the world's languages, or in any particular language? There are lots and lots of details that need to be filled in. But even at this very broad level, obviously created in order to fit this lecture in a single hour of presentation, there is essentially the opportunity to answer questions like: why do languages have the kinds of inflections you find, minor categories that you find and constructions in the general sense that you find? Thank you very much.

Typological Universals and the Semantic Map Model

Thank you very much! I'm very happy to be here. I'm glad that many of you have come. I know some of you are attending these lectures for the first time. So in my introductory comments, I'll try to explain what the topic of this today's lecture is, and also make a connection to the lectures that I gave before for the people who haven't attended the other lectures.

So the question I'm going to look at here today is syntactic categories. This is everything from categories like noun, verb, and adjective, or subject and object, to categories like indefinite pronoun categories that we'll look at, inflectional categories, and also categories of word meaning. The kind of thing I'm going to talk to you about now is something that Melissa Bowerman has talked about in her previous lectures and will probably talk about today, having to do with categories of word meaning. In all of these, you'll see what the issue is soon. But for now, what I want to point out is: for the kind of grammatical and syntactic categories I'm mainly interested in, like noun and verb and subject and object, they play an important role in the traditional model of syntactic analysis called the building-block model where we define constructions in terms of how they are made up of nouns and verbs and subjects and objects and so on [Lecture 2]. So the syntactic categories are used in this building-block model of syntax. The main thrust of the lectures I've given at Beihang University, the first five lectures, is that syntactic categories are language-specific. Syntactic categories are defined by the constructions in which they occur. I'm going to just take that as an assumption for now for those of you who are attending these lectures for the first time.

The approach to grammar that I've presented here in the last few lectures, Radical Construction Grammar, rejects the existence of syntactic categories as independent entities. The categories are defined by constructions and we use

All original audio-recordings and other supplementary material, such as any hand-outs and powerpoint presentations for the lecture series, have been made available online and are referenced via unique DOI numbers on the website www.figshare.com. They may be accessed via a QR code for the print version of this book. In the e-book, both the QR code and dynamic links are available, and can be accessed by a mouse-click.

© WILLIAM CROFT, REPRODUCED WITH KIND PERMISSION FROM THE AUTHOR BY KONINKLIJKE BRILL NV, LEIDEN, 2021 | DOI:10.1163/9789004363533_008

constructions as our starting point. Now to use an English proverb, we have to be careful not to throw out the baby with the bath water. The bath water is the building-block model of syntax that we want to get rid of. But the baby is syntactic categories that are used also to describe syntactic generalizations, general facts about English or Chinese or about languages in general, which is actually what I'm most interested in. So we want to find a way to represent grammatical generalizations. And the point I want to make here is—for those of you who have looked at syntactic analyses that linguists advocating different theories have used—that in fact there is no one best way to represent syntactic generalizations. So don't get fooled into thinking there is only one way to do it.

So as I said syntactic categories are defined by their constructional roles. We'll get an example right here. Take the category "transitive verb" in a language like English. The category of transitive verb is different from the category of intransitive verb. Each of them occurs in a different construction: the construction with a direct object and the construction without a direct object. And of course, many English verbs occur in just one of those constructions, so *touch* is only a transitive verb and *die* is only an intransitive verb.

Now, the traditional analysis of English says that transitive verbs and intransitive verbs also are both verbs, that's what the names imply. So why do we call them both verbs? The real reason that we make explicit here is that because verbs, transitive verbs and intransitive verbs occur in other constructions together. For example, the traditional definition of verb in English includes the ability to inflect for tense and agreement. Now in the modern sense of construction in construction grammar which I talked about in my first lecture, the ability to inflect is actually itself a construction: that is, it's a word root plus an inflection, and that particular inflection defines verbs in English. But from our perspective, what that really means is that there is yet another construction, this inflectional construction, that defines another role which we'll call MV for "morphological verb". And that role or category includes both transitive verbs and intransitive verbs as they are defined by the other constructions.

So how do we represent these syntactic generalizations in construction grammar? The usual way in construction grammar is to describe a taxonomy of more general and more specific constructions to capture grammatical properties of different degrees of generality. So for example, transitive verb includes more specific constructions like the particular verb *kick* as a transitive verb, and the particular verb *kiss* as a transitive verb [Figure 153]. So the fact that in both *kick* and *kiss*, the subject comes before and the object comes after, is captured by the fact that there is a more general construction "transitive verb" defined in English that includes subject before the verb and object after the transitive verb. Now if you look more closely of course, the actual structure of these

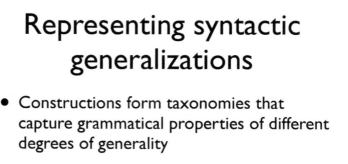

Representing syntactic generalizations

- Constructions form taxonomies that capture grammatical properties of different degrees of generality

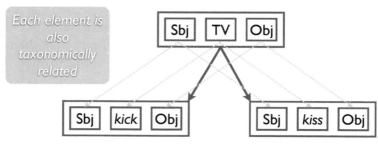

FIGURE 153

constructions is alike. That's what is important. So since each element of the construction—all these little boxes represent elements of the construction—are taxonomically related, the transitive subject in general is a more general category, and the subject of *kick* is a more specific category. It's the same with all the other elements.

Now construction grammarians have done more with this notion of taxonomic relations among the elements. So if we take a construction like question forms, WH questions, "What are you doing here?"—this is the analysis by Kay and Fillmore—you can see that we can get a pattern like this [Figure 154]. "What are you doing here" is what Kay and Fillmore call a "left isolation construction". But the left isolation construction itself consists of two parts: one is the question word and the other is a structure of the form that they called "subject auxiliary inversion". So here what we say is: this part of the construction is an instance of this more general construction that stands by itself. Ok, that's all fine.

So what do you have to do in Radical Construction Grammar? Remember, I said morphological verb is an element of another construction. Well, you can describe it in terms of transitive verb [TV], intransitive verb [IV] and then morphological verb [MV] [Figure 155]. And now here the element of this construction—transitive verb—and the element of this

Representing syntactic generalizations

- Elements of a construction can instantiate a construction themselves, e.g. WH questions (*What are you doing here?*; Kay and Fillmore 1999:18)—this is the nesting of constructions

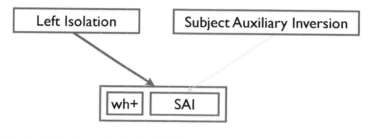

FIGURE 154

Representing syntactic generalizations

- To capture generalizations across construction-specific categories, one can allow an element of one construction to instantiate an element of another construction

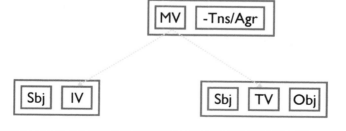

FIGURE 155

Another look at representing syntactic generalizations

- There are other representations that can capture the generalizations in a taxonomy

- For example, instead of a taxonomy...

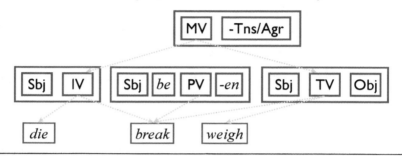

FIGURE 156

construction—intransitive verb—are represented as instances of an element of this higher construction.

Ok, so this is a way of using what they call taxonomies to capture general facts about the behavior of what we call verbs in English. And this is the common way to do it in construction grammar, including Radical Construction Grammar. The problem is, the facts of languages are messier than what I've just shown you. So most syntactic generalizations do not form these nice taxonomic hierarchies that you see. For example, many English verbs can be both transitive and intransitive, so they belong in both of those constructions. And this category overlap—verbs that are transitive and intransitive—this is a semantically coherent group of verbs as many linguists have pointed out. Then there are other verbs that are missing from other constructions. So for example, many verbs that look like transitive verbs, such as *weigh*, they occur in the active form with what looks like a direct object *160 pounds*, but they can't occur in the passive construction.

Ok, these are all basic facts of English. And they can be captured in a simple taxonomic hierarchy. Well, you can play around with it. If you look at this [Figure 156], here is a taxonomic hierarchy. And you can see we capture the fact that *break* can be an intransitive verb, it can be a transitive verb, it can be

Another look at representing syntactic generalizations

- …One could represent the generalizations spatially (with Venn diagrams)…

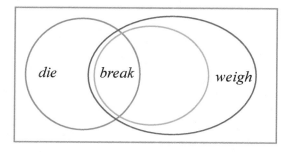

[____-TnsAgr]

[Sbj ____]

[Sbj ____ Obj]

[Sbj *be* ____ *-en*]

FIGURE 157

a passive verb. *Weigh* is a transitive verb; it takes an object but it's not a passive verb. *Die* is an intransitive verb, but it's not a transitive verb. And then of course they are all morphological verbs. So that's one way of representing the facts of English in a general fashion.

Another way of doing it is using what we'll call a "spatial model". And in the spatial model here I simply use what are called "Venn diagrams" to capture this fact [Figure 157]. So the red oval indicates that *die* and *break* can both be intransitive—they occur in this construction here [Sbj __]. The red line indicates any verb that can fill this role is in the red circle. The transitive construction includes *break* and *weigh*, so that's the blue oval. The passive construction includes only *break* of the examples we have here. And then the big brown box indicates all these constructions, all of these verb forms can be inflected. So that's another way of describing generalizations in English. I gave an example like this in my second lecture. The point that I want to emphasize to you is there's no one best way to do it. And so a linguistic theory that claims that there's only one way to capture syntactic generalizations is actually misleading.

John Bybee, a very well-known linguist in phonology, morphology and typology, and also a colleague of mine at University of New Mexico, has suggested another way to represent taxonomic generalizations in morphology, and

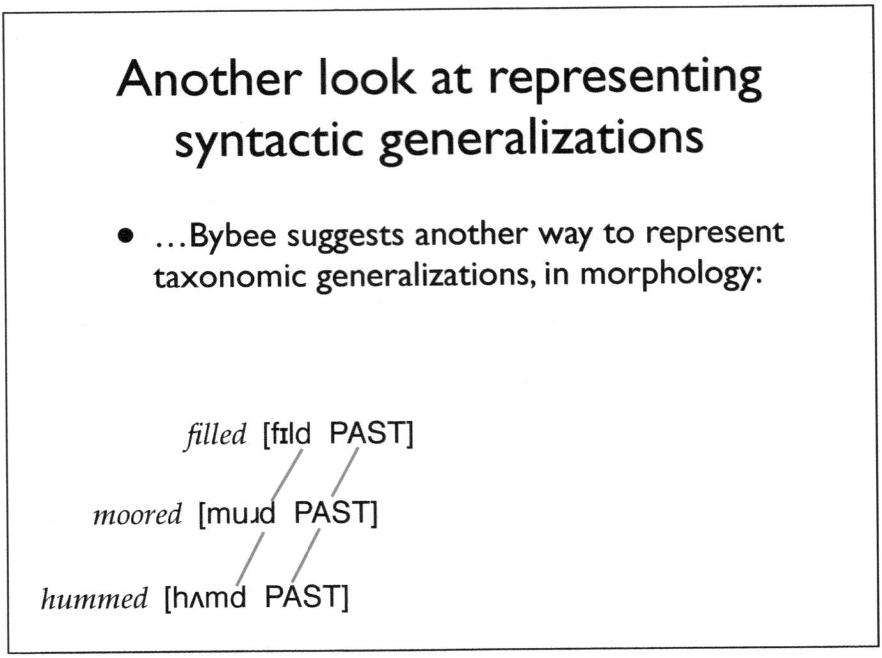

Another look at representing syntactic generalizations

- ...Bybee suggests another way to represent taxonomic generalizations, in morphology:

filled [fɪld PAST]

moored [muɹd PAST]

hummed [hʌmd PAST]

FIGURE 158

this is in terms of a network. So if you look here, you'll see that you have three different past tense verb forms: *filled*, *moored* and *hummed* [Figure 158]. If you represent their form and meaning—they are all past tense; here's the representation of form—they all have in common past tense meaning. They all have in common a -*d* suffix; their last phoneme is a -*d*. The red lines indicate this commonality. And the fact that these forms are linked and these particular parts of the construction are linked in this way shows that there is an association that speakers of English form between -*d* and past tense meaning. And that is the way that they abstract the past tense morpheme.

In this representation, a morphological generalization—past tense—is what we will call a connected region in a network of similarity relations. So these are all phonologically similar; these are all semantically similar. So we think of these as grouped, as similarity relations. Similarity is defined phonetically for the -*d* and it is defined semantically for the past tense.

Now generalizations can overlap with different networks of similarities, or they may not match perfectly. We can have exceptions, so we have *strung*, *spun* and *hung* [Figure 159]. They all have in common this schwa vowel, this /ə/ vowel. Then they have a nasal consonant but it isn't necessarily the same nasal consonant, so that's a dashed line. And their initial forms are also similar. They

Another look at representing syntactic generalizations

- Generalizations can overlap, or they may not match perfectly ("exceptions")
- Generalizations as connected regions in a space underlie the **semantic map model**

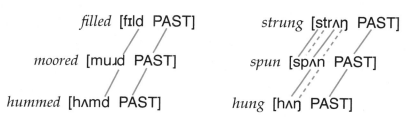

filled [fɪld PAST]   *strung* [strʌŋ PAST]

moored [muɹd PAST]   *spun* [spʌn PAST]

hummed [hʌmd PAST]   *hung* [hʌŋ PAST]

FIGURE 159

all express past tense. And in their famous paper from 1982, John Bybee and Dan Slobin argued this is a schema for a particular kind of irregular past tense in English that's actually still productive.

Now where I'm going to take this is: I've introduced this example to show you that you can use this kind of network structure to represent grammatical generalizations. And this notion of a network is what underlies what is called the "semantic map model". This is an example for those of you who have been attending the lectures. You've seen a lot of examples of word meanings by Melissa Bowerman where she uses the semantic map model to describe how different meanings are grouped together under single words in different ways in different languages. Here I'm going to give you examples that are mostly grammatical.

So typological theory has spent many years developing the semantic map model that's emerged in the last ten or fifteen years. So what we do is we compare the linguistic distribution of forms over meanings or functions across languages. Remember, the goal here is to try to find out what is universal about languages. The description of particular languages serves that goal but we need to compare languages to find out what is actually universal and what is specific to the way any single language organizes its categories. So for those of you

A simple example:
animacy and plural inflection

	Guarani (Tupian)	Usan (Papuan)	Tiwi (Australian)	Kharia (Austroasiatic)	Cree (Algonquian)
1st/2nd pronoun	né 'thou' peé' 'you'	ye 'I' yonou 'we'	ŋia 'I' ŋawa 'we [excl.]'	am 'thou' ampe 'you'	kīla 'thou' kīlawāw 'you'
3rd pronoun	haʔé 'he/she/it/they'	wuri 'he/she/it' wurinou 'they'	ŋara 'he' wuta 'they'	hokaṛ 'he/she/it' hokiyar 'they'	wīla 'he/she/it' wīlawāw 'they'
Human	tahaši 'policeman/men'	wau 'child/children'	wuɹalaka 'girl' wawuɹalakawi 'girls'	lebu 'person' lebuki 'persons'	iskwēsis 'girl' iskwēsisak 'girls'
Animate (nonhuman)	aŋuyá 'rat(s)'	qâb-turin 'Pinon imperial pigeon(s)'	waliwalini 'ants'	biloi 'cat' biloiki 'cats'	sīsīp 'duck' sīsīpak 'ducks'
Inanimate	apiká 'bench(es)'	ginam 'place(s)'	mampuŋa 'canoe(s)'	soreŋ 'stone(s)'	ospwākan 'pipe' ospwākanak 'pipes'

FIGURE 160

who attended the early lectures, the semantic map model is essentially distributional analysis, the basic method of syntactic analysis, extended to include meaning and crosslinguistic comparison.

So how does it work? I'm going to give you a crosslinguistic example [Figure 160]. Many languages differ in what kinds of words can be inflected for plural, what kinds of pronouns or nouns can be inflected for plural. And we can make a table showing the different types of languages that can be inflected for plural. In many languages including Chinese, only a limited number of words can be inflected for plurality. But the limited number of words varies from one language to the next. So you can see I've got here the different categories, first and second person pronoun, third person pronoun, human nouns, nonhuman animate nouns—like *rat*, *pigeon*, and *ant*—and inanimate nouns. Then on the columns I have different languages. So in Guaraní you only have separate plural forms for first and second person pronouns. In Usan you have plural forms for all pronouns. I think that's the same as the Mandarin system. In this Australian language you have plural inflections for pronouns and nouns referring to humans like a girl. In Kharia we have plural inflections for everything except inanimate nouns like *stones*. In Cree (and English as well) you have plural inflections or plural forms for all sorts of nouns.

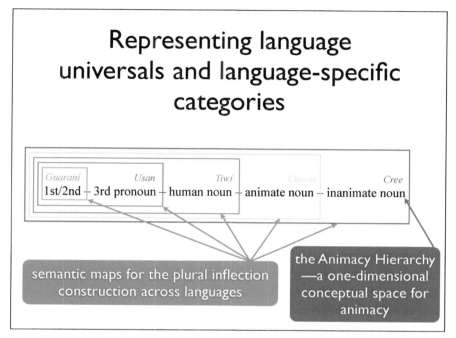

FIGURE 161

So you can see the languages fit a very regular pattern that's represented by the black line that cuts [across the table]. These [above the line] are all the forms that take plurals; these [below the line] are the forms that don't have plurals.

So, one way that a typologist represents this is by essentially an arrangement of the different classes of pronouns and nouns [Figure 161]. This arrangement is called the "animacy hierarchy". You can think it as of a one-dimensional "conceptual space": a way of organizing concepts that is a nice linear organization—a ranking. And then we can illustrate the different plural inflections in these different languages like this. So Guaraní is just first and second, so we have these boxes, a different color for each language, that indicate the range of plural inflections for all these languages. Ok, so you can see that we can describe the facts of different languages, the categories of plural inflection in different languages, on a single kind of template, namely this animacy hierarchy.

So now let's take a different example. This is one that's quite famous in typology. It's actually probably the first application of semantic maps. Depending on the kind of linguistics training you've gotten, you may or may not have heard about this problem. In languages like English we have categories that

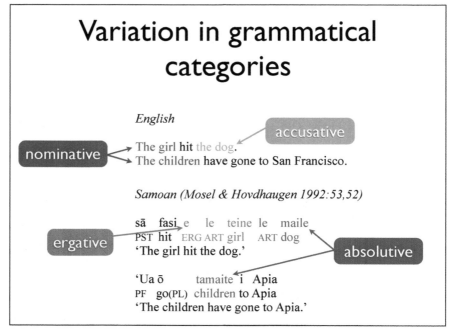

FIGURE 162

are traditionally called subject and object. Other terms that are used are the traditional grammatical terms from Latin: nominative for the subject and accusative for the object [Figure 162]. Well, this is a category that is similar in Mandarin. This is the category that most of us who speak languages like English and Mandarin think of as the basic and the only way to organize these grammatical roles.

But in fact a lot of other languages do it differently. So in a language like Samoan, only the transitive subject forms a category and what we think of as transitive object—"dog", in "The girl hit the dog"—and "children" in "the children are going to Apia", is a separate category called "absolutive". Now if you're seeing this for the first time in this language and you're here in the audience, you're going to probably think of this as being very strange. But quite a few languages do it this way. Now I'm not going to go into the details about this. I just want to point out that these categories are different.

Now there is one way that people try to deal with this problem. Let's take a language like Samoan or Tongan. These are closely related languages in Polynesia. They are similar: they both have these ergative and absolutive particles here. So some people really want to make every language have subjects

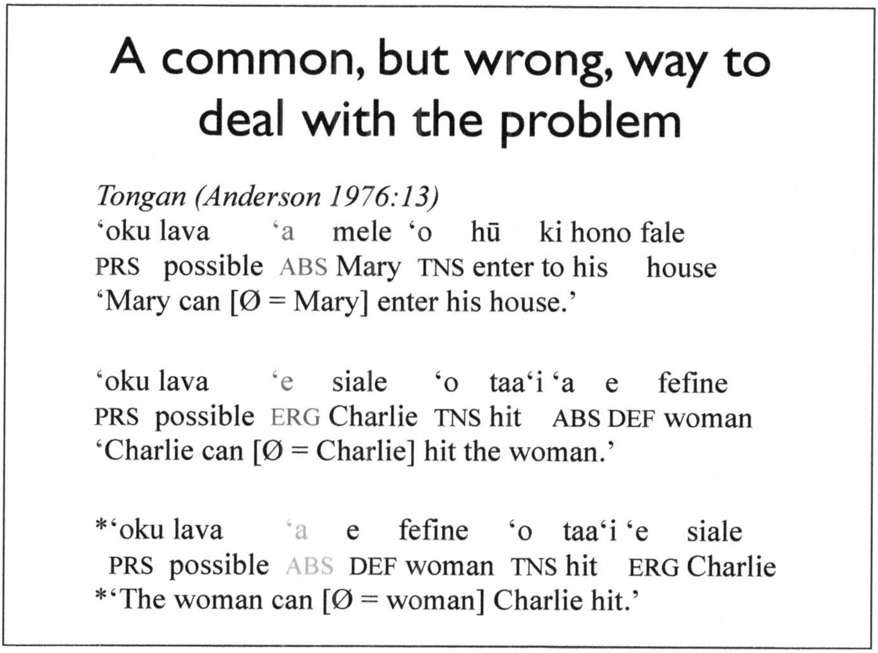

A common, but wrong, way to deal with the problem

Tongan (Anderson 1976:13)

'oku lava   'a   mele 'o   hū   ki hono fale
PRS possible ABS Mary TNS enter to his   house
'Mary can [Ø = Mary] enter his house.'

'oku lava   'e   siale   'o taa'i 'a   e   fefine
PRS possible ERG Charlie TNS hit   ABS DEF woman
'Charlie can [Ø = Charlie] hit the woman.'

*'oku lava   'a   e   fefine   'o taa'i 'e   siale
 PRS possible ABS DEF woman TNS hit   ERG Charlie
*'The woman can [Ø = woman] Charlie hit.'

FIGURE 163

and objects. They don't like ergative and absolutive, because of their beliefs about syntactic theory. They want to say that these categories are universal. So what they do in a language like Tongan [Figure 163] is they observe that there's another construction, the one where you use "can" or "is able to"—this verb up here [*lava*]—and then you have a complement, so it's very much like English: "Mary can enter his house". And the complement doesn't indicate there's a missing participant, and you have to interpret that as Mary. Now in a language like Tongan, also just like in English, you can say "Charlie can hit the woman". So "Charlie" is also understood, but you can't say "the woman can Charlie hit" where "the woman" is left understood, even though the woman takes the same particle here as you see up here. So in other words, in Tongan in this construction, "Mary", the intransitive subject as we would call it, works; what we call a transitive subject works, even though the expression of the case marking, the prefix or the preposition here, is different. And even though this one has the same preposition up here, it doesn't fit.

Ok, so this is taken from a classical article from the 1970s, so we are talking about a long time ago. And the typical argument is that, well, Tongan really does have subject and object, and this special construction with *lava* shows

The typological approach to "grammatical relations"

- More fine-grained categories:
  A = "transitive subject"
  P = "transitive object"
  S = "intransitive subject"

- A+S = nominative   P = accusative
  S+P = absolute   A = ergative

- These are conceptual categories
  (participant role clusters), NOT
  grammatical categories

FIGURE 164

that. So this is that common way of dealing with the problem: we found another construction that contrasts subject with object, so it looks like this is not really a weird language. But if you do that, you still haven't explained why this language also uses a special ergative preposition for transitive subjects. All you've done is added another fact about another language. Well, that's fine. We've seen that in any language, you have to capture the linguistic generalizations and there are different ways to do it. But what we really have in Tongan is two different generalizations that imply two different ways to organize grammatical relations. (For those of you who attended my earlier lectures, this is an example of the wrong way of looking at this, it's what I called methodological opportunism.)

So typologists take a different approach. Many typologists, when they come to subject and object, they accept that these categories are not universal. So the strategy since the 1970s has been to use a more fine-grained set of categories that we can use as a common denominator to describe differences in grammatical categories across languages. And, in particular, these definitions ultimately have to be based on the meaning of these particular categories.

So let's take this subject and object and ergative and absolute problem. The more fine-grained categories are expressed by these abbreviations [Figure

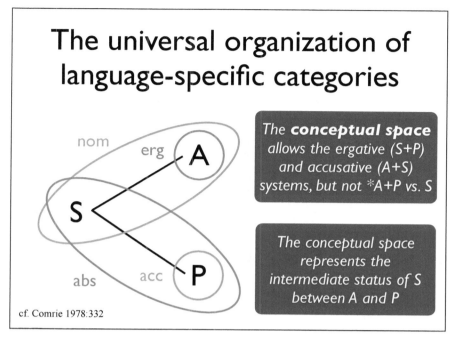

FIGURE 165

164]: A is a transitive subject, P is a transitive object, S is an intransitive subject. Then we can define nominative as A+S, accusative as P, absolutive as S+P, ergative as A—just transitive subject. So in other words, these common denominators allow us to describe these two different ways of organizing grammatical relations that we find in different languages. And I should emphasize that despite what you might read, these A, P and S are really ultimately conceptual categories. They are not grammatical categories. They're categories of meaning that ultimately have to be defined in terms of clusters of the roles that participants play in events—transitive events and intransitive events.

Ok, how is this pictured? It's very similar to what we did with the plural marking [Figure 165]. We have A linked to S—so A is transitive subject, S is intransitive subject, P is transitive object—we have A linked to S and S linked to P, with the black lines. Then for the English and Mandarin type systems, we have nominative as A+S, accusative as P. For the systems we saw in Samoan and Tongan, ergative is just A, and absolutive is S+P. And you can see Comrie is the first one to make these kinds of diagrams, back in 1978. So this conceptual space—that's the black, these three categories and then the links between them—allows the system where you have S+P group together, an ergative system. It allows a system where you have A+S grouped together. But

Indefinite pronouns (Haspelmath 1997)

- Haspelmath identified nine functions of indefinite pronouns for crosslinguistic comparison

(1) Specific known: a specific referent whose identity is known to the speaker (but not the hearer)
Masha met with **someone** *near the university.* [speaker knows who]

(2) Specific unknown: a specific referent whose identity is unknown to both hearer and speaker
Masha met with **somebody** *near the university.* [speaker has forgotten who]

(3) Irrealis non-specific: a referent (a manner in this example) which does not have a specific identity and exists only in a nonreal context
Visit me **sometime**.

FIGURE 166

it doesn't allow these two [A and P] to be grouped together, because there's no link. These links—these black lines—show that the intransitive subject is in a funny way intermediate between the transitive subject and the transitive object. And there are good semantic reasons for that which I won't to go into this morning. But this actually suggests that these semantic reasons show that speakers of different languages are sensitive to the fact that the intransitive subject role is actually in between the other two kinds, the transitive subject role and the transitive object role.

Now I'm going to look at an example in greater detail. This is an example of what are called "indefinite pronouns". "Indefinite pronouns" is not like a central category of grammar. So, linguists who were interested in making claims about what's universal in languages haven't really paid much attention to indefinite pronouns. That's probably not a bad thing. So Martin Haspelmath, a German typologist, wanted to look at indefinite pronouns, and he used this semantic map model.

So first we have to find the common denominator, and we have nine different functions of indefinite pronouns. I'm going to illustrate them here, but my main interest is in showing how Haspelmath used this to develop universal

Indefinite pronouns (Haspelmath 1997)

- Haspelmath identified nine functions of indefinite pronouns for crosslinguistic comparison

(4) Question: an unspecified referent in the scope of interrogation (especially polar interrogatives)
*Can you hear **anything**?*

(5) Conditional: an unspecified referent in the protasis in a conditional construction
*If you hear **anything**, tell me.*

(6) Indirect negation: an unspecified referent which is in a clause embedded in a negated clause
*I don't think that **anybody** has seen it.*

FIGURE 167

concepts and universal theories about indefinite pronoun categories. I'm not so concerned with the details of the definitions for now.

So there are nine functions [Figures 166–168]. The first function is "specific known". That's a referent whose identity is known to the speaker but not to the hearer. So if you say something like "Masha met with someone near the university", that "someone" is someone that I, the speaker, know but you don't know who that person is.

"Specific unknown", the second category, is one where it's unknown to both hearer and speaker. "Masha met with somebody near the university", the speaker has forgotten whom or never knew to begin with. And of course the hearer doesn't know either. I should mention for those of you who are interested in English, Haspelmath uses this difference between *someone* and *somebody* but it's not a sharp semantic distinction here.

The last is a non-specific context, what's called "irrealis" in semantic analysis, a referent of a particular time which does not have a specific identity and exists only in a nonreal context. So if I say to you "visit me sometime", that means some particular time. I'm making an offer. So I'm not talking about something that actually happened or is happening now, but something

Indefinite pronouns (Haspelmath 1997)

- Haspelmath identified nine functions of indefinite pronouns for crosslinguistic comparison

(7) **Comparative:** an unspecified referent occurring in the standard of comparison in a comparative construction
*The boy runs as fast as **anyone** in his class.*

(8) **Free choice:** an unspecified referent in certain contexts whose identity can be freely chosen without affecting the truth value of the utterance
*After the fall of the Wall, East Germans were free to travel **anywhere**.*

(9) **Direct negation:** an unspecified referent which is in the scope of negation in the same clause
*I noticed **nothing**/I didn't see **anything**.*

FIGURE 168

that might happen so it's not real yet. And we use *some* in English for that kind also.

"Question": "Can you hear anything?" So, under a question context you have a scope, you have an unspecified referent, and here we use an *any-* form in English, *anything*.

"Conditional": "If you hear anything, tell me." So in a conditional construction you have to use *any*. And these, of course, are two special kinds of unreal contexts, different from the one we saw before.

"Indirect negation": "I don't think that anybody has seen it". Here *anybody* occurs in the complement clause of *think* and it's *think* that is negated: "I don't think that anybody has seen it".

The "comparative": you can say "the boy runs as fast as anyone in his class", so you can have an unspecified referent that occurs in the standard of comparison in a comparative construction. So you can see we have all these different contexts that have unspecified referents.

"Free choice": there are certain contexts that are traditionally analyzed as free choice contexts in semantics. "After the fall of the Wall, East Germans were free to travel anywhere." So "free to travel" gives you a certain kind of, again, unreal context, talking about a general possibility. And here we use *anywhere* in English, the *any-* form.

Indefinite pronouns (Haspelmath 1997)

- Haspelmath analyzed the distribution of indefinite pronoun forms in 40 languages

	Rumanian:				Kazakh:			
	va-	*vre- -un*	*ori-*	*ni-*	*älde-*	*bir*	*bolsa da*	*eš*
Specific known	Y	N	N	N	Y	Y	N	N
Specific unknown	Y	N	N	N	Y	Y	N	N
Irrealis nonspecific	Y	N	N	N	N	Y	N	N
Question	Y	Y	N	N	N	Y	Y	N
Conditional	Y	Y	N	N	N	Y	Y	N
Comparative	N	N	Y	N	N	N	Y	N
Free choice	N	N	Y	N	N	N	Y	N
Indirect negation	N	Y	N	Y	N	Y	N	N
Direct negation	N	N	N	Y	N	N	N	Y

FIGURE 169

Then we have "direct negation", where now the relevant form is the object of negation. So, "I noticed nothing", so you can use the negative pronoun in English. Or you can use the negative particle and say "I didn't see anything", so you can use *any* in this context as well. You can see already in English, we have forms with *some*, forms with *any* and a form with *no* that are used in these different semantically defined contexts.

So Haspelmath looked at this in 40 different languages. I've given you two languages here on the screen with different pronoun forms, not in English, Samoan or any language you know, but four forms in Romanian, four forms in Kazakh [Figure 169]. I listed those nine contexts here in the rows, and the colours tell you when these forms are used—which context these forms are used for. So you can see there is overlap in the different contexts these are used in. And in particular you have forms that have a different range of uses in these two languages. And the same is true if you look at all 40 languages. So the question that comes up is what do they all have in common? Is there some kind of common semantic underlying basis, by which speakers of apparently all languages in principle organize their indefinite pronoun categories? It turns out that Haspelmath was lucky. Maybe he knew this in advance. But I can tell you from trying to do this with other categories he was lucky. He was able to find such a model, and he constructed a semantic map to show you this.

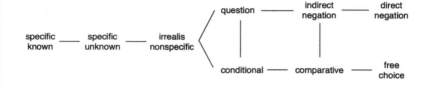

The conceptual space for indefinite pronouns

- Actually, it is a graph structure: what matters are the links, not the spatial arrangement

FIGURE 170

So, how did he do it? Well, the idea is: if you take two of these indefinite pronoun contexts and the same indefinite pronoun form is used in a particular language, that implies that the speakers conceptualize those two uses of the indefinite pronoun as being similar to some degree. And the more speakers and the more languages see the two categories of indefinite pronouns as similar, the closer together they are universally. So the idea is, we're going to simultaneously look at these nine uses of indefinite pronoun categories, these nine indefinite pronoun category uses; we are going to look at all the indefinite pronouns in all 40 languages and try to arrange those nine uses so that all languages respect the degree of similarity of these uses. And we'll call that a conceptual space [Figure 170].

As I said, Haspelmath was lucky: he was able to do it, and that's what he came up with. So what this shows is that the meanings that are directly linked are closer to each other, more similar to each other than meanings that are not directly linked. The meanings directly linked to each other are the most similar to each other. There's some degree of similarity here. The meanings on the far right are the most distinct, and certainly they're way different from the meanings on the far left. Again, it's what the mathematicians call a graph structure. What matters are the links, those black links you see, not the spatial

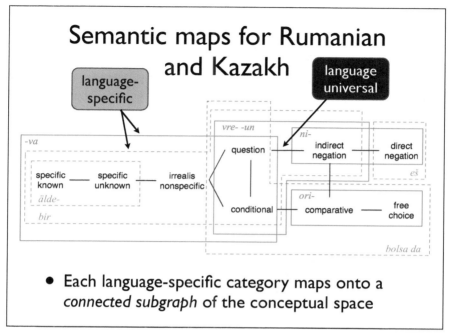

FIGURE 171

arrangement of the meanings. It is convenient to have a linear spatial arrangement. And if you come to hear my talk this afternoon at Tsinghua University [Lecture 8], I'll talk about that. But for now the main thing to see is that these links indicate the similarity relations between these different indefinite pronoun meanings or uses.

Now what we can do is we can take those Romanian and Kazakh pronouns and map them onto this conceptual space [Figure 171]. So the red solid boxes indicate the uses that these Rumanian categories have, and the blue dashed line boxes indicate the meanings that the Kazakh indefinite pronouns have. As you can see, they are quite different. You can't just reduce all languages to the same categories of indefinite pronoun. But you can map the pronouns of any language onto this conceptual space in such a way that if you follow this line around, like, say, this one [*bolsa da*], you get this L-shaped category. The uses here all are linked by the black lines. Likewise, if you take this Romanian category, *vre-* prefix plus *-un* suffix, you'll see that again, the uses that it includes are all linked directly by these black lines. So, when you say that the uses are all linked by those black lines, that indicates once again what the mathematicians would call a "connected subgraph". And that's what you want, because basically this layout says you can't have a category that includes the specific known and the irrealis non-specific, but excludes specific unknown. Or you can't have a category that includes direct negation and free choice if it doesn't also include indirect negation and comparative. You have to follow these lines.

So the other thing about the semantic map model is that the stuff in black, that conceptual space I called it, is language-universal. The idea is that these conceptual similarity relations are available to all speakers of all languages. But speakers are free to create grammatical categories in their language or lexical categories in their language that link together any of these meanings in any way as long as they respect these links, as long as it's a connected subgraph in mathematical terms.

So what does a semantic map model tell us? It allows for a language to have basically any categories it wants. We don't have to assume that all languages have the same number of categories, whether we are talking about subjects and objects or indefinite pronouns. But the semantic map model, at least in the good cases, shows that there are actually universals underlying this grammatical diversity that we find in languages. The other nice thing about the semantic map model is it allows us to clearly separate what's universal about languages and what's language-specific. So what's language-specific are the particular grammatical categories and lexical categories, and what's language-universal is the conceptual space. That [Figure 171] just repeats what I said, just emphasizes it. But here the main point is that the language universals are actually ultimately conceptual in character, while what's language-specific is grammatical, the actual formal categories that are defined by the words and constructions of the language.

Now that's very handy if you're comparing lots of languages, because you can't help but notice that languages have their own categories, because languages have their own constructions and they define the categories based on their constructions. I hope it's also handy for those of you who are working on a single language or studying the teaching of a language like English as a second language, because those aspects are universal, this range of meanings. So it's important, for instance, if you were to teach someone the use of indefinite pronouns in English, then it's useful to know that you've got these seven or nine meanings. The nine meanings are linked in the certain way they are. And then you can show people how those meanings are similar to each other and how those similarities are respected by the indefinite pronoun categories of English.

Ok, in the last section of this talk, I want to talk about parts of speech. This is one of my favorite topics, the one that led me to this approach of looking at grammatical categories as being language-specific, and of searching for universals that underlie them. It's also a central part of my model of Radical Construction Grammar. I talked about these at length in earlier talks [Lectures

Parts of speech

English

Object reference:	two hawk-s
Property reference:	its wid-th(*-s)
Action reference:	the elimina-tion/hunt-ing (*-s) of the lions
	I learned that archery is hard.
Object modification:	Sally-'s truck/the truck in the lot
Property modification:	a better/bigger/more effective mousetrap
Action modification:	the sleep-ing girl/the girl that I met
Object predication:	It's a hawk.
Property predication:	It's big.
Action predication:	It shrink-s in hot water.

The propositional act constructions form the basis of a crosslinguistically valid theory of parts of speech

FIGURE 172

2–3]. Most of the earlier talks were critical: I was trying to essentially criticize people that assume that there was a simple assumption that nouns, verbs, and adjectives are the same across languages, and languages either have those categories or don't have those categories. But in these earlier talks I also referred to universal patterns that underlie what you find. The fact is that languages are quite different. In fact this is a way in which Mandarin Chinese and Cantonese, the examples I'll use, are rather different from English.

So word classes are defined in language specific terms by whatever constructions the language has for expressing predication, modification and reference. These are all functions that are called the propositional act functions. So, word classes are language-specific; we shouldn't talk about nouns and verbs in English and Cantonese. We should talk about English Verbs in English, and Cantonese Verbs in Cantonese—and they are different categories—and then look at the kind of constructions that define those categories in those languages.

Nevertheless there are things in common. It's not completely different from one language to another. So let me start with English. Here again I'm going to use sort of basic examples. I've got some facts about English on the screen here [Figure 172]. The italics here, these refer to these common denominators. We're going to talk about how speakers of English refer to objects, refer to properties, refer to actions, and how they use object, property and action words as modifiers. And we are also going to look at how English speakers predicate object and property and action concepts. So these are things they have in common, and crosslinguistic research indicates that these are the crucial kinds of semantic categories that we can use as our common denominators. So notice that there is no noun, verb or adjective here. There are actually nine different categories we're going to look at. And that's not the entire list because objects, properties and actions, these are subsets of the total possible concepts that you can communicate in a language.

Ok, so that's the semantic side. That's our common denominator to compare languages with. On the other side are just a few facts of English about the constructions that they use. As you can see, it's color coded so that we have some things in green and some things in orange. The green things indicate inflectional possibilities, generally. This is really only a selected list because I want to fit all the information on one slide. But basically, if you refer to objects like a hawk, it has various inflectional possibilities in English including the ability to inflect for number. If you refer to properties, you have to do two things, one is this orange suffix, you have to add a suffix—some kind of abstract nominalization, it's traditionally called—and you can't inflect most of these abstract nominals for number. I'm oversimplifying the facts here, but my point is really that a more complicated story is the one we should go to. But just for presentation purpose I'm giving you a simper version of the facts.

If you want to refer to actions, you also have to add a suffix in most cases. Usually you can't inflect that for number. If you want to refer to actions like the object of *learn*, well, in English like many languages the object of *learn* is a whole state of affairs and that's often introduced by a word like *that* which is called a "complementizer". If you look at object modification, we have to use a possessive suffix or clitic, or we use a prepositional phrase. Property modification: we have a word like *big* and among other things you can inflect it for comparison, you even have special comparative forms for *good* and *bad*, or you use a periphrastic construction with *more* and *most*. If you want to modify with actions, you have to either use a participle form or some kind of relativizer. You don't have to use the relativizer, just like you don't have to use the complementizer, but you can use it. Object predication involves the copula—there's a suffix here—and also the indefinite article. Property predication, you have just a copula. Action predication: you don't have a copula, so nothing orange; but you inflect it as we observed earlier.

Ok, so these are a bunch of facts about English. How do we represent them in a way that allows us to compare English to other languages, including Mandarin and Cantonese? First, these constructions on the left—this is the point I made at the beginning of this slide—that's where we start from;

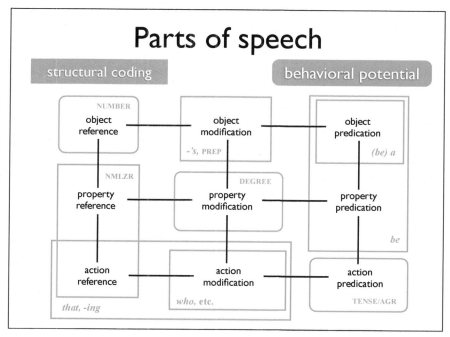

FIGURE 173

that's the common denominator. So this is what our common denominator looks like [Figure 173]. The rows indicate the semantic classes of the words we're interested in, objects, properties, actions; the columns indicate reference, modification, and predication. Now you remember, I color-coded those actual constructions in English. So the orange represents what typologists call structural coding. Those are constructions where you have an additional morpheme. The asymmetry between the presence and absence of an additional morpheme actually expresses the meaning of the construction, the meanings of that combination of property and reference or whatever. So you see that in English, you find these structural coding constructions off of this diagonal from top left to bottom right. So overt coding of these functions is found around the edges. Behavioral potential [green]: this is like the potential to inflect. So for the particular inflectional categories, you find them exactly in this diagonal [top left to lower right].

Now one of the things you see when you look at this example here is that it makes it look like in English it's easy to define parts of speech as word classes. That's the traditional approach, because these are nouns, verbs, adjectives, and then these are all special in some way. All of these categories are generally mutually exclusive. But there is something special about this diagonal from the top left to the lower right [Figure 174]. So that's the noun prototype [top

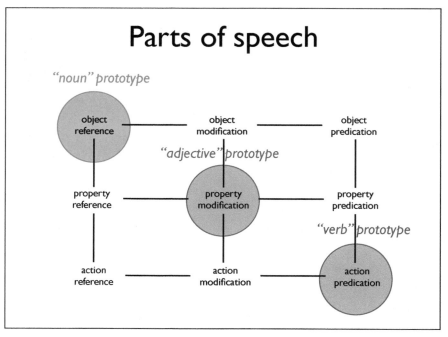

Parts of speech

"noun" prototype

object
reference

object
modification

object
predication

"adjective" prototype

property
reference

property
modification

property
predication

"verb" prototype

action
reference

action
modification

action
predication

FIGURE 174

left]—referring to objects; the verbs [lower right]—predication of actions; and adjectives [center]—using property concepts as modifiers. So intuitively, this corresponds to our functional prototype, of what it means to be a noun, a verb or an adjective. But this is basically defined on that conceptual space. So this is something conceptual, something special about the status of these points in the conceptual space. It's not something about the word classes of a particular language.

Now I'm going to look at a language that's a little stranger [Figures 175–176]. This is a language found in Africa, Lango. And it has two categories of properties. I bring this up partly because this is a language where the grammarian asks himself, does this language have adjectives or not? And what he found is that you have a kind of complicated distribution of grammatical facts about property words and action words in this language. So, for prototypical properties like "short", you have special forms for singular and plural, color-coded green because it shows an inflectional possibility available to this class of words [Figure 175]. However, even with these prototypical properties you have to have a particle when you use it for modification. This particular form does have some inflectional possibilities when it's predicated. So that makes it look less like an adjective in the traditional sense, but as we'll see, it's not really a problem from the universal sense. If you don't have habitual forms, like "I was

Parts of speech

Lango "core" properties :

Singular/Plural agreement stems: cèk/cègù 'short'

Attributive particle in modification: gwôkk à bèr 'the good dog'

Habitual predication—Subject agreement, no independent tone in Gerund: án àrâc 'I am bad'

Nonhabitual predication—Copula verb: án àbédò rác 'I was bad'

Lango "peripheral" properties: *same as core properties but no alternate Singular/Plural agreement stems*

FIGURE 175

Parts of speech

Lango actions:

Predication—inflect in Perfective, Progressive, Habitual aspects: àgíkò/àgíkô/ágìkkò 'I stopped/stop/am stopping something'

Predication—take Habitual tone: nénè 'he sees it'

Modification—take Attributive + Relative, Attributive, or zero: gwókk àmé/à/Ø òtɔ̀ 'the dog that died'

NB: properties may take Attributive + Relative (or zero), but Attributive + Relative is preferred for action modification

FIGURE 176

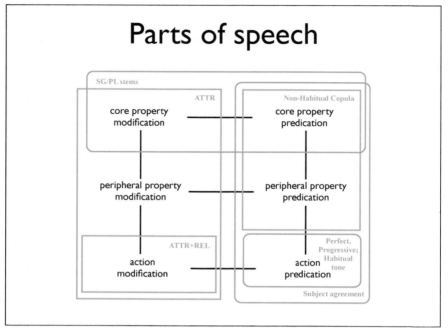

FIGURE 177

bad [on a particular occasion]", then you have to use a copula verb. Now there are other property words that don't work the same way. Well, they work almost the same way, but they don't have the special forms. They don't have the special singular/plural difference in form.

Now we can look at action words in Lango [Figure 176]. In predication they inflect for a bunch of different categories, the typical verbal inflections you think of. In particular, in the habitual form it takes a special tone pattern. In modification, it can take just the attributive particle, or it can take a combination attributive + relative particle, or nothing at all. That's what the grammar says. I contacted the author who told me that property words could also take all three of these options, but actions words are more likely to take this longer form, and property words are more likely to take the shorter forms.

So, let's now take a part of this conceptual space [Figure 177]. What we've done here is: we've got property modification for core properties and then I've added a role here for these peripheral properties that don't have singular/plural forms. Now let's look at the patterns. Here's the orange stuff, the structural coding, the overt expression. You can see that the attributive particle actually covers the whole range, though the attributive + relative is preferred for action modification. The copula is found for non-habitual forms only. When we look at inflection [in green], we see that it's also more complicated. You have singular/plural inflection extending whether both these property words are modifiers or predicates. All kinds of property words and action words have subject agreement, but only the action predications have the other inflections. So, when you look at this diagram, you can see there's not this nice clean separation of the green boxes and orange boxes.

So, what are the word classes in this language? Well, it's quite complicated. Essentially there're different word classes everywhere. All these different contexts work differently. But when you ask yourself, how did this fit with universals about how language is organized—predication, modification and reference—you see the same pattern. And the pattern is this: when you look at this diagonal from the upper left to the lower right, any of the green boxes—anything that indicates inflectional potential—includes this diagonal from upper left to lower right. And any of the orange boxes basically include at least the things on the other diagonal, so the unexpected combinations of semantic class of word and modification or predication. So, action modifications versus core property predications, opposite to what you expect. So the attributive particle extends all the way up this way, but the important thing is that it includes this category down here. That's the general pattern across languages. It's that behavioral potential will always include these prototypical categories, and structural coding will always include the non-prototypical categories, even if they get extended to be used more widely.

So now we can finish up with Cantonese. The reason I'm using Cantonese is: there was an article written by Elaine Francis and Stephen Matthews discussing the categories of Cantonese published in a prominent journal in England, the *Journal of Linguistics*, giving a lot of data. Stephen Matthews and Virginia Yip have also written a grammar of Cantonese, a reference grammar in English. So, for modification I'm going back to their reference grammar [Figure 178]. They argue that there are certain cases where you don't have any kind of modifying particle if the properties are an inherit characteristic of the noun, especially in fixed combinations. But it includes combinations like "white socks". The rest of the time modification uses this particle *ge*. It's coded orange since it's an extra morpheme to encode modification. In predication, property words always require an intensifier or degree modifier. Most of the time the degree modifier actually has some kind of meaning like "it's quieter here". But if you don't have a degree meaning, you have to put in a word that historically was a degree modifier originally. But the actual meaning of this phrase can be "your son is tall". Mandarin works similarly.

Cantonese action words [Figure 179]: well, this particle here [*ge*] is required. Predication, there's no copula. Another fact is the aspect particle here [-*jó*] does not change the meaning of the verb. If you say "I got some money" it still describes an action. If you, say, combine the particle with a word like *tall*, then

Parts of speech

Cantonese properties

Modification: zero if property is 'inherent characteristic of the noun', especially in fixed combinations (Matthews and Yip 1994:159): baahk maht 'white socks'

Modification: ge *if property is not inherent, or modified:* ji leng ge uk 'the most beautiful house'

Predication: always requires an intensifier/degree modifier; if intensifier meaning is not present, hóu *is used:* Nīdouh jihng dī 'It's quieter here.' Léih go jái hóu gōu 'Your son is tall.'

FIGURE 178

Parts of speech

Cantonese actions

Modification: ge *is required (Matthews and Yip 1994:110):* ngóh sīk ge yàhn 'people that I know'

Predication: no copula; aspect particle doesn't change meaning of verb: Ngóh ló-jó chín 'I got some money.' *Contrast:* Léih go jái gōu-jó hóu dō wo. 'Your son has gotten a lot taller.'

FIGURE 179

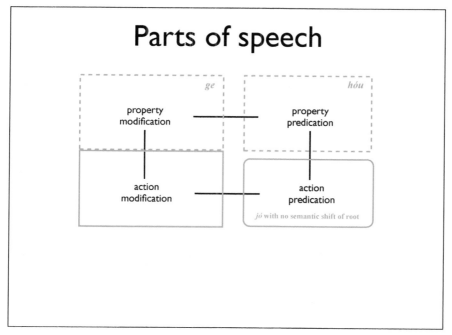

FIGURE 180

it now means not "to be tall" but "to have become tall". It changes the meaning from a state to a process.

So here's the subset of that conceptual space, just talking about properties and modifiers, actions, predications [Figure 180]. So here's the prototype, property modification [top left]. Here's the other prototype, action predication [lower right]. So at least some of the time you get this form [*hóu*] used without a degree meaning. For modification, at least some of the time you get this particle [*ge*] used even for property modifiers. And then here you have this particular aspect marker [*jó*] used without a change of the meaning only for action predication. So it seems to me it's an accurate description of the facts. And the thing to note here is you have one green box and it includes the lower right as you would expect. And you have two orange boxes and they include the lower left and the upper right. So this language actually conforms to the general pattern.

And even if you take the traditional view, which is that there is no copula for property predication and this particle is used for property modification, it's still true that the green box includes the prototype, so that construction includes the prototype, and the orange box includes the non-prototypical functions [Figure 181]. That's all that we claim languages do across the world. That's

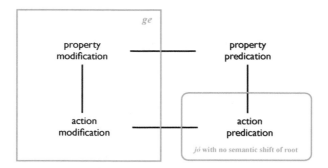

Parts of speech

- Even if we consider the "official" view of *ge* and *hóu*, Cantonese conforms to the typological universals of parts of speech

FIGURE 181

all you can claim; that's what the facts of the world's languages force you to conclude.

So the conclusions are: there are many different ways to represent grammatical generalizations. That's what I started with. Now grammatical categories pose a particular problem because they are so diverse from one language to the next, whether you are talking about noun/verb categories, subject/object categories, categories of words like indefinite pronouns, or the categories of word meanings that Melissa Bowerman has spoken about in earlier lectures. A fruitful way to represent grammatical generalizations about these grammatical categories is with a kind of network structure. That's what the semantic map model is. And the semantic map model cleanly separates what is language-universal from what is language-specific. That's something that's important to typologists who look at crosslinguistic comparison. It's important to people who are interested in syntactic theory and understanding what's universal about languages in general. And it also should be important to people that are interested in studying or teaching a particular language, to understand what would be the kind of universal common denominator that can form the basis of explaining how a particular language works to a language learner. Thank you very much.

Semantic Maps and Multidimensional Scaling

Thank you very much for coming. I know that many of you have attended the lectures that were given over the weekend at Beihang University. And some of you also attended the lectures this morning at the Beijing Forestry University. And I know that others of you are coming to these lectures for the first time. So I'm going to start by giving a little background about what this lecture is about, and also relate that to the things I have talked about before that you may not have heard.

This morning I talked about a thing called the semantic map model. This model is used in typology and is starting to be used in some other areas of linguistics, but mainly it's used by people working in cross-linguistic comparison. The reason this model has become attractive is that the first thing you notice when you start comparing different languages is that the basic categories are different from one language to the next. And the reason for that, I argued in the lectures this weekend [Lectures 2–3], is that the categories of languages are defined by the constructions that you find in that language, and since the constructions are unique to those languages, you shouldn't expect them to be the same from one language to the next.

So typologists have had to deal with this problem for a long time. And the semantic map model, which this slide describes here [Figure 182], allows us to represent facts about languages, about universals of conceptual structure, without assuming universal categories. So an old problem in typology is the fact that, in addition to languages with the western European style subject and object distinction, indicated by these green lines, there are languages with a distinction called ergative and absolutive, where the ergative marker is found only with the transitive subject—that's what the A stands for here—and the absolutive marker is found with what we would call intransitive subject and the transitive object.

© WILLIAM CROFT, REPRODUCED WITH KIND PERMISSION FROM THE AUTHOR BY KONINKLIJKE BRILL NV, LEIDEN, 2021 | DOI:10.1163/9789004363533_009

The semantic map model

- The semantic map model allows us to represent universals of conceptual structure without assuming universal grammatical categories

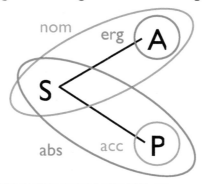

FIGURE 182

So many linguists for a long time felt this was a real problem in trying to develop universals of grammar. But it really isn't a problem, because what you can do is come up with a more fine-grained division of semantic roles—that's represented by these letters here. And that more fine-grained division of semantic roles allows us to be able to compare both systems with the nominative-accusative pattern and systems with the ergative-absolutive pattern. Then the other observation is that if you divide this up into these three different roles—so this is what's traditionally called transitive subject, intransitive subject, transitive object—if you divide up into these more fine-grained categories, then you also make another observation, which is that you don't find the system that categorizes or uses the same inflection for both transitive subject and transitive object and a different inflection for intransitive subject. That's represented by these lines here. The lines show the roles that it's possible to relate under a single case inflection. And the absence of a line here means you can't connect them there.

So this pattern here is called the semantic map model. You come up with more fine-grained categories—these represent the common denominator that you can compare from one language to the next. And then you link them together; and the links represent some kind of degree of conceptual similarity

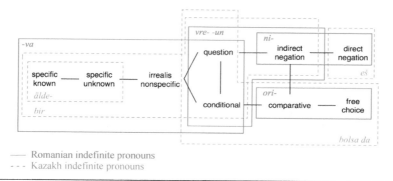

The semantic map model

- The semantic map model represents universal conceptual similarity relations between semantic functions (situation types)

——— Romanian indefinite pronouns
- - - Kazakh indefinite pronouns

FIGURE 183

between these roles. So we can talk about universal patterns here because the grammatical categories are construction-specific and therefore language-specific. So another point I'd like to make right now, for those of you who didn't hear the talk this morning [Lecture 7], is that the pattern that's in black—these fine-grained categories and the links that link them together—represent a pattern that's universal; whereas the patterns that are in green and red on the slide, those are language-specific grammatical categories. So we can say that for speakers of languages in general, human beings, the semantic roles that you find with the intransitive subject category are somehow conceptually intermediate to the roles found with transitive subjects and the roles found with transitive objects. So an important aspect of this, and the one I'm going to focus on today, is the relationship between what's language-universal and what's language-specific, particularly with respect to conceptual categories.

So here's another example that I am going to be using quite a bit [Figure 183]. This is from research by a German typologist, Martin Haspelmath, and it represents an analysis in the same semantic map model of indefinite pronoun meanings. He identified nine different indefinite pronoun meanings; those are the points here [specific known, specific unknown, etc.]. You don't need to worry too much about what those meanings are; I'm just using this example to illustrate. Then there are these links [the black lines], and the links represent essentially the minimum similarity relations that hold between these different meanings. And then Haspelmath did a study of forty languages. Here we have examples of indefinite pronouns from two different languages: Romanian and Kazakh. And these things which we'll call semantic maps actually outline which uses are found, or which meanings are found, with each indefinite pronoun in each language.

The important thing to notice here is that any particular indefinite pronoun in any particular language actually is used only for uses that are linked together by these lines. So you can see that this *"vre- -un"* thing, that's this red thing that goes around like that, so that pronoun form in Romanian is used for these three uses [conditional, question and indirect negation]. And that's ok, because these uses are linked. But just like the A, S and P, what you cannot have is an indefinite pronoun that's used both for direct negation and free choice and nothing else, because there is no direct link here. If you do have a pronoun that's used both for these functions, then it must include these other functions [indirect negation and comparative], to follow the links around. So this is the way in which this model limits the possible categories which are the grammatical categories in this indefinite pronoun domain. But of course, it allows lots and lots of different categories of infinite pronouns in different languages. So you are not restricted in the category. You are only restricted in this very broad sense.

Now there are a number of conceptual issues that arise with the semantic map model. So in what respect is this conceptual space universal, the meanings that are in black and the links that hold between them? And what sort of conceptual categories are universal? Those of you who have been following the lectures know that this is a topic that Melissa Bowerman has been discussing in several of her lectures. She talked about the Cognitive Primacy Hypothesis: that there are certain conceptual categories that are universal, available to all speakers and all learners of languages, children learning language; and that these categories were employed by children in learning grammatical categories of their own language. So Melissa Bowerman gave us a lot of examples showing that this is not going to work as a simple hypothesis. And so you might want to ask, well, what it is about these conceptual categories that might be universal? And then lastly, another important question is: when you see the model of conceptual structure I'm going to present by the conclusion of this lecture, you may be wondering what's the relationship between form and meaning, that is, what's the grammatical connection between form and meaning in languages based on that model. I'm afraid that I won't answer that question today, but if you are able to attend the lectures tomorrow morning which are at Peking University [Lecture 9], then I will talk about that there.

Well, it turns out that there are also some practical problems for the semantic map model. As I said, it's a good way to analyze what's universal and what's language-specific about grammatical categories. It allows grammatical categories to vary from language to language. Unfortunately, it's much harder to apply this model if you use more complicated data and many more languages, many more constructions than just three or four or five or nine. So even though the model is attractive, it's pretty much impossible to figure it out by hand comparing larger numbers of languages. Another thing is that there is no standard way to handle exceptions. So when you look at a lot of languages and a lot of data, you can see that some patterns are very widespread and others are rather anomalous: they're kind of rare, and they may represent something unstable. But the usual way that typologists look at it, which is a kind of the linguists' general perspective, is that it has to be a perfect fit. So we have to add a link any time we see two uses connected by a linguistic form in any language.

There's no notion of what the statisticians call "goodness of fit". The semantic map model is not mathematically formalized. I've had different opinions given to me by people who have more mathematical training than I do about this, but it sounds like it may be a very difficult problem, from the mathematical point of view, to formalize the semantic map model.

Another factor which some people objected to is that the spatial arrangement of these functions is arbitrary. All that matters is how those different uses are linked together. So even though I arrange it in sort of a linear fashion—those indefinite pronoun uses—just like Martin Haspelmath did, that linear arrangement doesn't necessarily mean anything. So we'll have to come back to that problem.

There is a solution here. And this is the use of a statistical technique which can handle more complex data. This is called "multidimensional scaling". And what I'm going to do in this lecture is I'm going to try to explain to you how it works. Because I believe that people—most of us, myself included—don't have a background in mathematical statistics. The work I've done is in collaboration with others who have that background. I think that's the route to go, if you aren't in a position to learn about the mathematics yourself. Younger people—younger than me—may have the time to do that.

So I'm going to talk a little bit about how I perceive this, how you understand how the method works, so it's not like I'm just waving a magic wand and showing you some facts about languages that are analyzed. And I'm also going to say a little bit about how to use statistics here. I know a lot of you won't do this, but

I would hope that from this you'll be able to understand or be able to look at an article that discusses statistics, like the work this is based on, and have some understanding of why the author analyzed it in this way and maybe even to question the author if you think he didn't do it in the right way.

So what is multidimensional scaling? It's a statistical method of analysis that produces a spatial model, so a model in one, two, or three dimensions or more, of similarity relations among data. So we'll see some graphs, or you're going to see dots, and the degree of similarity of the dots depends on how close together or how far apart they are in that spatial model. Luckily, it's mathematically well-understood and computationally tractable. This method's been developed over a period of over a hundred years. Multidimensional scaling is one of a family of techniques including factor analysis and principal component analysis (in case you've heard of those). It's a bit different. So the kind of method that you may have heard about in Melissa Bowerman's earlier talks on correspondence analysis handles the spatial dimensions in a slightly different way. I'm going to avoid dealing with that issue unless someone asks, because I'm sure it's going to be a challenge just to see how this method works by itself.

Ok, this is work I did together with a political scientist named Keith Poole. And we published a paper in a linguistics journal discussing this technique. He was the statistician who I worked with, because he's developed a very powerful algorithm for doing multidimensional scaling. So he is a political scientist and I am going to start by showing you how he does it because I think that would be easier to understand at first than the linguistics.

So imagine you want to analyze something like the United States Congress; that's what he works on. And you want to understand the patterns in which various US congressmen vote. So they vote yes or no on various legislative motions, laws and other things. And of course they sometimes vote yes, sometimes vote no; they vote differently from each other. There is a long-used informal description of people in the US Congress as being liberal or conservative. And also you can talk about them being liberal on social issues, but conservative on economic issues or vice versa.

So people talk about this informally. Can we actually measure this and talk about just how are the congressmen similar and different to each other? How do they map out in a spatial model of their political positions? Voting behavior is what they call nonparametric. Legislators vote yes or no on legislative motions. Sometimes you are absent, but we can ignore that actually for now. And we also think of legislators like US congressmen as having political stances. It's obvious: we just had an election, and people run for office based on their political stance, more liberal/conservative economically or socially or whatever.

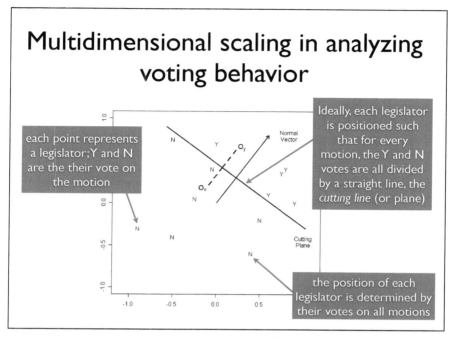

FIGURE 184

And we can represent this in a political space. Once they get in office, we can look what they do instead of what they say; we can look at how they actually vote instead of what they said they were going to do. And from that, you can see just how liberal or conservative they really are, when they are forced to take a stand.

So here is what a model would look like [Figure 184]. You can see these little Ys and Ns. Each of these points represents a legislator. The N here represents how this legislator voted on a particular occasion. So he voted no. These ones voted yes. In an ideal world if this was statistically perfect—a perfect fit—then you'd have this line here which indicates essentially the political orientation of the legislative motion, and then everybody on one side voted yes and everyone on the other side voted no. So this line, which is called the "cutting line", divides the legislators who voted yes or no on this particular bill.

So why are some Yes's over here, and this No is up there, and that No is down there, and that No is over there? Why are those people in those spaces? Well, that depends on how they voted on other legislative motions. So what you do is you simultaneously calculate, based on all of the votes that the congressmen make, where they fit in this dimension. And then we could say this dimension

Multidimensional scaling in analyzing linguistic behavior

- Linguistic distributional data is similar to voting data: meanings "vote" Y or N on whether they can be expressed by a linguistic form

	Rumanian:				Kazakh:			
	va-	vre- -un	ori-	ni-	älde-	bir	bolsa da	eš
Specific known	Y	N	N	N	Y	Y	N	N
Specific unknown	Y	N	N	N	Y	Y	N	N
Irrealis nonspecific	Y	N	N	N	N	Y	N	N
Question	Y	Y	N	N	N	Y	Y	N
Conditional	Y	Y	N	N	N	Y	Y	N
Comparative	N	N	Y	N	N	N	Y	N
Free choice	N	N	Y	N	N	N	Y	N
Indirect negation	N	Y	N	Y	N	Y	N	N
Direct negation	N	N	N	Y	N	N	N	Y

FIGURE 185

is, say, economically liberal and conservative, this dimension is socially liberal or conservative or whatever.

I should add that that's something that you, the political scientist, have to interpret. The statistical model, all it does is lay out the legislators and tells you how close or far apart they are, based on how often they voted together or voted on the opposite side of various laws. And then you have to look at it, and say ok, I see what's going on here: this dimension means economically liberal or conservative, and this dimension means something else. So, that has to be the political scientist doing the analysis. The statistics only tells you how legislators are similar or different based on their actual voting behavior.

And what do we do with language? Let me tell you a little story. I met Keith Poole because we were both on sabbatical at a research institute at Stanford University and it was interdisciplinary: people from different subjects. And each of us had to give a little talk about our research to the rest of the people in the group. So when Keith Poole presented basically the same thing I showed you on that last slide, I immediately recognized it as what you can see here on this slide [Figure 185]. If you see here, this is the same data from Romanian and Kazakh put in a table. I showed you this table this morning [Lecture 7]. The Yes's indicate that this form can be used for these different indefinite pronoun functions, this form can be used for these functions and so on. So as the bullet point says, you could think that these linguistic meanings (the functions down the side), so to speak, vote yes or no, whether they can used with that particular linguistic form. Or in a more accurate way, think of it so that speakers, when they choose to express that meaning, so to speak vote yes or no, by choosing to use a particular form and not another form. So it has to do with how speakers express meaning in form.

And once you make this connection, then you can see how this works. Now we can use this technique to look at linguistic data. So that's the kind of the first thing to think about when you look at statistics. There's lots of different statistical techniques out there, and you have to ask yourself: which is the one that's appropriate to use? And this is the reason why this particular technique is useful for looking at grammatical categories across languages and their uses.

So functions or meanings are like these political stances of legislators: they are represented by their position in conceptual space. Forms have meanings based on the range of functions they are used for. I'm not going to go on about this. But they define the similarity relations among meanings in the conceptual space.

So here are those nine indefinite pronoun functions where we have done a multidimensional scaling analysis [Figure 186]. I will say a little bit more about how it happens. But it's essentially the same idea. The positions of these things are based on whether or not linguistic forms group these functions together or not. So, one of these points is a particular situation type, a particular meaning or function of the pronoun.

Then you can take a language like Romanian; that was one of the example languages [Figure 187]. Then we have those four Romanian indefinite pronoun forms. Then you can see the lines divide it up, so on this side are the functions you can use with this form. On the other side are functions you can't use with this form. And there is a line here for this other form and a line here for that form and a line here for the last form. So those lines together help you position these points grouping together the ones that have the same form and keeping apart the ones that require a different form. So those lines represent a language-specific indefinite category. And you have to think of it as if the line came all the way across, and divided the space into the functions that can be used for the forms and the functions can't be used.

So this is what happened to the semantic maps. We have those semantic maps in the old style diagrams which are like squares or funny shapes that group together different uses. Here a semantic map has to be a straight line that cuts through this. That's because this is a Euclidean geometric spatial model. So the idea is: you want to get these cutting lines—these straight lines

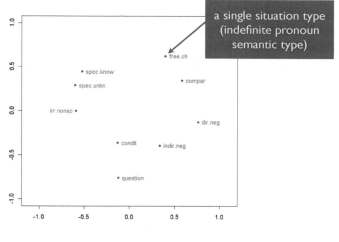

A spatial model of conceptual similarity among indefinite pronouns

FIGURE 186

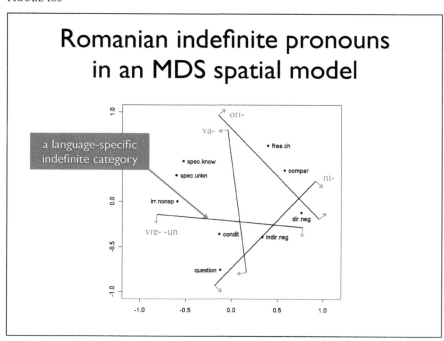

Romanian indefinite pronouns in an MDS spatial model

FIGURE 187

dividing uses—and arrange all the lines and arrange all the dots representing the uses in such a way that you can find a straight line for any language category that would have the uses that the form is found for on one side and uses it's excluded from on the other side.

Another important point: this is a statistical point that is often lost on linguists, because linguists aren't used to thinking in this way. The conceptual space, that spatial model with the points that have all the meanings, it's only interesting if it's low-dimensional. That's because if you add dimensions, it weakens the constraints on possible cutting lines. If we added a third or a fourth dimension, then basically every use could be similar to every other use on some dimension. Well, that's not terribly helpful. It doesn't really constrain the possibilities much. Now it's possible that there is no pattern: languages really can just group meanings together in any old way. The reality is, at least for the cases that I've investigated, that that's not true. There is always some kind of limitation that shows that there is some structure to our conceptual space, to the relationships between concepts.

Ok, I mentioned before that we have to have goodness of fit. No statistical model is perfect. It is only an approximation to help you understand complex data that you cannot analyze by hand. So the way this works in statistics is you have to have some kind of measurement of how good the fit is. Now, in multidimensional scaling in particular, you try to model all this cross-linguistic variation in different dimensions. So you try to force the model to be just one-dimensional, just a line, or two-dimensional—that's what I showed you before—or you can have a three-dimensional model as well. And then what you do is you ask yourself: how well does the one-dimensional model fit the data? How well does the two-dimensional model fit the data? How well does the three-dimensional model fit the data? And you have to have some way to measure that [Figure 188]. The statistics that my colleague Keith Poole uses: one is correct classification, so how well does the data correctly divide up the uses that are found on one side and the uses that are excluded on the other side. And there's another measure [APRE] I won't go into for now. It's another way of measuring essentially how good the model is. I can talk about it later if people want.

The fitness statistics indicate a two-dimensional model is best. And this is where you're probably thinking, what? What about a three-dimensional model? It's perfect: 100% correct classification. Well as I said, this is where statisticians and linguists tend to think differently. If you add a third dimension, as I said, that makes the model weaker. There are too many different ways that meanings could be similar. So you want a stronger model. So, even a model that is not perfect might be better than a model that is perfect. After all, if you

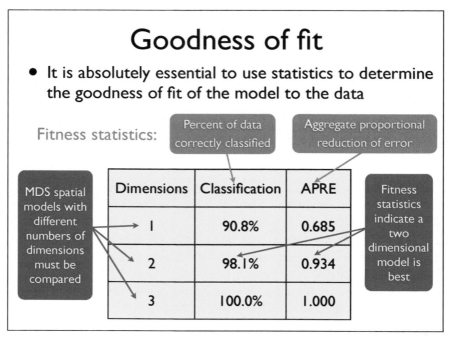

Goodness of fit

- It is absolutely essential to use statistics to determine the goodness of fit of the model to the data

Fitness statistics:

	Dimensions	Classification	APRE	
MDS spatial models with different numbers of dimensions must be compared	1	90.8%	0.685	Fitness statistics indicate a two dimensional model is best
	2	98.1%	0.934	
	3	100.0%	1.000	

Percent of data correctly classified

Aggregate proportional reduction of error

FIGURE 188

add enough dimensions, you'll eventually get a perfect model. So what really matters is you have to compare these numbers and see if adding another dimension really makes the model fit better. Now going from 90.8 to 98.1 is a big jump in fitness. Going from 98 to 100: even though it makes the model perfect, you are not gaining a whole lot by adding a third dimension. And the same is with this other measure: from 0.685 to 0.93 is a big jump. 0.93 to 1.00: even though that is perfect, it's not a big jump. So again, adding a third dimension only improves your model a little bit, and it makes the model a lot weaker. So we'll stick to two dimensions.

Ok, the next thing to think about with a statistical model is it's always a good idea to check it against some data where you know what the answer is already, to make sure that you are actually getting a sensible result. In this case we have a study that Haspelmath did by hand, and we can compare what he discovered with what this statistical model will show us [Figure 189]. So that is what he discovered. As I said before, in the traditional semantic map model, what matters are these links. The links are what matters, and you can see that it's roughly linear. It's a complex thing on the right hand side; it looks like it almost could be a one-dimensional model, but it's not good enough to be a true one-dimensional model.

Comparing the semantic map model to MDS spatial models

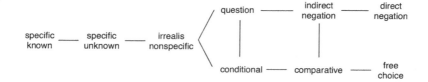

- In the semantic map model, what matters are the links, not the spatial arrangement (it is a graph structure, mathematically)

- This conceptual space is more or less "linear"

FIGURE 189

Comparing MDS and semantic maps

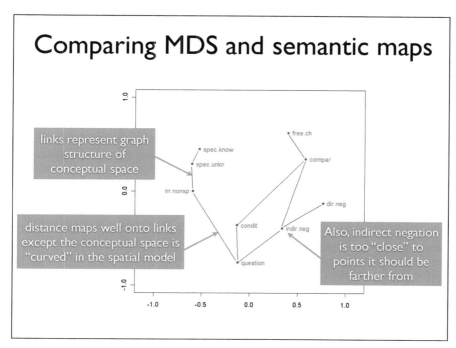

FIGURE 190

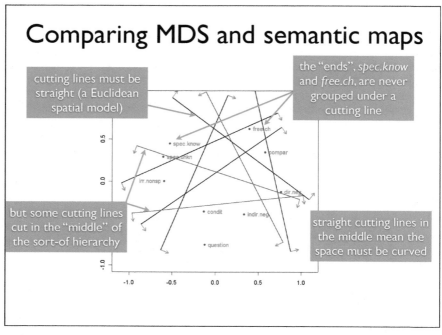

FIGURE 191

Ok, let's take that semantic map, the spatial model represented by the locations of these dots. And now let's put in the links that were in the semantic
map model [Figure 190]. So as you can see, it looks pretty good. Distance in the
spatial model corresponds pretty well to links on the model except that this
conceptual space is sort of curved in a horseshoe shape. So that's one problem we want to look at: why is it different from what Haspelmath did? The
other thing is that if distance really mattered, this dot here representing indirect negation ought to be a little bit further out, because it looks too close
to conditional and there is no link in the semantic map model. So the whole
model would look better if this was out a little further. So I'm going to address
both these questions here, and illustrate some things about multidimensional
scaling with this.

Ok, so let's look at this diagram [Figure 191]. This shows you some of the
lines that represent indefinite pronoun categories in specific languages. So remember I said the cutting lines have to be straight: so the semantic maps are
straight lines cutting the space in half. However, some cutting lines cut in the
middle of this sort of hierarchy—I will illustrate this with a simpler example in
a moment—and the straight cutting lines in the middle mean the space must

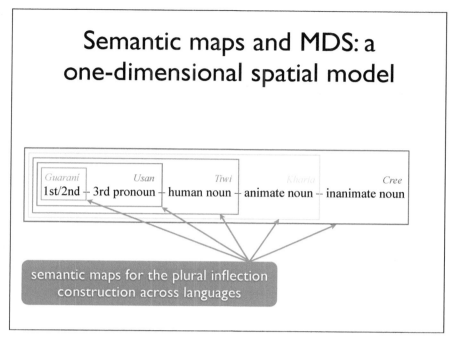

Semantic maps and MDS: a one-dimensional spatial model

Guaraní	Usan	Tiwi	Kharia	Cree
1st/2nd – 3rd pronoun – human noun – animate noun – inanimate noun

semantic maps for the plural inflection construction across languages

FIGURE 192

be curved. You probably don't understand that; I'm going to show you with a simpler example.

Ok, let's consider something that really is a simple hierarchy. This is an example I used this morning [Lecture 7; Figure 192]. It has to do with how different languages use the plural inflection. Languages vary as to which pronoun or noun categories allow plural inflection. So English allows anything. Mandarin Chinese actually is quite limited in when you use the plural inflection. So if we compare different languages, we can see that on the whole, there is a nice scale that shows you the semantic map. So this is the semantic map model. The different categories are linked by these lines, the black lines here, and then these boxes represent the semantic maps.

If you want to translate this to a multidimensional scaling model, I don't even have to bother to plot it. It's very simple [Figure 193]. You have a one-dimensional model here and then you have these cutting lines. And the reason for that is that all of these plural categories include every semantic category of noun and pronoun to the left. So if you have a cutting line here, it includes everything to the left—a cutting line here, everything to the left. So a nicely linear arrangement works fine.

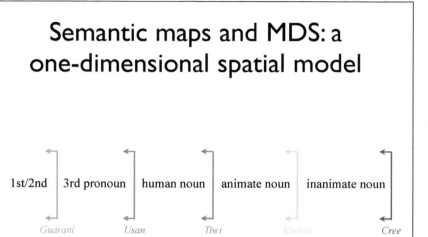

Semantic maps and MDS: a one-dimensional spatial model

| 1st/2nd | 3rd pronoun | human noun | animate noun | inanimate noun |

Guaraní   Usan   Tiwi   Kharia   Cree

Since all semantic maps include the leftmost end of the Animacy Hierarchy, the Hierarchy can be represented in one dimension

FIGURE 193

Now I'll give you another kind of example. This is what's called the grammatical relations hierarchy, or the noun phrase accessibility hierarchy [Figure 194]. It was first discovered by the typologists Bernard Comrie and Edward Keenan back in the 1970s. And their claim was: if you look at relative clause constructions in different languages and ask which grammatical relation can you form the relative clause on, the following generalization holds. So here's a hypothetical example. So here is the generalization: a relative clause construction covers a continuous segment of the accessibility hierarchy. So this blue box goes all the way to the left, the brown box goes all the way to the right, but the red box includes the two grammatical relations in the middle and the little orange box includes just the indirect object relation that's also in the middle.

If you want to convert this to a multidimensional scaling model, the cutting lines have to be straight. So the only way you can do this is to have our grammatical relations hierarchy a little curved, then you can put a cutting line in here, a straight cutting line that includes only the indirect object, and a straight cutting line that includes only the direct object and the indirect object [Figure 195]. So that's why the conceptual space, the spatial model for the indefinite pronoun is curved: it's because there are some indefinite pronoun categories that include only uses in the middle of that roughly linear arrangement.

Semantic maps and MDS: a curvilinear model

Subject	Dir. Object	Ind. Object	Oblique

NP Accessibility Hierarchy: Keenan and Comrie argue that a relative clause construction covers a continuous segment of the Accessibility Hierarchy

FIGURE 194

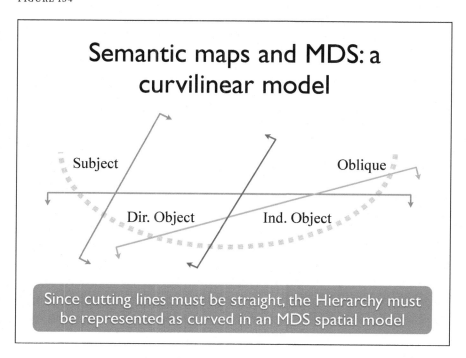

Semantic maps and MDS: a curvilinear model

Subject

Oblique

Dir. Object

Ind. Object

Since cutting lines must be straight, the Hierarchy must be represented as curved in an MDS spatial model

FIGURE 195

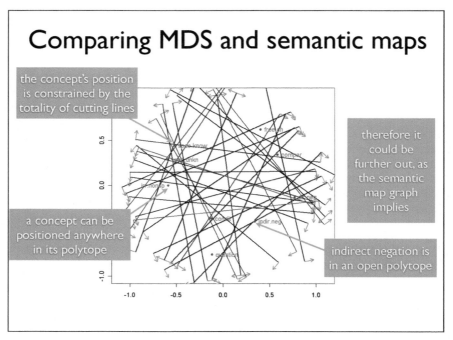

the concept's position is constrained by the totality of cutting lines

therefore it could be further out, as the semantic map graph implies

a concept can be positioned anywhere in its polytope

indirect negation is in an open polytope

FIGURE 196

Now if we compare multidimensional scaling and semantic maps [Figure 196]: this is every cutting line; all of the data from the 40 languages that Haspelmath looked at. As I said, you have to put every concept in a position so that the cutting lines will be right. So something like this dot, this usage here [spec.know], is extremely constrained: it can only occur right in here; this one [condit] can occur only right in here; this dot [irr.nonsp] could have occurred anywhere in this general region; this one is very limited. So, the computer program that constructs these spatial models, it has to put the dot somewhere inside this shape which Keith Poole calls a polytope. It's limited by that, sometimes it is really constrained. Other times there is a little bit of room: this dot [irr.nonsp] could have been [further] down here.

So then we have indirect negation. You can see that its position is not very constrained. It could be way down here. And remember, that was the dot that was a little too close to the other ones, I said, compared to the semantic map model. But the reason that the multidimensional scaling computer program put it there is because it could have put it further out, but the algorithm just sticks it in as close as possible. So this thing could actually be out here somewhere [coordinates 0.8, –1.0]. That's probably a more accurate description. So this is a reminder that statistical models are only approximate, but they can be very useful, because they can analyze much more complicated and messy

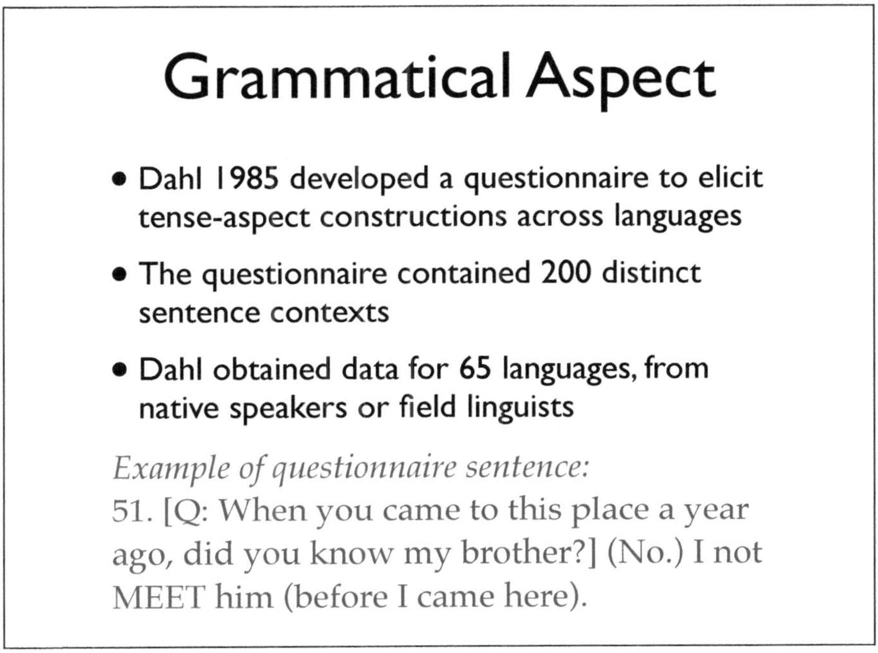

Grammatical Aspect

- Dahl 1985 developed a questionnaire to elicit tense-aspect constructions across languages
- The questionnaire contained **200** distinct sentence contexts
- Dahl obtained data for **65** languages, from native speakers or field linguists

Example of questionnaire sentence:
51. [Q: When you came to this place a year ago, did you know my brother?] (No.) I not MEET him (before I came here).

FIGURE 197

data than we usually can analyze by hand. And that's very important, because the linguistic point I want to make at the end of this talk, you can only really see it and appreciate it if you look at really complex data sets. If you look at simple data sets, it's not so obvious; it's less easy for me to persuade you about this point.

I'm going to show you briefly another example [Figure 197]. This is actually the most difficult data that we analyzed, and it shows a different kind of spatial model. Another typologist, Östen Dahl, in a ground-breaking work from 25 years ago, developed a questionnaire to look at tense-aspect categories or constructions across the world's languages. He ended up getting data on 200 different contexts, 200 different sentences with different tense-aspect meanings in 65 languages. He got his colleagues who were either native speakers or field workers on particular languages to give him the data. 200 distinct contexts, 65 languages. So here is an example. The setup question is: When you came to this place a year ago, did you know my brother? And the response is no; and then Dahl didn't want to inflect it in English to give away what English tense-aspect structure is. So he just put it in capital letters—the verb—and then asked the native speakers in the questionnaire to provide the sentence with the tense-aspect construction that you would find for that context, where the context is explained here.

Example: Dahl's Pluperfect

Rank no.	No. of categories	Examples
1	20	901, 1382
3	19	1392
4	18	891
5	17	481
6	14	491, 1291
8	13	521
9	10	511, 1061
11	7	671, 681, 1011
14	6	461, 611, 1441
17	5	431, 451, 621, 631, 1132, 1431
24	4	391, 1012, 1062, 1771, 1781, 1791

FIGURE 198

Well, in English, in this case you would have the pluperfect. I would say "I had not met him before I came here". At least, that's the answer I would give, if someone gave me this questionnaire. I don't know what you'd say in Mandarin. So you can think for yourself what you might say. And then do it for 199 other contexts. Well, 25 years ago when Dahl did his research, we didn't have powerful personal computers, we didn't even have very powerful mainframe computers. So, first he coded this data, using the construction as a whole. So he would code differently even the constructions that we know are semantically related, like present progressive and past progressive.

What Dahl did is a little different from what we are going to do. He identified a set of prototypes for tense-aspect constructions. So these are grammatical constructions in the world's languages. So he used some kind of clustering program to identify constructions that had the same range of uses and that were used for similar questionnaire questions. And then he looked more closely at those sentence contexts, and ranked them by the number of the languages that contained that context.

So here is an example [Figure 198]. Here is the pluperfect category. This is one of Dahl's crosslinguistic constructions. And what this means [under "No. of categories"] is: these example sentences [901, 1382] were found in 20 of the

Dahl's tense-aspect prototypes

Tense-aspect prototype	Letter code	Cluster size
Perfective	V	136
Quotative	Q	10
Perfect	F	67
Experiential	X	10
Pluperfect	L	29
Future	U	45
Predictive	D	7
Progressive	O	35
Habitual	H	13
Habitual-Generic	G	14
Habitual Past	S	5
Past Imperfect	R	43

FIGURE 199

pluperfect constructions that he identified across the languages in his sample. So that was the most languages that you found [i.e., rank no. 1]. This particular sentence [1392]—these are the codes indicating the sentences—was found in 19 languages. So this sentence got a rank of three, because these two sentences [901, 1382] were tied for first place. This sentence [891] got fourth place, used in 18 of these pluperfect constructions; and so on down the list. So you can see, some of these sentences were thought of as really central: some uses seem really central to the pluperfect. These sentences down here [at the bottom of the table] were less central to the pluperfect.

First I should mention, we're very grateful to Östen Dahl who took this 25-year-old data, which it is very difficult to remember what the coding was all about, and he gave it to us and answered lots of questions about how he coded the data, so that we could process it. There were actually essentially 250,000 pieces of data, if you treat every questionnaire question as one piece of data, for all the languages. So that means we had to interpret these data.

The first time we did it, there were 200 dots; and that's not very helpful. So what we did was we gave these dots letter codes based on Östen Dahl's clusters, so the pluperfect got a letter code, the progressive got a different letter code and so on [Figure 199]. Now there are some cases where Dahl did not posit a

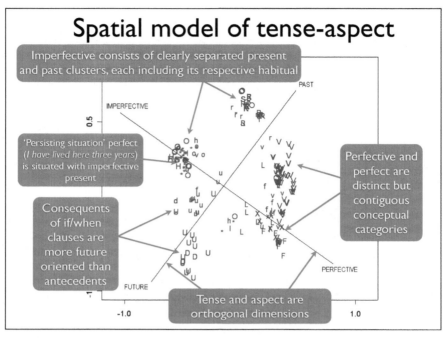

FIGURE 200

prototype category. So any sentence that didn't follow any prototype, we give it an asterisk. Then we had a way of dealing with the sentences: because some sentences were found in more than one of these crosslinguistic categories that Dahl presented, we had to choose one. You don't need to worry too much about the details. These are the letter codes that we used, so pluperfect, we give it L, because P was already used. Actually P is not used, too many categories of P. So we had all these letter codes for the different categories.

So that's what we mapped here [Figure 200]. This may look messy to you, though you can see the letters tend to group together, which is a good sign. The first thing to notice about this is that this spatial model, it's a two-dimensional model—the statistics give you that it's the best fit—but it's quite clear that when you look at the actual sentences, this is the tense dimension from past up here to future down there. This is the aspect dimension from imperfective over here to perfective over there. Ok, now when you do statistics, you see this, all right, the statistical analysis shows you that tense and aspect are different semantic categories. Well, we already knew that. But it is a good thing that the model actually shows us that; so that gives you some feeling that this is a good model.

When you start looking more closely, then you start discovering that the model tells you things that linguists or semanticists who study tense and aspect disagree about and it suggests some answers. So for instance, for most of you who have studied the category of aspect in semantics: linguists who work on aspect say that the perfective and perfect are very different categories. Well, they are different categories. The perfective contexts are up here and the perfect contexts are down here for the most part, but they form a continuum. So they are closely related even if you can differentiate them. On the other hand, the imperfective here has a clear separation between present tense imperfective and past tense imperfective. So it shows that many languages make this distinction. Moreover, the present tense habitual, so something like "I run in the park every day", is associated with the present tense specific, "he is running in the park ". Past tense "he used to run in the park", past tense habitual, is associated with simple past, "he was running in the park".

Another type of example is future orientation. If you look at these, the really good futures up here are "the train will arrive at 6 P.M."—those are down here, that's the D for predictive. This separation shows that if you have a conditional sentence like "If Melissa goes to the Forbidden City tomorrow, I will go too", you'll notice that the "if" sentence in English didn't have the future—it said, "If Melissa goes"—the consequent clause do have the future—"I will go too". Even though if it really happens, both of the events would be the same time: in the future. But the second event, the consequent event, is basically defined on the basis of the first event. And sure enough, the consequents are down here, and the antecedent ones are up here. Lastly, again, for those of you who have studied aspect, the English perfect construction can be used for a special use called the persisting situation. An example of it is "I have lived here three years." That means I lived here three years and it means I'm still living here, so persistent to the present. Well, this analysis puts that usage of the perfect over here and the other perfect uses are down here. That suggests that this is actually rather different from the other uses. And indeed many languages do not include that usage in their perfect construction.

You can do a more detailed analysis of this. I have a forthcoming book[1] on essentially the semantics of aspect and argument structure, in which I go through in gory detail almost all these little points here, all 200 of them, and discuss more fine-grained aspects of the analysis. So this is a case where we can take incredibly complicated data, with lots of problems in analyzing it. There is no way that you can figure this out just by looking at it, Dahl himself used a computer program 25 years ago. This is I think a more sophisticated program than he used and it gives us interesting results about things that linguistic semanticists have been debating about for many years.

---

1 Croft, William. 2012. *Verbs: Aspect and causal structure.* Oxford: Oxford University Press.

Now I'd like to turn in conclusion to spatial adpositions. I'm going to come back to the question now: what is universal here? When you go back to this model of tense-aspect, there's some sense in which this is universal. That is, these are all questionnaire contexts, so these are all sentences that express a certain kind of tense-aspect meaning. And you can see this arrangement here. And the arrangement is universal in a sense that any speaker measures the similarity of different meanings in this way and uses that in order to construct the categories of their language, the tense-aspect categories of their language, you know, a cutting line goes like this and another cutting line goes like that or whatever. So how do we interpret this conceptual space? What sort of structure is there in the conceptual space? And how do languages use it? Well this is much too complicated an example to use. I'm going to use one that is a little easier and that's spatial adpositions.

Those of you who have heard Melissa Bowerman's lectures earlier in the series will recognize these examples, because the data I'm using here from a paper published by some of Melissa's colleagues at the Max Planck Institute at Nijmegen in the Netherlands—the data was based on a set of pictures of spatial situations that was developed by Melissa Bowerman and Eric Pederson, who is now at the University of Oregon. So this set of pictures of spatial situations was constructed to represent situations commonly expressed by English *on* and *in* and some other similar situations. The data that we analyze here was discussed in a paper published by Stephen Levinson, Sérgio Meira and other colleagues from Nijmegen. And they looked at the data found in these languages. So they showed these pictures to speakers of these languages and ask them to describe the location of a particular object that is pointed out. And then what they did was they analyzed the uses of spatial adpositions: prepositions, and postpositions or case affixes. They also performed a multidimensional scaling analysis. The algorithm that they used, to make a long story short (I'm skipping some slides here), the algorithm they used is not as powerful as the one that Keith Poole developed. So we reanalyzed the data using Poole's algorithm.

So here is an example of the kind of pictures that they used [Figure 201]. These are the first six pictures in the data set, the stimulus set that Melissa Bowerman and Eric Pederson developed. Just to illustrate some examples, these I shamelessly ripped off from Melissa's own handouts from earlier this session [Figures 202–204]. So these were six pictures that Melissa picked out in her lectures [Figure 202]. And this is how English would typically categorize these: all of these scenes on the left are expressed by *on*, and just that picture on the right would be expressed by *in*. If we compare Dutch [Figure 203]: Dutch actually has three propositions that divide things up a bit differently. And she also gave the example of Berber where you have two forms and there's actually overlap in this particular scene [Figure 204].

FIGURE 201

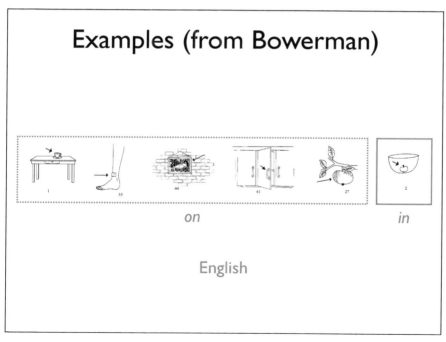

FIGURE 202

Examples (from Bowerman)

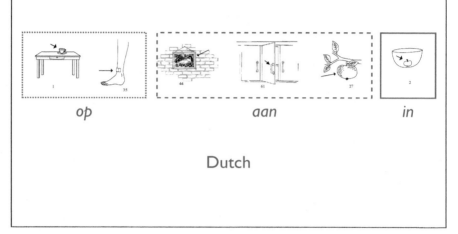

op   *aan*   *in*

Dutch

FIGURE 203

Examples (from Bowerman)

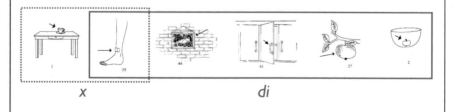

x   *di*

Berber

FIGURE 204

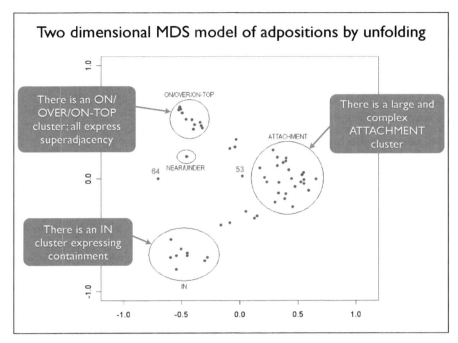

Two dimensional MDS model of adpositions by unfolding

There is an ON/OVER/ON-TOP cluster: all express superadjacency

There is a large and complex ATTACHMENT cluster

There is an IN cluster expressing containment

ON/OVER/ON-TOP

ATTACHMENT

NEAR/UNDER

IN

FIGURE 205

Now I'd like to say, these are only six pictures out of the 71. Melissa selected these six pictures because it seemed to represent a kind of hierarchical arrangement of a more "on"-like relation and a more "in"-like relation. But there are 65 other pictures in the stimulus set. And Levinson et al. collected data for all 65 pictures. Melissa Bowerman and Eric Pederson have also collected the data for these pictures from a much larger set of languages. But I'll just be talking about this nine language sample [Figure 205].

Ok, Poole's algorithm is called an "unfolding algorithm". This is what came out of it. The labels for these clusters are labels that were given by Levinson, except this particular one happens to lump together two clusters that were in the original study, so you have "on/over" and "on top": some kind of superadjacency relationship that could involve contact or not. This is a large and complex cluster that includes attachment. So for instance in English we would say these pictures here [Figure 202] are "on the wall", and that represents not just surface contact, but also the pictures being attached to the wall in some way. And we also in English say that a fruit like an apple is on the tree, on a branch. That is the attachment relation. There is also an "in" cluster expressing containment there.

Now, let's go back to the Cognitive Primacy Hypotheses that Melissa Bowerman discussed. The idea there was that there are some basic conceptual

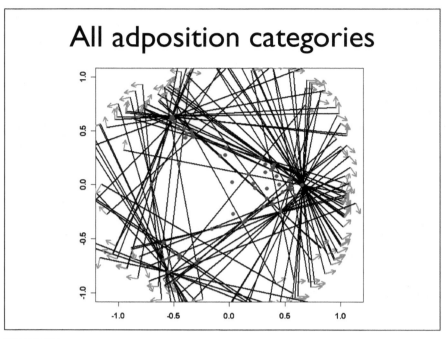

All adposition categories

FIGURE 206

categories that speakers use in constructing the grammatical categories of their language. And the description I've given you so far makes it look like this analysis suggests that's true: we have some kind of superadjacency concept, some kind of attachment concept, and some kind of containment concept. One might assume that's what it shows. But I would like say that's not the right analysis. Those clusters simply illustrate the coherence of the conceptual space. The pictures that were designed in this stimulus set describe spatial relations that speakers tends to think of as similar. And that's why you get the clusters. And the similarity seems semantically motivated, so that's why we can name the clusters the on-cluster, the attachment-cluster or the in-cluster.

But they are not linguistically relevant per se. Instead, what's relevant is the individual situation types represented by each of those 71 spatial relationships in those 71 pictures, and their conceptual relationship to each other that's represented geometrically by distance and angle in those diagrams.

This is what all the adposition categories look like if you superimpose them on the spatial model [Figure 206]. As you see, it's a big mess. In particular, a language-specific category, you remember, is a cutting line; but they cut through these conceptual clusters. So you can't just say that the speaker has some kind of innate knowledge of the attachment relationship and they

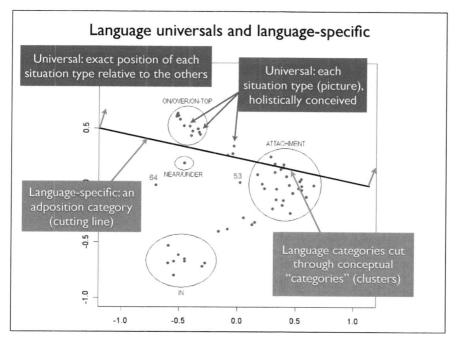

FIGURE 207

use that to figure out the grammatical categories of their spatial adpositions. They really have to know the exact positions of these different spatial relationships, these different situation types. They have to know these are up here, and these are down here. And only these are included in this particular language category.

So what's universal [Figure 207]? It's not these big clusters or these names we give to these big clusters. But what's universal are very specific situation types. Remember I said at the beginning that the insight of typologists for the semantic map model was to come up with a more fine-grained division of uses and then compare how languages express those usages in linguistic form. Well, this is really fine-grained. We have 71 different spatial relations represented by these pictures, all in a domain that in English is covered by only two prepositions, *on* and *in*. And yet this model had a very good fit. I didn't show you the statistics, but it has a very good fit. So that means all of these dots, all of these different situations, are very precisely located. And it's the exact positions here, the exact spatial position and the different kinds of conceptual similarity relations that they represent, that's what's universal. So don't go away from this [lecture] thinking that I've shown that there is an "on" concept, an "attachment" concept and an "in" concept. No; I've shown you that there is this

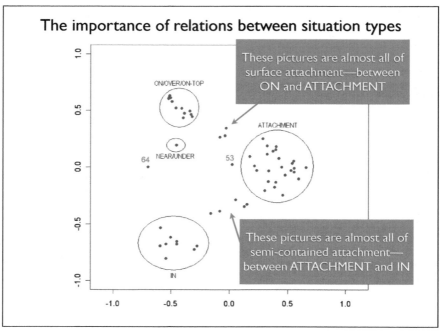

FIGURE 208

complex spatial relationship and a lot of very specific situation types can be positioned here on this space.

But now let's examine this a little more closely [Figure 208]. I'm just going to examine bits of it. There are a few pictures that go between these two clusters. If you look closely, they're almost all "surface attachment". It's kind of like the bandage on the leg example that was in the pictures that Melissa Bowerman had. So they are actually conceptually in between "on" and "attachment". The pictures down at the bottom are what I'll call "semi-contained attachment". They represent something that looks between "attachment" and an "in" relation.

So let's look at that a little more closely [Figure 209]. So these are the pictures that are there in between the attachment-cluster and the in-cluster. The ones that are closer to the in-cluster have a figure—the thing that's being located, that's indicated by the little arrow—that's partly contained in the ground. So the cork is partly in the bottle; the cigarette is partly in the man's mouth. So the thing that it's in has an opening, and that opening is where that the figure is located. But it doesn't have a hole; it doesn't go all the way through. If you look at the ones up here, the figure either is a hole or creates a hole in the ground object, the other object. But at least in the case where it creates a hole, it can extend beyond the ground. So it's not really containment. It kind of goes

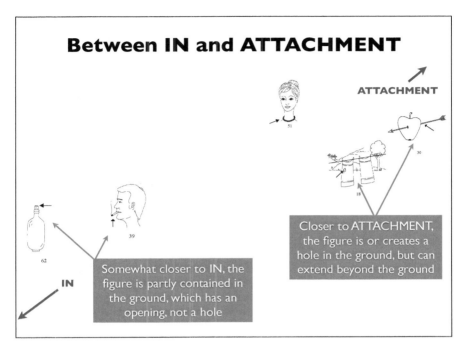

Between IN and ATTACHMENT

ATTACHMENT

Closer to ATTACHMENT, the figure is or creates a hole in the ground, but can extend beyond the ground

Somewhat closer to IN, the figure is partly contained in the ground, which has an opening, not a hole

IN

FIGURE 209

through the object. But it's not really attachment, either. There is some sense of attachment, in that when the arrow is stuck through the apple, it's going to be stuck in the apple.

Ok, so that's what's going on in between the clusters. Now, let's look at the in-cluster in more detail [Figure 210]. So these are the pictures you see in the in-cluster. And I'll tell you right away, the generalization, the semantic pattern I'm going to show you doesn't perfectly match here. But remember this is a statistical model that's essentially guiding us in understanding the conceptual structure of the spatial domain. It's not a perfect model. What you see over here is the figure [47, 60]; the ground encloses the location of the figure, but it doesn't envelop it. You get up here [14, 54, 67], it is starting to envelop the figure more: this bird in the hole in the trunk, and the rabbit in the cage and the box in the purse. But here the object still sticks out and you've got like, you know, still a whole open side. You get up here [71] and the figure is almost entirely enclosed by the ground, so it is really even more contained than below. And these [2, 19, 32] don't fit where you'd expect.

But on the whole, you can say that there is a pattern. There is a gradient of increasing envelopment of the figure by the ground as you go from down here to up here. That's the only thing that's really universal. There are no particular sharp lines here. There are degrees of spatial relationship, envelopment in this

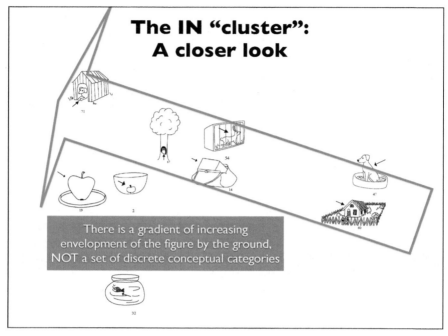

FIGURE 210

case, between the figure and the ground. And it's that degree of relationship that is pushing the spatial model there. So this [top left] is the extreme end of the "in" category. These [center] are still in-like but not as in-like as these, and these [lower right] in turn are not as in-like as these. So there are no conceptual categories that children are taking to the learning process. There's instead a kind of understanding of spatial relations that's gradient, that children could be bringing to the language learning process.

If you look at "on top", the on-cluster [Figure 211], it is not quite as good. But still, the best "on" cases are ones where we have a small figure on a large horizontal surface which is at the top. When you get down here, the figure is not quite on the top, but is on a nice horizontal surface. And if you get down here, you get more of a covering relation between the figure and the ground. So it's a less clear gradient. But my point remains the same: there aren't just discrete conceptual categories that are innate. Instead, there is a sort of a general understanding of spatial relations and the kind of dimensions of variation in spatial relations that we see. It's not a set of discrete conceptual categories.

So, to conclude, grammatical categories are not universal. This is the point I started with today; those of you who attended the other lectures know that I have been trying to make the point for several lectures in a row.

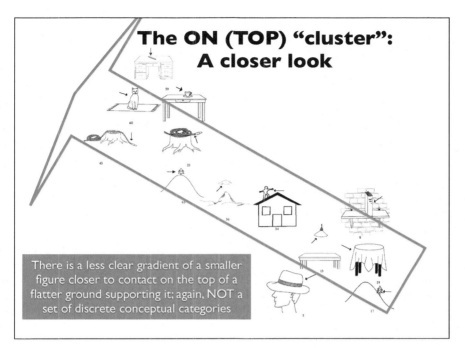

The ON (TOP) "cluster": A closer look

There is a less clear gradient of a smaller figure closer to contact on the top of a flatter ground supporting it; again, NOT a set of discrete conceptual categories

FIGURE 211

So, grammatical categories are language-specific and construction-specific. There's too much diversity when we look across languages and even within languages. Nevertheless, grammatical categories are constrained by the structure of this conceptual space. This structure of conceptual space is hypothesized to be universal in the typological sense of that term, but it does not consist of universal conceptual categories. Instead, it consists of particular situation types and their relationships to each other that are represented spatially using this statistical method that I've described here today. So, that's the kind of theoretical linguistic point I want to make here: not only are grammatical categories variable across languages—i.e. there is no set of universal grammatical categories; there is no set of universal conceptual categories, either. There is just a well-behaved range of variation in conceptual space. The multidimensional scaling analysis allows us to find out what dimensions of this variation in the spatial domain seem to be important when the speakers are learning and using the grammatical categories for spatial relations in their language. And it limits those kinds of spatial relations, but it isn't a small set of conceptual building blocks.

So, I will say a few things here; this is more trying to sum up all the lectures I've given so far. (I do have more to say tomorrow, so this is not the grand finale yet.) The syntactic generalizations that I started with this morning [Lecture 7] capture similarities between instances of syntactic structure, so similarities between say, different indefinite pronouns, different spatial adpositions. This is the stuff I talked about this morning: there are different ways to represent generalizations; the kind of traditional ways of using taxonomic relations are actually not very good for this very complex variation we find. So network structures like the semantic map model, or spatial models like the multidimensional scaling that I've shown you this afternoon, handle better the complex cross-linguistic and language-internal variation that I've shown you. However, I just want to remind you, the statistical analysis is just a tool. They still require the analyst to identify what properties give rise to the similarity measure: what kind of spatial properties are actually governing the structure of that spatial arrangement that the statistical analysis produced. We still have to go in and look at all those situation types and how they're arranged with respect to each other and figure out what kind of semantic or conceptual dimensions do they represent in a conceptual space. Thank you very much.

Exemplar Semantics and the Model of Grammar

Thank you all for coming. I know it's difficult to get through Beijing traffic and be here by eight o'clock in the morning, and I appreciate all the efforts that you have made. I know that some of you are hearing these lectures for the first time and have not heard the previous lectures in the series of lectures I've given here. So I would like to say a little bit of introduction to situate my lecture today in the context of the lectures that I've given before, both for those of you who haven't heard those lectures and those of you who have already heard them.

This is the slide I used in my last lecture towards the end [Figure 212]. In the lectures I was giving in this past week, my focus of attention has been on the fact that grammatical categories are extremely diverse across languages. And the reason for that is that grammatical categories are defined by the constructions in which they occur. And then I turned my attention to looking at the semantic basis of these categories, what is the range of functions that a particular role of a construction or a particular word has. And I've looked mostly at crosslinguistic evidence, namely looking at the grammatical diversity of categories across languages. What sort of semantic common denominator can we use as a basis for describing different categories in different languages? And I started with a famous example from typology, using the categories of transitive subject, transitive object and intransitive subject—typologists label these A, P and S—to show that we could use them to distinguish between ergative languages and nominative accusative languages like English and Mandarin [Lecture 8].

Then we looked at more fine-grained categories. I gave examples from research by the typologist Martin Haspelmath on nine different functions of indefinite pronouns, and I examined them in detail. But then it turned out that if we were going to look at more complex patterns across languages, we had to use some more advanced statistical techniques. So for instance, the diagram you see on the screen is a piece of the representation of the semantic

 All original audio-recordings and other supplementary material, such as any hand-outs and powerpoint presentations for the lecture series, have been made available online and are referenced via unique DOI numbers on the website www.figshare.com. They may be accessed via a QR code for the print version of this book. In the e-book, both the QR code and dynamic links are available, and can be accessed by a mouse-click.

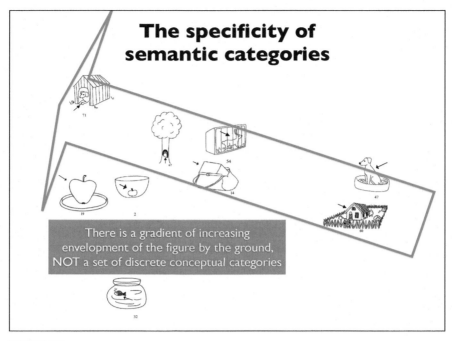

The specificity of semantic categories

There is a gradient of increasing envelopment of the figure by the ground, NOT a set of discrete conceptual categories

FIGURE 212

categories for spatial relations. The data, the actual pictures that you see here on the screen, are pictures that were designed by Melissa Bowerman, one of the other presenters of lectures here, and Eric Peterson, her colleague. The data was collected by Stephen Levinson and other people at the Max Planck Institute for Psycholinguistics, from nine different languages. There are a total of 71 pictures that represent 71 slightly different spatial scenes. So the statistical analysis shows you that all of these scenes are positioned in this conceptual space in a particular way. And the positioning in the conceptual space indicates that these 71 scenes, or at least the ones you see on the display right now, are all actually somewhat different crosslinguistically. In other words, from a crosslinguistic perspective, you compare grammatical categories of spatial relations across languages. All of these different scenes are treated slightly differently. So yesterday I argued that in fact the semantic categories have to be incredibly fine-grained to the point that we can distinguish some of these different situations [Lecture 8].

The arrangement of situations in this conceptual space, the geometric arrangement, actually is significant. These are relations that we think of as involving spatial containment. But what we have is a gradual change from the categories in the lower right, where the figure (the things that the arrow is pointing to, the thing that's being located) is only slightly surrounded by the ground, which is the fence down here, or this little pool for the dog. And then as you go further to the left, you get a gradual increase in how much the reference object (the ground object) envelops or surrounds the figure. So that is the semantic dimension that seems to be relevant for the subtle crosslinguistic difference between how speakers express this scene, these scenes and the scenes over here [from right to left in Figure 212].

So this points to a model of grammar as a relationship between form and meaning, such that linguistic form—of course a particular construction, so that's already kind of very specific in the syntactic form—the linguistic meaning is also very specific, and then we have to represent a syntactic category or a spatial word as covering a range of different situations, and we have to keep these situations distinct. That's if you want to propose that there is some kind of universal basis for these semantic categories and relationships. The only way you can find some sort of universal patterns here is to look at extremely fine-grained distinctions among situations, and then look at the dimensions of semantic variation, such as the degree of envelopment in the case of these spatial relations, that will link together these situations.

So the question here is—and this is the question that Melissa Bowerman has been asking in her lectures—is: well, ok, children learning a language and adults using a language, use these categories. And as Melissa Bowerman's research has shown, these categories are influenced by the language around you. So you have to figure out what the categories are. And notice that in the semantic representation here, these really fine-grained situation types, speakers still have to build categories out of them, the grammatical categories of their languages. But still, those categories have to respect the structure of the conceptual space, the semantic relationships between these very specific situation types. So a question we can ask is: Where does this come from? Is this something innate: that is, something that has to do with our cognition that we're sensitive to the degree of envelopment of the ground over the figure? Or is it something that we somehow can learn, either through language or through other means?

I will not be able to fully answer this question today. But I would like to show you some evidence that indicates that in fact the pattern that we see crosslinguistically may also be manifested in a single language, if we look at that language in the right way. And so you don't have to assume that the kind of conceptual space we see here is innate. There may be something there that's cognitive, independent of language, but it's not necessarily just given to human beings to begin with.

Ok, so I said I've got this very particularistic view of grammar. The idea here is that we're going to go from not just particular situation types, but we are going to go down to the actual individual instances of language use, individual utterances, and look at their form and look at their meaning, and talk about what's the relationship between form and meaning in actual language use. Now in this lecture that I'm giving this morning as well as the lecture that I'll be giving this afternoon at Beijing Foreign Studies University, I'm going to be actually showing you that my work here is inspired by research in phonology of all places. And so what I'm going to be doing is taking some models that were first developed in phonology and suggesting that similar models are important for our understanding of grammar, that is, the relationship of grammatical form and meaning.

So, today, my starting point or my inspiration is going to be a movement in phonology called "exemplar phonology". What is exemplar phonology? Well, it basically focuses on variation in language. So the variation we see in language in phonetics, is something that's only been discovered in the last 50 or so years. That is, the advent of instrumental phonetics—ways to measure how people actually pronounce things—has demonstrated that variation in language use is ubiquitous. Within a language and even within a single speaker, the phonetic realizations of phonemes are variable. And then across languages, the phonetic realizations of supposedly the same phoneme were actually different. So just because you see the phoneme [a] or [e] from one language to the next, doesn't mean you can pronounce it like a native speaker does. And anyway there is no one way to pronounce like a native speaker does, but there is a range of variation that you also have to be able to master.

So here is an example of this. The first example is just one of many you get from reading Peter Ladefoged and Ian Maddieson's book called *Sounds of the World's Languages*. Every single page of this book has examples like the one I'm giving you. Of course what I'm giving you, I like it because I'm a native of California and I also lived in Britain for a long time, so this difference is something which I wasn't really aware of, but it's apparently there. So California English speakers use true interdentals—I'm a Californian, so *think* (/θɪŋk/); while British speakers use dental fricatives, so it'll be more like /θɪŋk/, with the tongue behind the teeth. So here is a very subtle difference. And most people who are comparing English and American accents wouldn't even notice. I didn't notice it, for instance, living in England. But the other point to make is that Californian English speakers and British English speakers aren't completely regular on how they use the language. Some of them use the other variant. So both of them are variable, but the proportions differ, and that's how you distinguish these two dialects.

Janet Pierrehumbert, who is the chief advocate of the exemplar approach to phonology, writes "there is no known example of two languages with literally identical phonological category systems." So this is the same point I have

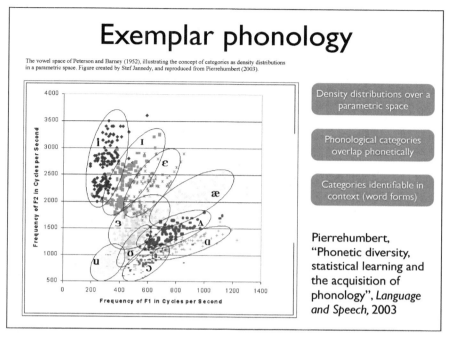

FIGURE 213

been making about syntax—there is no known example of two languages with identical syntactic category systems. Nevertheless in the phonological domain, these different phonological category systems are built on a common phonetic space. That's what instrumental phonetics shows you. So, for instance, in this diagram taken from one of Janet Pierrehumbert's papers—Janet Pierrehumbert kindly gave me the color version of this table—you can see the productions by an American English speaker of the vowels of American English [Figure 213]. And you can see from the different colors, dots and crosses and so on, that in fact any given phoneme is produced in a highly variable way. There is even overlap, so that in the phonetic space, some phonetic realizations of one phoneme are phonetically the same as those realizations of another phoneme.

So Pierrehumbert argues that the way you describe a phoneme, a phonological category, is in terms of a density distribution over a parametric space. So the parametric space is the vowel chart, the first and second formants. As you can see, I mentioned already that phonological categories overlap phonetically. And the categories are identifiable in context. So do you know when you hear something that you are listening to an /æ/ and not an /a/? It has to do with the words. And I'll be coming back to this theme, actually, in this afternoon's lecture [Lecture 10].

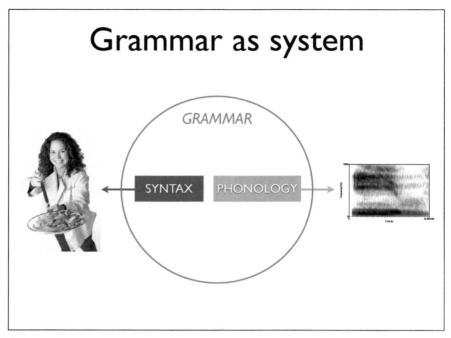

Grammar as system

GRAMMAR

SYNTAX   PHONOLOGY

FIGURE 214

So now let's look at the perspective from syntax [Figure 214]. The usual view of grammar is as a system. So we have syntax and phonology in the speaker's head. These are the grammatical systems. And we think about these being the real grammar and everything else is outside. So phonetic realization is outside. On the right is a spectrographic analysis of the name "Stephanie". And likewise in syntax, the meaning that's expressed by words and constructions is also out-side. So we look outside and here we have a picture of a Stephanie who I found [on a Google image search], a cook in Chicago.

Now usage-based grammars, the standard usage-based model which is widespread in Cognitive Linguistics, takes the same perspective, which is starting from comprehension. You start from a particular construction or a particular word, and you identify its range of uses. So for example in a study done in *Cognitive Linguistics* (the journal) of the Dutch preposition *door* which translates as "through", you see a diagram here that lists a bunch of different schematic situation types that represent different uses of *door* and their re-lationships to each other, their semantic relations to each other [Figure 215]. So when I was preparing this slide for the first time I ever gave this, I started looking through the literature and I didn't find a good usage-based study that actually started from actual tokens of use. They were all more abstract like the

Usage-based grammar

- Usage-based approaches are comprehension oriented: they start from a particular construction and identify its distribution over uses

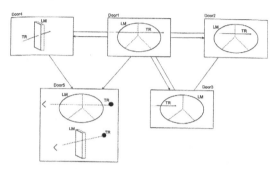

Image-schematic representation of polysemy network for the Dutch preposition door
(Cuyckens 1995:197)

FIGURE 215

one we saw that gave abstract schemas to describe different uses of this Dutch preposition. So we really want to move to actual exemplars of use.

The comprehension approach doesn't give us the relationship among different constructions used for the same function. So we saw that this Dutch preposition had five different uses, but we do not know whether there are other Dutch prepositions that can be used to express the same meanings. Also frequency isn't really calibrated. So if we actually did a corpus based study of this Dutch preposition *door* and discovered that one of those uses was much more frequent than the others. That might be a real fact. But it might just be because, overall, that situation type is expressed more commonly. So the fact that it's expressed more commonly with *door* is just a symptom of the fact that it's expressed more commonly overall compared to the other uses of *door*.

So I propose a model which I'm calling "exemplar semantics", which is basically the usage-based model, but turned around. First, we are going to start with actual particular situation types. Someone asked me yesterday about this term "situation type". Well, I should really say actual specific situations in which language is used. Now in principle, as I said, you could do this in the standard usage-based approach, this comprehension orientation. But the big change we are going to make is: we are going to take a production orientation [Figure 216].

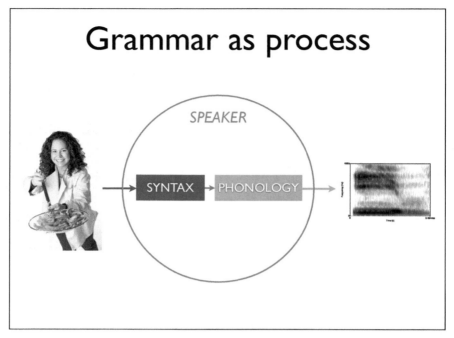

Grammar as process

FIGURE 216

This is what I have been calling verbalization in earlier talks [Lecture 6]. You're starting from an experience that you want to verbalize in a particular linguistic form in an utterance. So, exemplar semantics analyzes what specific linguistic forms are used to express a particular situation: a semantic exemplar. So now instead of thinking of grammar as a system, we are going to think of grammar as a process. The process starts with an experience we want to communicate, its syntactic expression, phonological translation and then some kind of actual phonetic verbalization. So you can see the direction is the same all the way across. The verbalization direction is the same as the phonological direction. So that's the process we are interested in. It's a harder one to analyze, but that's what makes it more interesting.

Now if you want to do exemplar semantics, it is harder than exemplar phonology, the kind of research that produces that phonetic graph that I showed you earlier. First, it is not clear what counts as the same semantic situation, the same experience being verbalized, since every situation is unique. It is easier to determine what counts as the same phoneme, because you think of it in terms of the words that the phonemes occur in. Also it is easy to sample a significant number of exemplars of a particular phoneme, because most phonemes occur at a high rate of frequency in an utterance. There are lots of examples of /a/ or /d/ in English, for instance. The same semantic situation recurs much more

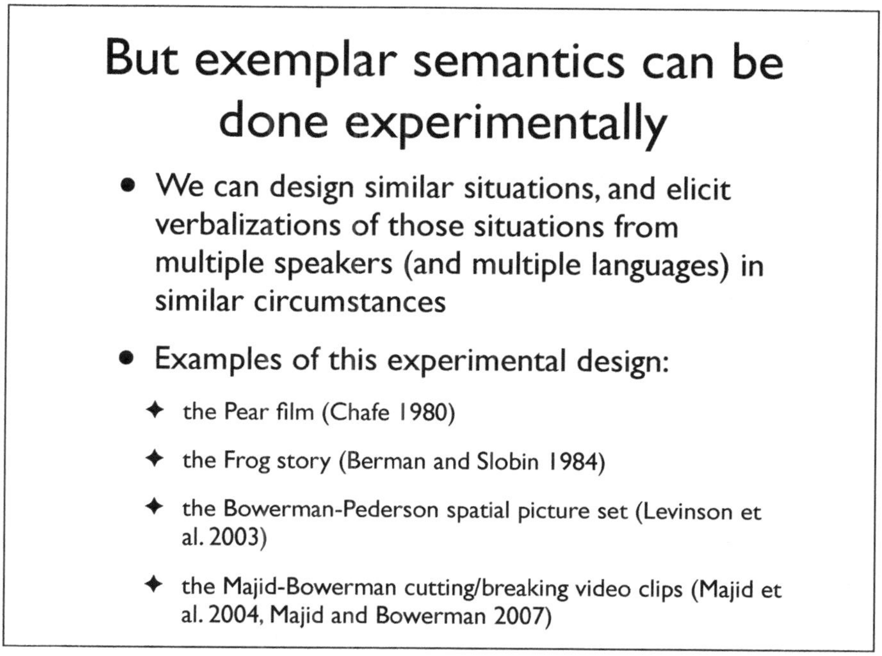

But exemplar semantics can be done experimentally

- We can design similar situations, and elicit verbalizations of those situations from multiple speakers (and multiple languages) in similar circumstances

- Examples of this experimental design:

  ✦ the Pear film (Chafe 1980)

  ✦ the Frog story (Berman and Slobin 1984)

  ✦ the Bowerman-Pederson spatial picture set (Levinson et al. 2003)

  ✦ the Majid-Bowerman cutting/breaking video clips (Majid et al. 2004, Majid and Bowerman 2007)

FIGURE 217

rarely. If you want to have a hundred tokens of the same semantic situation, you're going to have to record an awful lot of language use.

But exemplar semantics can be done experimentally [Figure 217]. We can design similar situations, and elicit verbalizations of those situations from multiple speakers—and multiple languages too—in similar circumstances. So there are numerous examples of this experimental design: between my lectures and Melissa Bowerman's lectures especially, we've seen a number of examples of this. One of the first is the Pear film by Wallace Chafe which I'll be using as my source of data here. Another is the Frog story, the picture book that those of you who came yesterday saw Melissa Bowerman show you. Another one is the Bowerman-Pederson spatial picture set. That's the one that was illustrated in the first slide this morning [Figure 212]. I discussed that in some detail yesterday [Lecture 8], and Melissa Bowerman discussed that in some of her lectures beforehand. Finally, there are also these video clips of different kinds of cutting and breaking events, developed by Asifa Majid and Melissa Bowerman; and Melissa Bowerman gave examples of those video clips a couple of days ago in her lectures.

So as I said I'm going to be using here the Pear film, or rather I'm going to be using the set of transcriptions of narratives of the Pear film that were collected by Chafe and published in his book on the Pear Stories in 1980. So this film came out of the research project that I talked about, Chafe's model of verbalization from the 1970s. The film was actually filmed by a professional filmmaker that was hired by Chafe to investigate interesting questions in the verbalization of experience. Once the film was made, in this particular case it was shown to English speaking UC Berkeley undergraduates in the 1970s. So these are actually people who must have been at my age at the time. And since then of course it has been shown to many other people in many other languages, including Mandarin. After the speakers viewed the film, each speaker was asked to describe it to an experimenter. And they were told the experimenter had not seen the film before. So each person who saw the film was put into the same situation, describing the film to a stranger who hadn't seen it before. So that experimental design maximizes similarity of situation for the speaker. As I said, the film has been shown to speakers of many other languages.

Now how many of you have actually seen the Pear film? Ok, I'm going to show you the Pear film now. It is about seven minutes long ...[1]

So that's the Pear film. So you can see there is sound, but there is no speaking. Of course that was designed for the purpose of allowing them to show this film to people who spoke other languages for crosslinguistic comparison. Ok, so there were twenty undergraduates who described this film and the descriptions were published in the 1980 work. And I used that as the basis of the analysis I'll be showing you in the rest of the lecture.

So the first thing is, let's look at these scenes [Figure 218]. Now I gave the scenes a kind of letter-number code, so D5. You don't have to worry about that. That is just a way to identify particular scenes. You could break down the verbalizations that all the speakers used. It's pretty easy way to identify them as describing or verbalizing specific scenes in the film. And roughly there is a large scale of organization, A, B, C, D, E, and within them, each number indicates more specific scenes. So you probably remember the scene from the film you've just seen. The numbering on the side there, that's the numbering I gave. So these are the speakers [in the left-hand column]; there were twenty speakers. Not everybody verbalized this particular scene, as you can see. But that's the number. And then the second number refers to the intonation unit, prosodic unit, as the speaker produced it. So this [the last two lines of column 1] means that speaker 11, in intonation units 66 and 67 in this narrative, describes this particular scene.

So as I said, there were 20 speakers. So here is another set of what they said [Figure 219]. Take a quick look of what they said. The main point is, you look at this and you say, ok, how did speakers verbalize the scene? Every speaker

---

1   https://www.youtube.com/watch?v=bRNSTxTpG7U.

Verbalization of Scene D5

1,75	[.45] he when he turns around his hat flies off.
2,65	[1.05 [.55] and uh] it turns out she [.7] from what I could understand she grabbed his hat.
3,20	[.9 [.7] uh] he loses his hat,
6,33	[.6] and his hat flies off,
7,49	{cross}=and she knocks the hat that he's wearing off on the ground,
8,28	[.7 [.1] a--nd] his hat falls off,
10,93	[.5] and apparently he [.9] I think by the breeze,
10,94	. . his hat sort of gets [.7] blown off his head=
11,66	[.5 . . And [.3]] his hat blows off,
11,67	[.55] when they cross,

speaker   intonation unit

FIGURE 218

Verbalization of Scene D5

12,108	[.8] also,
12,109	. . before he fell over,
12,110	[.2] his hat blew off.
12,111	[.25] While he was still looking at the girl.
13,57	and she brushes off this little hat that he has on,
13,58	[.7] and so his hat . . comes o--ff,
14,70	. . lost his hat,
15,62	[.8] and he checks [.3] and his hat flies off also.
17,99	[.35] The little boy {creaky sound} . . that was on the bike,
17,100	had been wearing a hat.
17,101	[1.3 [.55] A--nd [.3]] in the [.55] i--n passing the little girl,
17,102	it had . . fallen off.
18,34	so that his [.6] his hat flies off.
19,57	his hat comes off,
20,25	[.35+ and [.35]] somehow she took his hat.
20,26	. . Not on purpose but [.8] it came off.

FIGURE 219

does it differently. There are no two speakers that say exactly the same thing. Notice this is a very different perspective than we normally take about meaning. When we take a comprehension perspective, we say, ok, here is a sentence, this is what it means. But when you take a verbalization perspective—a production perspective—here is the scene, and how do people express it, suddenly you see there's a huge amount of variation in how people describe scenes.

So in other words, there isn't a simple one-to-one mapping from a particular scene and meaning, even when we restrict ourselves to a very specific scene in the film. So that is the first point. Every verbalization of every scene is unique in this entire corpus of twenty people describing a film with about 40 or 50 scenes. Now you can break down the verbalizations into their component parts (and I'll talk about that in a moment): lexical categories, particular kinds of argument structure constructions, and other constructions they use. And even there, as we will see, variation is pervasive. There are some cases where all the speakers who verbalized the scene used the same verb, but that's not very common.

So now I want to analyze this variation. So what we've done is: by turning it around and looking at what speakers actually do, how they use their language to express a particular situation, suddenly we see that there's a huge amount of variation within a language. And my theme is going to be this: the variation is governed by the same principles that govern variation across languages.

So how do we analyze this variation? This particular slide [Figure 220] is taken from the talk I gave on Sunday afternoon [Lecture 6]. And the question I had to deal with then was: in the construction grammar framework, how do you count constructions? How do you decide what kind of constructions a language has? And I said that Chafe's verbalization model, elaborated, provides a framework in which we can talk about the constructions in a language. Well that framework is of course a framework based on how speakers verbalize experience as a general process, a general cognitive process. And it also provides a basis for taking the constructions in a single utterance and breaking it down into [component] constructions.

So to summarize very quickly, since I can't really go into all the detail I'm afraid, for those of you who weren't there: Chafe says the first thing you do when you have a whole experience like the Pear Stories film—and I'm simplifying and pretending this is done in sequence but you all know this is not the way human mind works—but basically the first step is what we call subchunking. So that's essentially breaking up the Pear story film into the scenes that we saw. Then you do propositionalizing. That's breaking it down into the individual participants in the scene and the things that happened to them from one scene to the next. And that's mainly captured in argument structure

Analyzing variation via verbalization

Taking it apart...	...and putting it back together again
Subchunking/Focusing of consciousness	Cohering (Flow of consciousness)
Propositionalizing	Structuring
Relating it to prior experience...	...and re-establishing its unique specificity

Categorizing	Particularizing:
	    Selecting (Instance)
	    Situating (Grounding, Orientation)

FIGURE 220

constructions. Once you've got your individuals and events and other properties, then you can categorize them using linguistic categories: nouns, verbs and adjectives that you as the speaker have used in prior utterances to describe similar individuals, properties and actions.

Ok, that was Chafe's model. And then I added to this the stuff that gives you a lot of the grammatical structure. So once you come up with categories, you're still talking about a particular pear-picker, a particular boy, a particular pear, so we need to have some way to specify that grammatically. And to make a long story very short, the kind of constructions we usually find in noun phrases and prepositional phrases perform that function. Structuring means once you've taken a situation apart, a subchunk apart into the event and its participants, you have to put it back together again, both to specify who did what to whom in the scene, and to impose a particular discourse/information structure packaging or perspective on the participants in the scene. Lastly you have some kind of cohering construction, how you link one scene to the next, using clause linkage, coordination, subordination, or simple sequence of sentences, or reference tracking devices using some kind of pronouns or nouns and null anaphora as they call it, to indicate that you are tracking the same participant from one scene to the next. And that also helps to weave together the different

Analyzing variation via verbalization

| | | Categorizing | | | Particularizing | | |
| | | | | | Situating | | |
	BOY	GIRL	HAT	EVENT	HAT	EVENT:Time	EVENT:Mood
1	–	–	hat	fly off	Poss	Pres	Decl
2	–	–	hat	grab	Poss	Past	Decl
3	he	–	hat	lose	Poss	Pres	Decl
6	–	–	hat	fly off	Poss	Past	Decl
7	–	she	hat	knock off	the ... that he's wearing	Pres	Decl
8	–	–	hat	fall off	Poss	Pres	Decl
10	–	–	hat	get blown off	Poss	Pres	apparently
11	–	–	hat	blow off	Poss	Pres	Decl
12	–	–	hat	blow off	Poss	Past	Decl
13	–	–	little hat	brush off	this ... that he has on	Pres	Decl
13	–	–	hat	come off	Poss	Pres	Decl
14	–	–	hat	lose	Poss	Past	Decl
15	–	–	hat	fly off	Poss	Pres	Decl
17	–	–	it	fall off	Prn	Pluperfect	Decl
18	–	–	hat	fly off	Poss	Pres	Decl
19	–	–	hat	come off	Poss	Pres	Decl
20	–	she	hat	take	Poss	Past	somehow
20	–	–	it	come off	Prn	Past	Decl

FIGURE 221

scenes you verbalized, and therefore give the listener an idea of the whole. In this case the whole is the Pear Stories film.

So this allows us to take one example, the example that I just gave you, and start talking about the constructions, the words and constructions there [Figures 221–222]. So the subchunking and propositionalizing are just the initial breakdown of the scene into parts which we then categorize linguistically and then re-assemble. So what I've got here is categorizing [Figure 221]. So these are the participants in the event (BOY, GIRL, HAT). And you can see that there is a fair amount of variation, even when you start breaking down the scene, in how they express that event; I won't go into the details. Then the particularizing, the situating of events: the situating of the hat was basically identifying a particular hat, and most of them identify it as "the boy's hat", "his hat". Sometimes they use more elaborate expressions to specify that: "the hat that he's wearing", "this hat that he has on". Then you have to situate the event that took place in time. And then, as you can see you've got present tense; but you've also got someone who used the pluperfect and a number of speakers who have used the past, so again there is variation there. The mood of the event: mostly declarative, but then you've got *apparently*, an adverb that

Analyzing variation via verbalization

	Structuring				Cohering		
					Reference Tracking		Clause Linkage
	AGT	PAT	EXP	OTH	BOY	GIRL	
1	–	Sbj	–	–	–	–	*when he turns around*
2	Sbj	Obj	–	–	–	–	*and it turns out*
3	–	Obj	Sbj	–	Prn	–	Ø
6	–	Sbj	–	–	–	–	*and*
7	Sbj	Obj	–	Loc→Obl	(Prn)	–	*and*
8	–	Sbj	–	–	–	–	*and*
10	–	Sbj	Obj	Force→Obl	–	–	*and*
11	–	Sbj	–	–	–	–	*and*
12	–	Sbj	–	–	–	–	*also, before he fell over,*
13	Sbj	Obj	–	–	–	Prn	*while he was still looking at the girl,*
	–	Sbj	–	–	–	–	*and so*
14	–	Obj	Sbj	–	Ø	–	Ø
15	–	Sbj	–	–	–	–	*and… also*
17	–	Sbj	–	–	–	–	*and in passing the little girl,*
18	–	Sbj	–	–	–	–	*so that*
19	–	Sbj	–	–	–	–	Ø
20	Sbj	Obj	–	–	–	Prn	*and*
	–	Sbj	–	–	–	–	*but*

FIGURE 222

indicates something a little more complicated, and *somehow* near the bottom. So, again not every speaker did it the same way.

Now the next slide [Figure 222] is a little different from what you had in the handout because the structuring side I had on the handout, I did it in a wrong way. I did it in a comprehension way, starting from the grammatical roles and saying what semantic roles they've built. This time I've got it in the right way, I put the semantic roles up (AGT, PAT, EXP, OTH) and looked at what grammatical roles they are (Subj, Obj, Obl). So, as is common in English and other languages, agents are, when they are expressed at all, they're expressed as the subject; patients are expressed in different ways; and the experiencer, who is affected by the entity, is expressed in different ways. But you really should be looking at the purple rows all the way across, since those are argument constructions. So instead of looking at subject and object one at a time, you should be looking at the combination. Finally cohering—reference tracking: most of the time in reference tracking, if the participant is expressed at all, it's a pronoun or zero (in the case of speaker 14). Clause linkage: you can see a lot of them simply use coordination with *and*. But then also some use subordinate clauses to link the current event to a prior event in the narrative.

Ok, so this is just to illustrate variation. Now let's analyze some particular cases. Oh, first we have a possible explanation that I'd like to actually reject. So one possibility is to say—and this is a very Cognitive Linguistic type of explanation—one possibility is to say: what speakers are really doing is conceptualizing the scene differently in each case, even if each speaker is describing the same scene under similar circumstances. So the variation we have observed is not in the process of verbalizing the experience, but in the alternative construals of the scene that different speakers are producing.

Well, I don't think that's entirely wrong, but I think there are some important problems with this kind of explanation. And to see these problems, you have to think in terms of what we verbalize for. We're communicating with other people, the listener. It's an interactional phenomenon; it's not something going on only in the speaker's head. So the hearer cannot read the speaker's mind. That's the fundamental thing. That's why we use language: we can't read each other's minds. So the hearer doesn't really know what the speaker has to say. Now it is true that these scenes can have alternative construals. But given that that's true and the hearer of course knows that, the hearer cannot be certain of the construal that's intended by the speaker. So you might think, well, the language that the speaker uses should tell the hearer what the construal ought to be. But that's not entirely true either, because the speaker uses language based on past use of language that the speaker knows about. The hearer understands language based on past experience with those same words and constructions that the hearer has been exposed to in his lifetime. But those are two different things. The speaker's knowledge about their language is not the same as the hearer's knowledge about their language. And anybody who doesn't believe that, just teach a class and have your students do an exercise and exam and then read the kind of responses you get, and then you discover just how much the hearer's interpretation can differ from the speaker's intention.

And lastly, each experience that's being communicated is unique and different. So take this Pear film. The speaker has never seen the Pear film before, that exact combination of the participants and events. And the hearer hasn't either. So both of them have to rely on their common ground, their shared knowledge of past experiences with picking pears and kids on bicycles and stealing baskets and so on, in order to communicate and understand this event. So all of this suggests that there's not the purely cognitive construal such that the listener automatically reads the mind of the speaker as to what the construals ought to be. And that explains the variation.

I'm going to suggest an alternative explanation here. All of what I have just said shows that there is a fundamental indeterminacy in the communication process. However, as we know from a lot of psychological evidence, speakers

Second mention of referents

- How referents are verbalized after they are introduced in discourse
- Two types of verbalizations: possessive pronoun; definite article

1,16   and he [.3] dumps all his pears into the basket,

6,10   and dumps the pears into a basket.

FIGURE 223

are very good at tracking frequency information about the experiences they have, including the language they hear. So the speaker and hearer are tracking the frequency differences in these alternative verbalizations. So you can think of what these twenty speakers said, the variation in what they said, as variation that language learners are exposed to. They are learning language, immersed in the speech community in a naturalistic way. And what I'm going to show you with the data in the next few slides is that those frequency differences that the speakers can track demonstrate that speakers are sensitive to subtle semantic differences in individual scenes. Sound familiar? The whole point of the lectures I gave yesterday [Lectures 7–8] was that if you look cross-linguistically at variation in categories across languages, the speakers are sensitive to subtle semantic differences in individual scenes. That's my last bullet point.

Ok, so now let's look at some examples that I've studied. Some of the data was presented in a paper that had a different function. I'm going to talk about that other function, the diachronic or historical processes, this afternoon. Here I'm going to focus on the implications of this, what we think about speaker's knowledge of their language. So what I'm going to look at here is how referents are verbalized after they are introduced in discourse [Figure 223]. In English, in this particular set of data, there are two types of verbalizations: possessive

FIGURE 224

pronoun, "he dumped all *his pears* into the basket"; or definite article, "and dumps *the pears* into a basket". That's two different speakers describing the same scene.

Here's a table showing the frequency of verbalization of the definite versus the possessive pronoun [Figure 224]. There are also others, I won't worry about that. Here I actually did summarize across scenes: all the scenes where the tree was mentioned, the goat was mentioned, the ladder, and so on. The color coding indicates where are the higher percentages; I didn't put percentages in here. So you can see there are differences. But the differences form a pattern. If the referent is more animate and more alienable—in the grammatical category of alienable possession (possession that's usually specified by ownership)—then you are more likely to get a definite article. Referents that are less animate, more likely to be possessed, get the possessive pronoun. So in other words we see that there are subtle differences that are reflected by the frequency differences.

Other subtleties: the ladder is less likely to be owned by the pear picker. So this is cultural knowledge or cultural stereotypes that Americans have, a pear picker is an employee. Ok, so because it is less likely to be owned by the pear picker, speakers are less likely to use a possessive pronoun. The bicycle is more

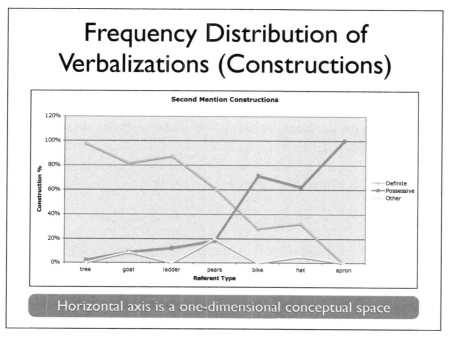

FIGURE 225

likely to be owned by the boy, the cyclist—again cultural knowledge—hence it's more likely to take the possessive pronoun. More complex: you have inter-action with the event verbalization. There's the scene where the three boys found the hat and gave it back to the kid. If they verbalize the scene with *give*, they used the possessive pronoun "gave his hat", whereas if you verbalize it with a different verb, you are more likely to get the definite article.

So what are the implications here for syntactic and semantic representa-tion? First, there is no simple one to one mapping between form and meaning. We can't just say with a particular noun type, or semantic type of object, you're going to use the possessive pronoun or the definite article. Most speakers could use either one for any of the objects that were in the Pear film. Instead, the mapping is a frequency distribution of forms for each function. So for the goat, the boy, the tree, the bicycle, you want to say how do you express the second mention of those? Well, the answer is a frequency distribution, something that the speakers track and is a part of their knowledge about their language. Now these functions are arranged in a conceptual space; I won't go into the busi-ness about the unimodal frequency distribution. Since we're looking at all the verbalizations, we don't have this problem about how to measure frequency. We've got all the data, so we can compare the frequencies.

Unintended human events

- Events with a human participant that does not intentionally bring about the action

- Three variants: subject = human; subject = other; existential

2,67   and then he . . crashes into a rock.

11,68 [1.2 [.25] and [.65]] his bike hits into a rock,

7,53   [.25] and the pears all [.45] spill on the ground,

3,21   a--nd . . there's a stone in the way,
3,22   so his bicycle falls over,

FIGURE 226

So here is a graph showing this [Figure 225], arranged on the bottom from left to right, to roughly the ones where you're most likely to get the definite article over to the ones where you're most likely to get a possessive. So the horizontal axis in this graph is basically a one dimensional conceptual space, from essentially "less likely to be possessed" on the left to "more likely to be possessed" on the right.

Another example [Figure 226]: unintended human events. You saw several events like the boy losing his hat, where the boy didn't have control over the outcome of the action. It wasn't certainly something that the boy intended. In the Pear Stories you had three different argument structure constructions or information structure constructions used: three variants characterized by whether the subject was the human—the human who didn't intend the action—the subject was something else; or an existential construction. So, subject was a human: "he crashes into a rock". The subject is something else: "his bike hits into a rock", "the pears all spill on the ground". And the existential construction, "there's a stone in the way, so his bicycle falls over".

Let's do the same frequency table [Figure 227]. Here now I divided up each individual scene. So there were actually six different scenes where there was an unintended human event, obviously something that Chafe must have been interested in when he scripted the film. But the choice of undergoer as subject

Frequency of verbalization in unintended human events

Events more likely to be under control of human being

	Und-Sbj	Oth-Sbj	Exist	Other	Total
D8. Cyclist falls/ bike falls	15	2	0	2	19
D7. Cyclist hits rock/ bike hits rock	14	5	3	0	22
A4. Picker drops pears/ pears drop	1	2	0	0	3
D5. Cyclist loses hat/ hat flies off	2	11	0	0	13
G4. He's missing a basket/basket is missing	2	12	5	0	19
D9. Cyclist spills pears/ pears spill	2	17	0	1	20

Events less likely to be under control of human being

FIGURE 227

or other as subject varies from one scene to the next. So the scenes where you are more likely to get the undergoer as the subject are the ones where again, a sort of stereotypical expectation is that the human being should have more control over the action—basically the cyclist operating his bicycle or the pear picker with the pears—whereas you are more likely to get something else as the subject in the events that are less likely to be under control of the human being: losing a hat, missing a basket (obviously), spilling the pears.

Again we can map this out and roughly rank the situations from the ones where there should be more control by the human to those that have less [Figure 228]. So what we have here is a dimension of likely or plausible human control over the action, but the action's outcome is contrary to that control. And it has grammatical effects. Again, not in the sense of: if the human has control, you make the human the subject; if they don't, then they don't make it the subject—but rather a frequency difference: you are more likely to make the human the subject, if the human is expected to have control; you're more likely to make something else the subject if the human is not expected to have control.

The third example I'm going to give you is scenes verbalized with the verb *see* [Figure 229]. What I did here was I picked out every scene where at least one speaker used the verb *see* to verbalize the event. It turned out there were

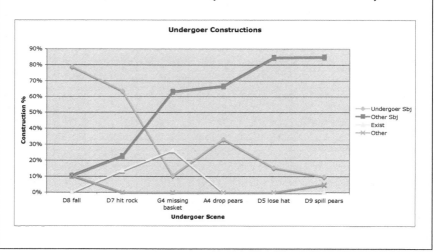

FIGURE 228

Scenes verbalized with *see*

Scene C3

5,15   And he sees . . the pears,
5,16   so he stops=

Scene E4

5,40   And they see,
5,41   [.7] him on the ground,
5,42   with all these [.5] pears strewn out all over the road,

Scene F1

1,103   [.6] And then . . they walk . . the three boys walk down the road and they
        see-- . . the kid's hat.

Scene G4

4,59   . . And he looked down,
4,60   . . saw that [1.05] he was missing a basket.

FIGURE 229

Frequency of verbalization of SEE scenes

	look at	see	come/run across	find	notice	discover	realize	Total
C3	2	4	0	0	0	0	0	6
E4	0	7	0	0	0	0	0	7
FI	0	3	3	7	2	0	0	15
G4	2	3	0	0	10	3	1	19

- C3 is more likely to be construed as durative
- E4 is more likely to be construed as inceptive
- FI is more like a finding situation type
- G4 is a cognition, not perception, situation type

FIGURE 230

four such scenes. And I've given you examples of the speaker using *see* for each scene. So the first one is "and he sees the pears, so he stops." The next scene: "And they see him on the ground, with all of these pears strewn out all over the road." The next scene: "And then they walk. The three boys walk down the road and they see the kid's hat." Last scene: "And he looked down, saw that he was missing a basket."

Let me mention something right now. You'll see in the first three sentences, if you look beyond the verb to the argument structure construction, you'll see that *see* has a direct object. If you look at the fourth example and again you look beyond the verb, you'll see that *see* has a complement, "he sees that he was missing a basket". And in fact it's not really a perception verb in that context, it is recognition, so a cognition verb.

But let's look at the way other speakers verbalize these scenes [Figure 230]. So you have *see* there [in column 2], and then you have a lot of different verbs that are used, at least in some cases, as well as the verb *see*, and in different frequencies. So scene C3, the first one, is more likely to be construed as durative, and that's why you get *look at* as an alternative. Scene E4, where the boy goes and sees the pears, is more likely to be construed as inceptive. He comes to see something; it appears in the boy's field of vision. F1 is more like a finding situation. *Find* is actually the most frequent verb, and then you have other verbs

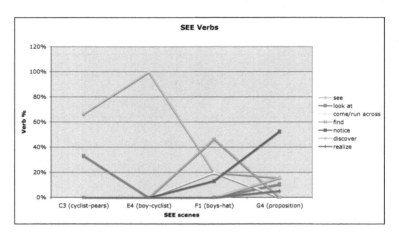

FIGURE 231

like *come* and *run across*. G4, as I mentioned, is a cognition, not a perception, situation type.

Well, as I said, the speaker can recognize that by looking at the syntax of the verb, what's combined with the verb. But the speaker could also figure that out by just looking at the alternative verbs being used. First, by far the most frequent verb for that scene is *notice*. *Discover* and *realize* are also used in this scene and no other scene. So you don't even have to look past the verb. If you have this variation in verbalization, a speaker can immediately see that the range of variation shows you that this is the cognition use, which is possible with English *see*, unlike the other three scenes which are all perception. So here is the frequency distribution to show you just what that looks like [Figure 231].

Some more semantic subtleties: the first scene that had *see* is the one that's more likely to be durative. It's a complex scene where the cyclist comes by, sees the pears, stops and gets off his bike. Well, in fact, I don't know if you remember, I don't even remember, what the order of the events was. Did the boy see the pears and then stop, or did the boy stop and then see the pears? Well, speakers varied as to which order they thought these events took place. If it's stop plus see, however—stop first—then "look at" is more likely to be used, or

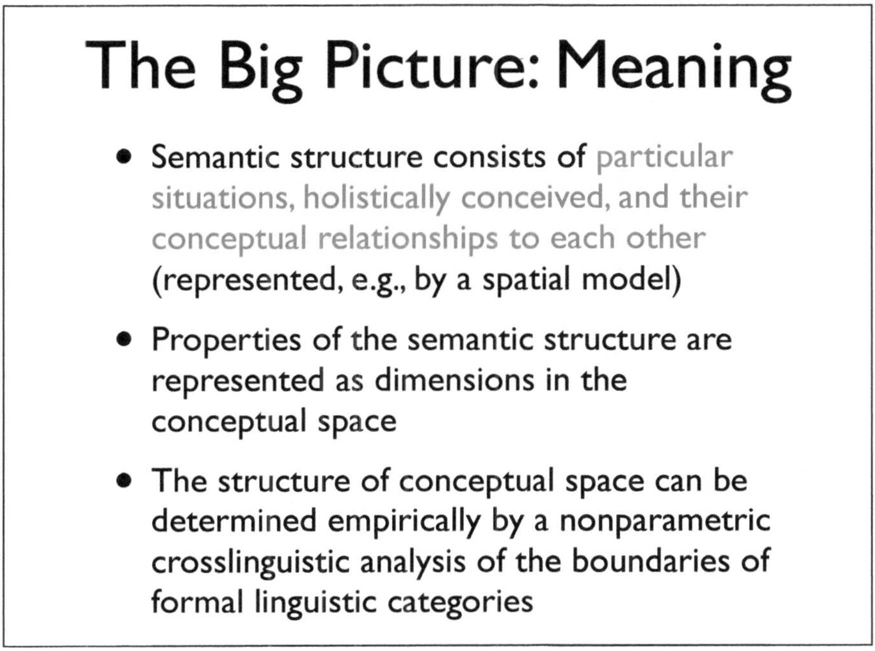

The Big Picture: Meaning

- Semantic structure consists of particular situations, holistically conceived, and their conceptual relationships to each other (represented, e.g., by a spatial model)

- Properties of the semantic structure are represented as dimensions in the conceptual space

- The structure of conceptual space can be determined empirically by a nonparametric crosslinguistic analysis of the boundaries of formal linguistic categories

FIGURE 232

is used, because that's durative. Stopping is a punctual event, then you see the pears, that's duration after that punctual event. If the sequence is the other way around, you get two punctual events, one is "comes to see the pears" and then "stops". And then you use *see*, which in English is more likely to have this inceptive "come to see" alternative semantic construal.

So let's go back to that issue of construal. I was critical of that analysis but I do think it's not entirely wrong. So do these different expressions imply different construals? Well, the point I've been emphasizing in this talk and the previous talks is that human beings know the rich detail of particular situations. So they have all this very fine-grained knowledge of differences between particular situations, and the complex, rich structure and detail of each situation. That detailed knowledge about events, and also the cultural knowledge that frames our knowledge of particular events or our experiences of particular events: that detail provides us with a potential for alternative construals to different degrees. So what we know about aprons and bicycles give us a potential for expressing this or construing it as a possessive relation or a nonpossessive relation to different degrees. And we saw that's reflected in what speakers actually did. As I said, they're reflected in the frequency distribution of alternative verbalizations.

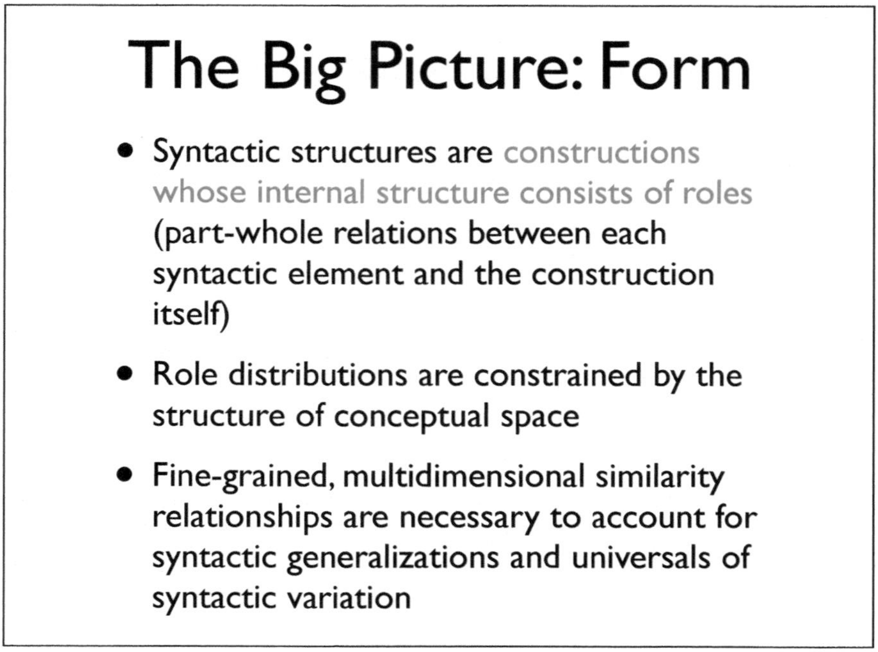

The Big Picture: Form

- Syntactic structures are constructions whose internal structure consists of roles (part-whole relations between each syntactic element and the construction itself)

- Role distributions are constrained by the structure of conceptual space

- Fine-grained, multidimensional similarity relationships are necessary to account for syntactic generalizations and universals of syntactic variation

FIGURE 233

Now I come to my concluding points about what is the big picture here [Figure 232]. Semantic structure (this is linguistic semantic structure, what corresponds to meanings of forms) consists of particular situations, holistically conceived (that is, their full rich detail) and their conceptual relationships to each other, which could be represented by a spatial model of a conceptual space. So properties of the semantic structure are represented as dimensions in the conceptual space, like degree of envelopment of the ground object over the figure in containment. The structure of a conceptual space can be determined empirically by crosslinguistic analysis, using the boundaries of the formal categories, the actual grammatical categories of particular languages.

Form [Figure 233]: this is going back to my earlier lectures. Syntactic structures are constructions whose internal structure consists of particular roles that are filled, and those roles define grammatical categories. The distributions, that is, the kind of things that you find in these grammatical categories, are constrained by the structure of the conceptual space I just described. And this was the theme of my talk about syntactic space: syntactic constructions are also holistically defined, and they have rich detail, lots of different syntactic and morphological properties. And you need to come up with a kind of multidimensional model of the similarity relationships among different

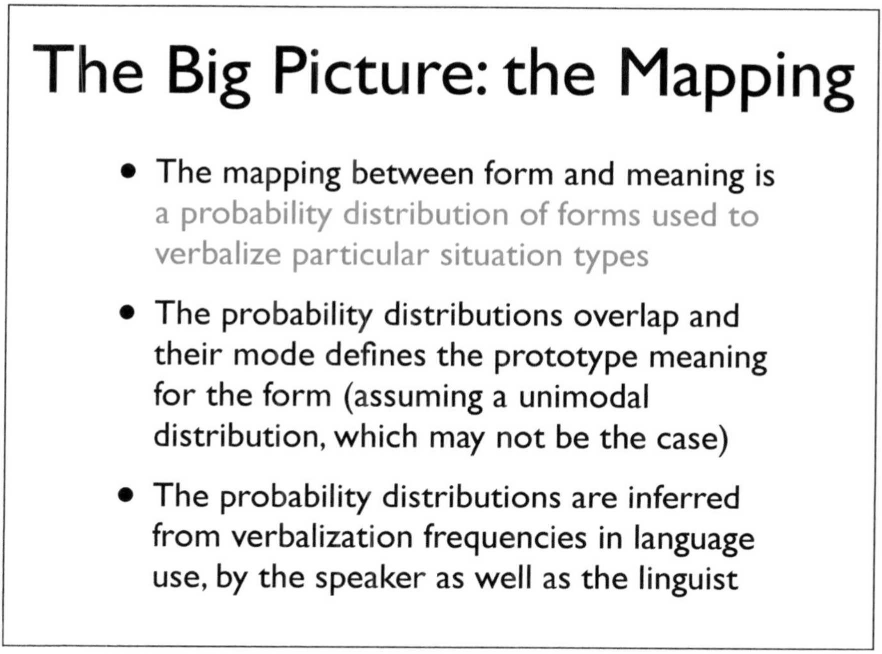

The Big Picture: the Mapping

- The mapping between form and meaning is a probability distribution of forms used to verbalize particular situation types

- The probability distributions overlap and their mode defines the prototype meaning for the form (assuming a unimodal distribution, which may not be the case)

- The probability distributions are inferred from verbalization frequencies in language use, by the speaker as well as the linguist

FIGURE 234

constructions in order to account for syntactic generalizations and language universals.

Finally, the mapping between form and meaning [Figure 234]. The mapping between form and meaning is a probability distribution of forms used to verbalize particular situation types. That was the main thrust of this morning's lecture. These probability distributions overlap; we saw that. And their mode, that is, the high point in those graphs I showed you for any particular construction, define the prototype meaning for the form, assuming there is a mode. And the probability distributions are inferred from verbalization frequencies in language use, by the speaker as well as the linguist. Obviously with these Pear Stories examples, I was the linguist, analyzing the frequency distributions and making inferences about the dimensions of semantic structure that were important to speakers. But that's just me as an empirical scientist trying to guess what the speaker is doing. The speakers are doing the same thing. They are listening to language, hearing how it is used, hearing variation in how the people around them verbalize different experiences, and then using that to develop an understanding of the language. So that's the sense in which I'd like to say that the semantic structure doesn't have to be completely given to you innately, the semantic structure underlying conceptual space. There is actually variation in how language is used around speakers—in a monolingual speech community even—that gives them evidence about what's important, what there is to pay attention to in semantic structure, and the kind of general semantic dimensions that are relevant for understanding and learning grammatical categories. Again I'm not denying that there might be some innate aspects to it about what kinds of semantic dimensions speakers turn to. But I'm just saying that it doesn't have to be all innate, a lot of it can be learned. Thank you very much.

From Construction Grammar to Evolutionary Linguistics

Thank you very much for coming. I know that a lot of you have been following the lectures since the three of us came to Beijing. And others of you are joining the lecture series for the first time, some of you who are students here at Beijing Foreign Studies University.

The lectures that I have been giving have been on the topic of construction grammar. Construction grammar is a model of representing syntactic structure in Cognitive Linguistics. I spent most of the lectures discussing a particular version of construction grammar which I have proposed, called Radical Construction Grammar. In this model, I have focused my attention on how much diversity there is in grammatical constructions across the world's languages. In the last three talks that I have given yesterday and this morning, I focused on the relationship between form and meaning. And I argued that when we look at meaning, we also have to respect essentially the diversity of languages and how they pay attention to meaning. And that in fact, when we look at the analysis of the meaning of linguistic forms, we have to take an extremely fine-grained perspective on that, to describe the range of very specific kinds of situations that human beings express in language. And I concluded by arguing for essentially a radical version of what's called the usage-based model in Cognitive Linguistics, the idea that the linguistic knowledge that speakers have is derived from language use. But in fact, perhaps not so much derived, but added up in the sense that speakers actually can pay attention to and track the frequency of the use of different linguistic forms for situations that are expressed in language.

So, in some sense I've wrapped up on that, on the first nine lectures that I gave. But all of that discussion was based on looking at language from a

All original audio-recordings and other supplementary material, such as any hand-outs and powerpoint presentations for the lecture series, have been made available online and are referenced via unique DOI numbers on the website www.figshare.com. They may be accessed via a QR code for the print version of this book. In the e-book, both the QR code and dynamic links are available, and can be accessed by a mouse-click.

synchronic perspective. Now I'm going to turn my attention to looking at language from a diachronic perspective. And so this last lecture will be a bit different from the other three. I'm going to start from the endpoint of my first nine lectures, this usage-based approach to linguistic knowledge, and then situate this in a broader model of essentially human linguistic behavior and the social context of linguistic use. Obviously I have only one hour here, so there will not be any details. I will focus my attention on some of the kinds of linguistic problems that I talked about in previous lectures. But I will be painting a very broad picture, and that's what I call "evolutionary" linguistics.

I should start by saying that the usage-based model itself is diachronic in its character because the language use that the speaker has changes over time. When the speaker learns a language and comes to use a language, in the usage-based model the idea is: through the speaker's lifetime, their knowledge of language is evolving, is changing. So all we are really doing here is taking what the speaker is doing in his or her lifetime and then embedding it in a speech community where there are lots of speakers whose lifetimes overlap and extend for much longer than any one person's lifetime.

Ok, so that's my little introduction. So the approach that I have been advocating is exemplar semantics or exemplar grammar. And this is the idea that speakers' knowledge of language is actually influenced by every single usage they have. So every time they hear someone use a particular expression to express a particular kind of experience, that essentially influences their knowledge of language. And in my last lecture, I emphasized how speakers contrasted different frequencies of forms and that reflects subtle semantic differences in the situations they communicate. And it also influences their knowledge of the language, how the language is used, and the different constructions in the language and the different words in the language that are used to express meaning.

So I want to stay with this exemplar-based view. An exemplar is a particular occasion of use of language, like me talking right now, that influences your knowledge of English. But now I'm going to take the view that exemplars are what are called "replicators". So the exemplar model of grammar is basically a kind of usage-based model. It represents linguistic knowledge as the frequency distribution of particular constructions across the situations or meanings for which they are used. That's what I talked about this morning [Lecture 9].

So this knowledge is based on language use to which the speaker has been exposed. Think of yourself in terms of your native language, which is Chinese for most of you, and think about it in terms of your own way of learning the language where essentially you are exposed to people using the language around you. You started using the language yourself as an infant or as a child growing up. And so your knowledge of language is based on what you have been exposed to, which is going to be different from what your neighbors were exposed to, even if you think of yourselves as speaking the same language.

So how does language use actually work? Well, essentially you have kept track of past uses of language in your mind. And any time you want to say something new, you are going to be using words and constructions and sounds that you have used before. That process is what we are calling "replication". Replication means you're making a copy of a sound, or a word or construction—that's what I'm doing right now—sounds, words and constructions that I've used before on previous occasions. And these sounds, words and constructions are used to communicate recurrent experiences. So any time I use the same word to describe something, like *word*, that's because the thing I'm trying to communicate to you is something I've talked about before, and other people in the English speech community have talked about before, and verbalized it with the word *word*.

Now replication in language use isn't always perfect. It leads to language change. So you see change in the forms used to communicate particular meanings. Some of you who have been on this planet as long as I have, perhaps, will have seen the changes that have taken place in your own language, the language that you think of as Chinese or English or whatever. You can observe these changes. Sometimes they happen very rapidly as with vocabulary; sometimes more slowly.

So now we have to look at this process. So we're thinking now about the usage-based model in language use in terms of replication: the repeated use of forms to express similar meanings. So in order to understand this use, we have to use or develop a theory of replication in change. Well, there is one out there that's been used by biologists for over 150 years. And that's the theory of evolutionary change. And this is the one that I'm going to be describing here, applied to understanding how language works.

So I'm going to give you a little introduction to evolutionary change [Figure 235]. Now all of us think of it in terms of something that originated in trying to describe biological evolution: the evolution of species. But in fact you can abstract away from the particular example of biological evolution which occurs through replication/reproduction of organisms, and talk about replication of anything that happens to be replicated, including linguistic expressions. So evolutionary change is change by replication, as opposed to inherent change. Sometimes things change just by themselves. There is no new object. It just transforms itself in some way or another, so, for instance, a child growing up. Replication is when you make some kind of copy as illustrated diagrammatically with those red squares.

Evolutionary change

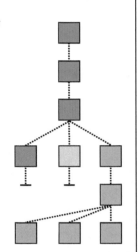

- Evolutionary change is change by **replication**, as opposed to inherent change
- Evolutionary change is a **two-step process**:
  - ★ *Generation of variation* (*creation of multiple variants*)
  - ★ *Selection* (*propagation/ extinction of variants*)

FIGURE 235

Now an important aspect of evolutionary change that biologists emphasize, and it's important for linguistics as well, is that evolutionary change is a two-step process. The first step is "generation of variation". So you're creating linguistic form, say, or any kind of form that's different in some way. And you usually get variation, a range of differences. And the second step is "selection": where some variants get propagated and others go extinct, as you see with the little boxes on the right.

The model I'm presenting was developed by a philosopher of science who sadly died just about month or so ago, David Hull. And he called it the General Analysis of Selection (GAS) [Figure 236]. Because, if any of you know a little bit about the theory of evolution, you know that evolution precedes by what they call "natural selection" in biology. Again we can talk about selection in general.

So we've talked about replicators, the things like linguistic forms, or biological species, or actually genes in biology. So we're going to define it in this abstract general way: as an entity that preserves most of its structure in replication. So when I speak, I use words and so on; they keep most of their structure, enough hopefully to be recognizable.

But there is another entity that's involved, and this is the entity that Hull calls an interactor. This is an entity whose interaction with its environment—you

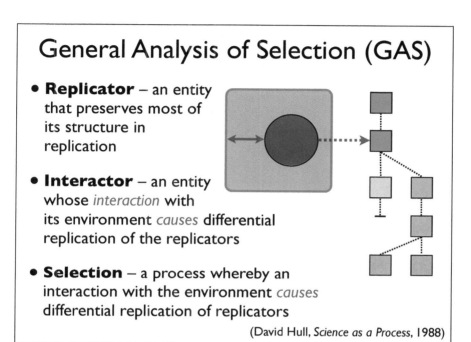

FIGURE 236

should think of it as that brown square—causes the replicators to be differentially replicated. So there's another entity here, the interactor [the blue circle]; this is all very abstract, but I hope you can get the basic idea. And it's actually something that that interactor does that causes that differential replication. So it does have to happen in some way. And selection is simply that process whereby the interaction with the environment causes differential replication of replicators. Differential replication means some replicators get propagated and others do not.

So how does this work in biology [Figure 237]? The interactor is an organism, like this elk. The environment that the interactor interacts with is the ecosystem, conspecifics (that's the other members of the same species) and as a result of the success in survival or failure in survival of the interactor in the environment (that's the interaction with the environment, does it survive or not), it will cause the replication of the genes. So that's the kind of basic biological model. This is not the only way in which selection happens in biology, but since we are all interested in linguistics, I'm not going to worry about that. It's the basic case which can function as a starting point for our discussing language.

So how does this work in language change [Figure 238]? Basically, as I've said already, every time we talk, we replicate tokens of linguistic structure: not

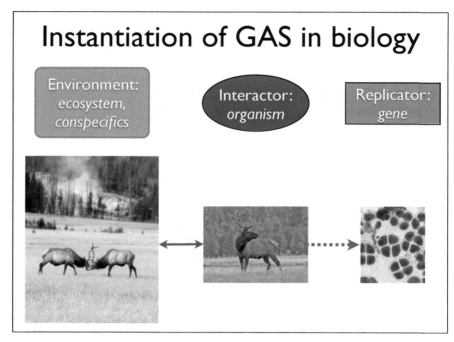

Instantiation of GAS in biology

FIGURE 237

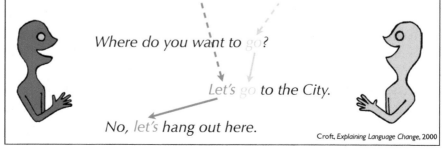

An evolutionary framework for language change

- Every time we talk, we *replicate* tokens of linguistic structure—**linguemes**—in utterances Social cognitive linguistics

- The process of communication, i.e. perception and production, generates *variation* in replication Exemplar semantics

Where do you want to go?

Let's go to the City.

No, let's hang out here.

Croft, *Explaining Language Change*, 2000

FIGURE 238

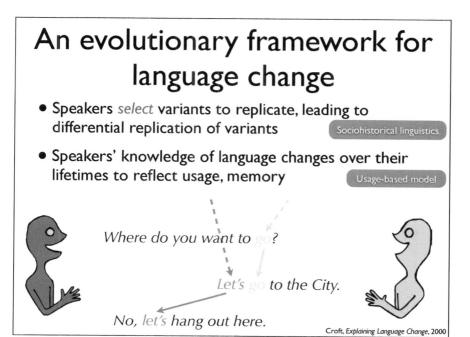

An evolutionary framework for language change

- Speakers *select* variants to replicate, leading to differential replication of variants — Sociohistorical linguistics

- Speakers' knowledge of language changes over their lifetimes to reflect usage, memory — Usage-based model

Where do you want to go?

Let's go to the City.

No, let's hang out here.

Croft, *Explaining Language Change*, 2000

FIGURE 239

just a word like *structure* in the abstract but my particular pronunciation and use of the word *structure* right now. That's a single token of that form. And I've coined the term "lingueme" to describe this in a book of mine, which is called *Explaining Language Change*.

So this process occurs in conversation, in social interaction between human beings. And that's an area which I call "social cognitive linguistics". I'm calling it that just for two silly reasons. One is that I wrote a paper with that title, and the second, this is a cognitive linguistics forum. It's really about pragmatics, but it's pragmatics with a cognitive side to it. It's not just what's going on in social interaction, but what we are understanding about our own cognitive processes and intentions, and what we interpret the other persons' intentions and desires and beliefs to be.

So that process of communication, that is the perception and production of utterances, generates variation in replication. Now I talked about that this morning [Lecture 9], when I talked about exemplar semantics, and I will talk about this again later on in this lecture.

Then speakers select particular variants to replicate, which leads to differential replication of these variants [Figure 239]. That's what people work on in sociohistorical linguistics. This is about how we study the kind of processes that leads one variant to be preferred and propagated in a speech community

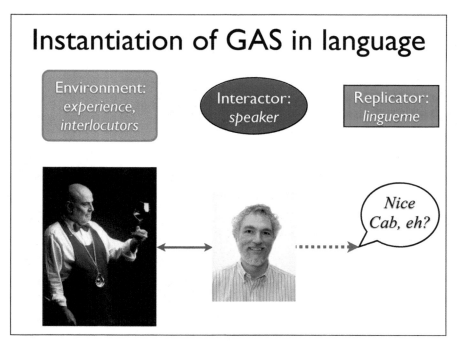

FIGURE 240

while other variants disappear. Again I won't talk about this, though I have done some research and mainly some mathematical modeling of this process in the evolutionary framework. But since this is a cognitive linguistic forum, I'm not going into any more detail on that. The last point is worth remembering, which is that when you think about the speakers, their knowledge of language changes over their lifetime; this reflects the usage—what they hear, how they hear language being used around them—and also their memory. It's also a cognitive process: how you organize that knowledge that you've learned from language use in your mind, how easily you remember or forget various aspects of language. And that's also a part of the usage-based model.

So that's the evolutionary framework for language change. So how does this work in language [Figure 240]? The interactor is a speaker. The environment is some kind of experience I want to communicate and the person I want to communicate this experience to. And then the replicator is the actual expression that I might produce on a particular occasion. So the two crucial elements here are the speaker, who of course is the person who uses the language, the person who is learning language. And the speaker is the one whose understanding of language, and therefore the mechanism for replicating language, evolves over his or her lifetime.

Now some of you in this room know about research that has been done on language and social cognition. So this evolutionary framework for understanding language presupposes all the social cognitive prerequisites for language proposed by philosophers such as David Lewis and Michael Bratman, and psycholinguists such as Herbert Clark, Michael Tomasello and others. Some of these elements are things like the notion of joint cooperative activity, common ground or shared knowledge, joint attention or salience, what are called coordination devices, including convention, which in turn includes linguistic convention. Again, I could give a whole talk about that. That's the pragmatic side of why we talk: what's the circumstances under which we produce utterances. But I'll just take all of that for granted for now, so that I can focus on the linguistic effects of this process.

Now I've given a lot of talks, so I discovered at least in the West, as soon as you use the word *evolution* in your theoretical discussion, suddenly, everybody is interested. You get invitations to all sorts of unusual conferences, interdisciplinary conferences and whatnot. And people who are not linguists, which of course is the vast majority of the world, suddenly get interested in your work. But they also seem to think—and many linguists also think—that what you are doing is you are making analogies from biological evolution to language change. Well, biological evolution is a very complex process. I've only given you the crudest and the most basic description of the process. Language change is also a very complex process, if you start bringing in everything: not just what happens to linguistic forms but how speakers use these forms and how their usage evolves over time. So you cannot just make analogies, because you'll find analogies and you'll find disanalogies, things that don't match. And you won't know what's an important analogy and what's an accident; and what disanalogies you can ignore and what ones you might have to worry about.

So GAS is a general theory of change by replication, as I said to start with [Figure 241]. For example, there is no relationship here about how a replicator gets you to an interactor in the General Analysis of Selection. This is something that trips up people who try to apply evolutionary models to language change, because in biology there is a very important relationship here. Genes, when the organisms reproduce, those genes gave rise to the new organism: daughter organisms. But there is nothing quite like that in language. So that means biological development—development of an organism from when it's born—is not quite the same process as language learning. And thank goodness, that's not a part of the general analysis of selection, because they don't work in the same way. I won't go into the details; I'll just assert that they don't work in the same way.

GAS is **NOT** an analogy!

- GAS is a *general theory of change by replication*

- For example, there is no replicator → interactor relationship in GAS

- Development in biology ≠ language learning

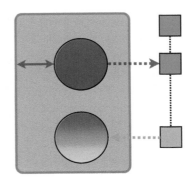

- And in fact, they are not alike: there is nothing like genotype → phenotype in language; lingueme replication can feed back to the same speaker ("Lamarckianism"), etc.

FIGURE 241

Well, I have a little time, so I'll talk a little bit about this. There are some things I talked about in an article I did in a journal of philosophy and biology. It's one of these invitations I got from starting using the word *evolution*. What's going on in language change, and also in biological change, is that speakers are interacting with a constantly changing environment. The kinds of experiences you want to communicate are changing all the time. Every experience you want to communicate is unique. Likewise, the people you interact with are changing, and the social structures that you are part of—as a child, as a student or as an adult: both are also changing over time. So the environment that helps determine your choices of language to use is changing constantly. And so the evolutionary response to this has been a very flexible structure. And one of the things you discover is—something that cognitive linguistics spends a lot of time describing—is how flexible language is in conceptualizing the world and communicating experiences.

Some people ask, well, what kind of progress do we see? There is no real progress in biological evolution. And there is no real progress in language too. The reason for that is: language has evolved as a general purpose communication system. So on the whole, we can find ways to talk about just about anything we want to talk about. If something new comes up, we can find ways to

Replication lineages

- Replication processes lead to **lineages** of replicators

- In biology, lineages define categories of evolutionarily related replicators, such as the jaws of reptiles and mammals

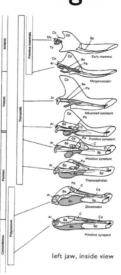

left jaw, inside view

FIGURE 242

talk about that as well. So what you see when you look at language changes in different languages: it's going through the same old cycles evolving from one kind of grammatical system to another, to another, and then back to the first. And you see this happening over and over again if you look at a lot of languages.

But another factor is that it seems like language is very unforgiving to inter-actors: miscommunication can have serious consequences, to put it in linguistic terms. So evolution turns out to be very conservative. And so you can see again, similarities between biological evolution and language change probably have to do with these general properties of the environment. So for instance, those of you who have studied English, you know that the English auxiliaries like *can* and *will* have a special syntax. Well, that special syntax is left over from Middle English. It's a historical relic. It's what they call a "vestigial trait". Languages also tend to reuse existing material rather than to create whole new things from scratch. So, for instance in some dialects, that English third-person singular -*s* in "He walks", which hardly has much function any more: it's now been reused to express aspectual distinctions like habitual. And then some-times, if you have a complex construction, you get something, that's from a processing point of view a little problematic. It gets carried along because it

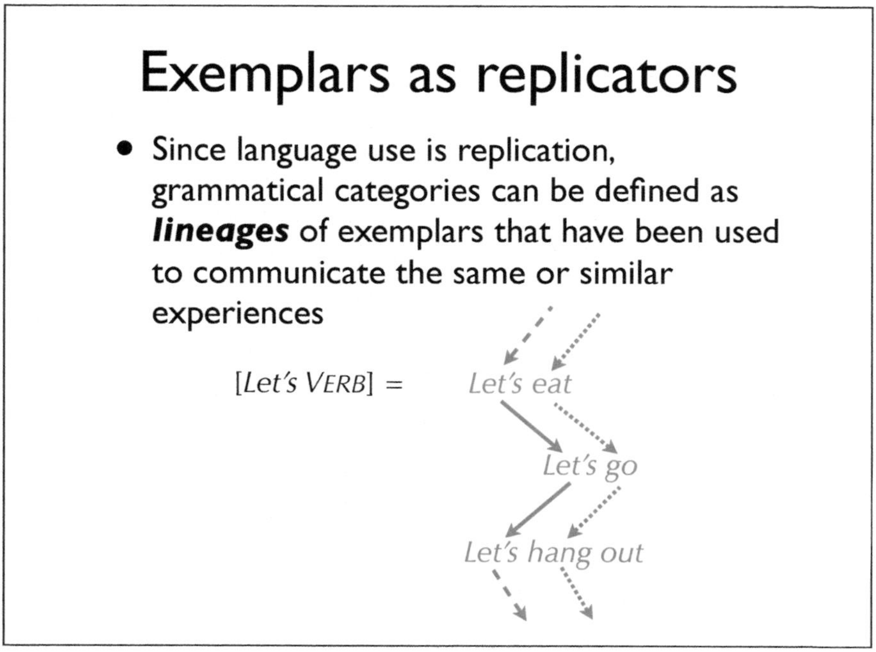

Exemplars as replicators

- Since language use is replication,
  grammatical categories can be defined as
  lineages of exemplars that have been used
  to communicate the same or similar
  experiences

[*Let's VERB*] =   *Let's eat*

Let's go

Let's hang out

FIGURE 243

takes too long, it's too complex to unpack the construction. So in an expression like *brother-in-law*, the plural, or at least the old plural, is *brothers-in-law*. The plural is inside the word, very inconvenient place for it to be located. That survives because, as I said, evolution is very conservative. People do say *brother-in-laws* now. So you do get change taking place here.

Ok, now I want to start focusing more specifically on the properties of linguistic structure that you might conclude from the basis of this evolutionary approach. Replication processes lead to lineages of replicators [Figure 242]. So you think of yourself, you and your mother and your grandmother and your great-grandmother, you are all replications. This is a lineage, like a family lineage. And there will be a family resemblance in the appearance and personality between you and your parents and your bothers and sisters and your children when you have them. Now in biology, you have lineages like this one for the jaw of reptiles evolving into the jaw of mammals. Lineages define categories of evolutionarily related replicators. So just like you are related to your great grandmother, so the mammalian jaw is related to the reptile jaw.

I'd like to suggest that we look at linguistic categories in the same way. Since language uses replication, we can think of grammatical categories as lineages of exemplars that have been used to communicate the same or similar

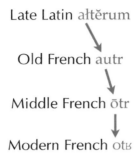

Sound lineages

Sounds (sound changes)

Late Latin ałtĕrum

Old French autr

Middle French ōtr

Modern French otʁ

FIGURE 244

experiences [Figure 243]. So every time I keep using the word *structure* over and over again, I'm creating a lineage. So are the other people who are speaking English and using the word *structure*. And so we can think of the category that's defined by the word *structure* as a lineage of all these different uses that have been made. And so it's not just that the uses form a kind of family resemblance. They actually form a family tree. There's an example: the "Let's VERB" construction is actually a lineage. So when we talk about semantic categories as being of the family resemblance type, we should be taking this metaphor a bit more literally I think.

So these linguistic category lineages are out there in language use. They are not inside the speaker's head. It's part of communicative interaction. That's the sounds I produced that you interpret in a certain way, and then on the basis of that you will use the same sounds to express the same words or meanings in the future. So these lineages, since they're not inside the speakers' head, the lineages can extend long after any individual speaker is dead. That's of course what historical linguists traditionally study.

So a sound lineage is what they call "sound changes". So here we have a sound change, the one that's in purple, from Latin to Old French, Middle French and Modern French [Figure 244].

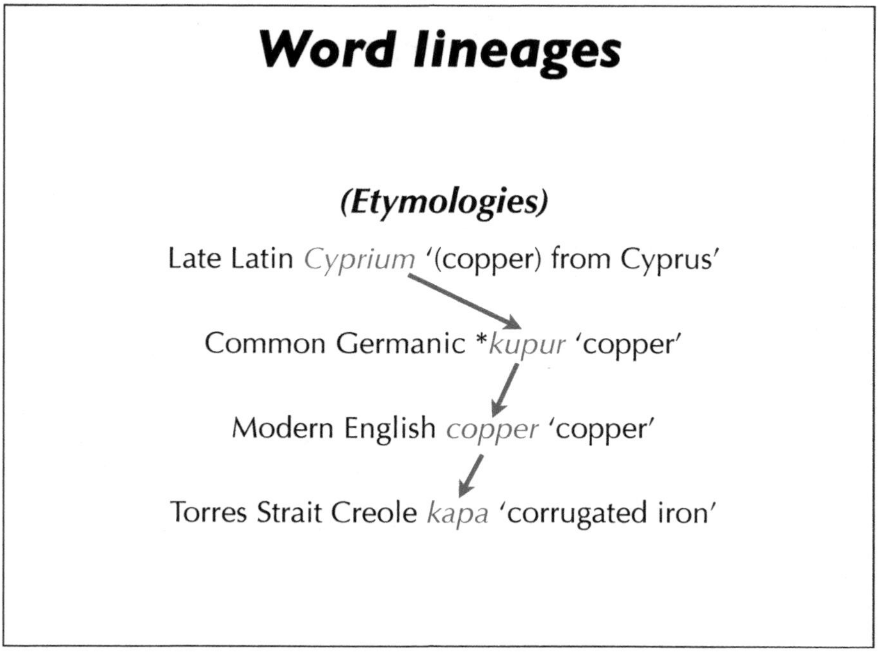

Word lineages

(Etymologies)

Late Latin *Cyprium* '(copper) from Cyprus'

Common Germanic **kupur* 'copper'

Modern English *copper* 'copper'

Torres Strait Creole *kapa* 'corrugated iron'

FIGURE 245

Word lineages are what historical linguists call an "etymology" [Figure 245]. You take a word—here we have a word that started in Late Latin: it got borrowed into the Germanic languages. And you can see continual evolution of both form and meaning through Modern English and also into a Creole language, an English Creole spoken in Australia.

Lastly, we have construction lineages [Figure 246]. This is what grammaticalization theorists like Bernd Heine called "grammaticalization chains". This is perhaps the single most famous, most heavily studied grammaticalization chain. It's how in Latin a construction that uses the auxiliary verb *have* followed by the infinitive form of the verb—"have these things to sing"—comes to mean future: "I will sing". And then the auxiliary gets suffixed to the verb form, so in the modern Romance languages like French, "I will sing" is a single word. This is a grammaticalization chain, showing the grammaticalization of the Modern French future.

Ok, so that gives you the basic model. Now I'd like to focus on how the variation is generated. Remember that evolution is a two-step process: it involves the generation of variation and propagation through a speech community. I won't say much about the latter, because I want to focus on language use and how variation is generated [Figure 247]. So we have mechanisms of variation. There's a process that's called "teleological". This means that speakers

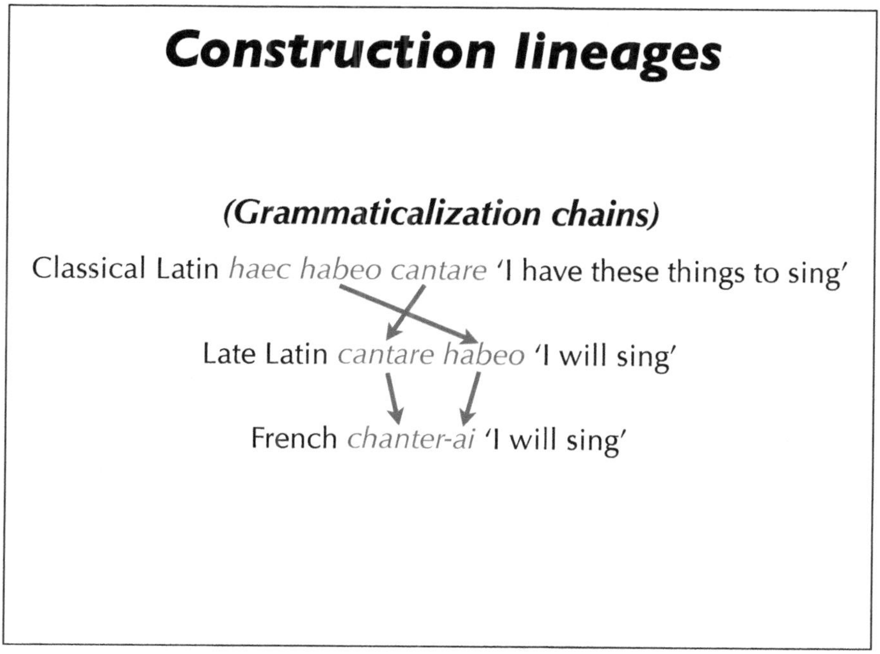

Construction lineages

(Grammaticalization chains)

Classical Latin *haec habeo cantare* 'I have these things to sing'

Late Latin *cantare habeo* 'I will sing'

French *chanter-ai* 'I will sing'

FIGURE 246

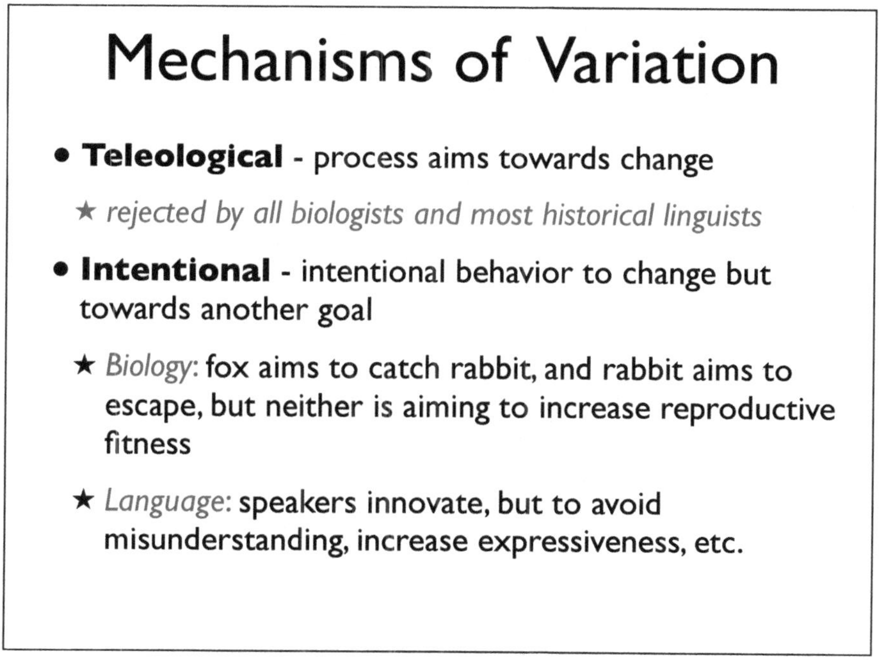

Mechanisms of Variation

- **Teleological** - process aims towards change
  - ★ *rejected by all biologists and most historical linguists*

- **Intentional** - intentional behavior to change but towards another goal
  - ★ *Biology:* fox aims to catch rabbit, and rabbit aims to escape, but neither is aiming to increase reproductive fitness
  - ★ *Language:* speakers innovate, but to avoid misunderstanding, increase expressiveness, etc.

FIGURE 247

essentially intend to change the language for the sake of making change in the language, for making the linguistic system more symmetrical or something filling in a gap. These are hypotheses that have been proposed by historical linguists as recently as fifty years ago. But most modern historical linguists reject these kinds of changes and biologists certainly reject those changes. If you read historical linguists who actually think about the problem of how does language change get started, most of them propose mechanisms that we can call "intentional". So speakers intentionally say something different but they do it with a purpose, some kind of social purpose. So for instance, to impress somebody, to make yourself understood, to avoid being misunderstood. There is a very nice book by a German linguist named Rudi Keller called *On Language Change* that discusses some of these kinds of processes.

Biologists also have to worry about this problem. So animals do have intentional behavior. A fox wants to catch a rabbit, and the rabbit wants to escape. Well, the end of result of this is going to be reproductive success or failure for the fox or the rabbit. But they are not trying to improve their reproductive success or failure: the rabbit is just trying to avoid being eaten, and the fox is trying to get dinner. So likewise in language, speakers are doing something novel but they are doing it for purposes that have to do with social interaction. So as I said, if you read most historical linguists, this is the kind of explanation for how variation happens that they will give.

More recently, some linguists have proposed what I call "nonintentional" mechanisms of variation [Figure 248]. This is based on the hypothesis that most of the time we are trying not to change our language, because we are trying to follow the linguistic conventions of our speech community, because that's the most likely way you will be properly understood. If you start playing around with language, you will risk not succeeding in communicating. So speakers aim to conform to linguistic convention, but change happens anyway because of the nature of the communicative process. As I shall show you, the communicative process is complex and messy and it's hard not to change language even if you try to avoid it.

And there seem to be two kinds of processes involved here. First, speakers have to produce variation in utterances. And then listeners or hearers have to reanalyze the utterance structure and replicate this reanalyzed form. Now the next examples give you a kind of artificial distinction between these two categories, these two types of change, but it's a bit of an oversimplification. So in this work, I'm going to show you examples from sound change, because in sound change this theory has been developed to a greater degree. I've tried to apply these concepts to grammatical change both in the book and in more

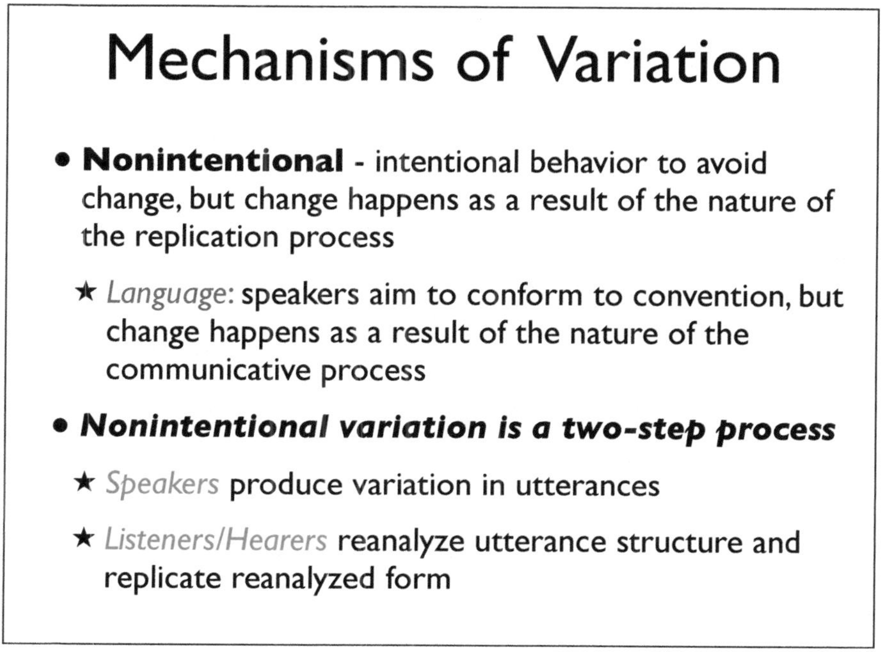

Mechanisms of Variation

- **Nonintentional** - intentional behavior to avoid change, but change happens as a result of the nature of the replication process

  ★ *Language:* speakers aim to conform to convention, but change happens as a result of the nature of the communicative process

- **Nonintentional variation is a two-step process**

  ★ *Speakers* produce variation in utterances

  ★ *Listeners/Hearers* reanalyze utterance structure and replicate reanalyzed form

FIGURE 248

recent publications. So, I'm going to first give you the examples from sound change and then look at the examples from grammatical change.

So what you see here [Figure 249], this is a diagram that those of you who attended the lecture this morning saw [Lecture 9]. This is from a phonetician named Janet Pierrehumbert. Actually the data is from a very old study; you can see the reference at the top, from 1952. But Janet Pierrehumbert and her postdoc created a nice pretty diagram to show you this. So what you have are the vowels produced in English, the standard phonemes are indicated there, /iː/, /i/, /e/, /æ/, /ə/, /ʌ/, and so on. So those are the things we think of as the sounds of English which you may have learned when you were learning English as a foreign language. But you can see that speakers, even though they may be aiming to produce distinct sounds, distinct phonemes, they don't succeed very well. They actually end up producing a whole range of different exemplars of sounds, this whole range here [labelled 'i']. And sometimes they go a little further out.

So what Pierrehumbert argues is that the phonetic realization of sound categories is variable. She concludes that sound categories—phonemes—should be represented as a density distribution of exemplars over this parametric

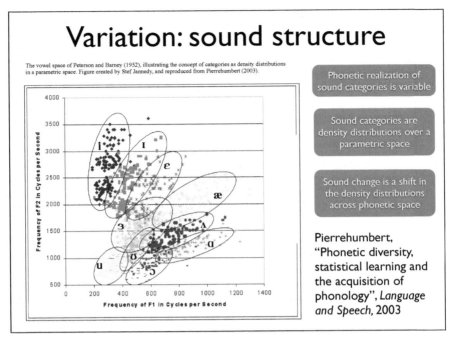

FIGURE 249

space, the space of the first and second formants, which is a standard way that phoneticians represent vowels.

So if we have sound change, sound change is a shift in those density distributions across phonetic space. So if we say that a vowel /e/, a vowel in English that has come to be pronounced as /i/ by some speakers in some dialects, what we mean is that distribution of occurrences of /e/ have slid up to be more like /i/ in that phonetic space.

Also it happens there is an interesting study that was made: the Queen of England makes a radio broadcast every year. Well, the Queen of England has been around for a long time now, over fifty years—same person, different years. So some phoneticians managed to get their hands on the recordings of these radio broadcasts from the 1950s to the present, and compared how this one same person's speech changed. Well it turns out, even though the Queen is probably about as conservative speaker of English as you can imagine, her sound system did change a little bit over this time, reflecting changes in the London area, the London accent. And one particular change is the final vowel in *happy*. So the quote says, "The fact that the Queen's pronunciation of the final vowel in *happy* changed gradually over the decades of her adult life can be captured using incremental updating of the density distribution for the vowel

Listener: Sound Change

Table 22.2 Probabilities of identification of initial consonants as /p/, /t/, /k/ in the columns of the stimuli in the rows

	Heard →	/p/	/t/		/k/
Spoken ↓	/pi/	.46	.38	p > t/_i	.17
	/pa/	.83	.07		.11
	/pu/	.68	.10		.23
	/ti/	.03	.88		.09
	/ta/	.15	.63		.22
	/tu/	.10	.80		.11
	/ki/	.15	.47	k > t/_i	.38
	/ka/	.11	.20		.70
	/ku/	.24	k > p/_u	.18	.58

Notes: Values on the diagonal (with borders) represent correct judgments; those off the diagonal are misperceptions. The average rate of misperception is .173. Confusions that occurred at much higher rate than this are given in italics.
Source: Winitz et al. (1972)

Ohala, "Phonetics and historical phonology", *Handbook of Historical Linguistics*, 2003

FIGURE 250

which is imputed to her cognitive system." This is Pierrehumbert's interpretation of the results of that study.

What's the role of the listener in sound change? Obviously even in the case I gave you before, if the sound actually changes, it's because the listener interprets that density distribution to have changed its centre, so to speak; that the actual target sound has changed its position. But there are other ways in which a listener can re-interpret sounds, and they have to do with aspects of the perception of sounds. John Ohala at Berkeley has made a lot of proposals in this regard. And this is an example from one of his articles [Figure 250]. This is a perception study comparing different vowels after different stop consonants, so take the vowels /a/, /i/ and /u/ after the consonants /p/, /t/ and /k/. So you have /pi/, /pa/, /pu/, /ti/, /ta/, /tu/, /ki/, /ka/, /ku/. And in the perception study, he wanted to see how well speakers could recognize the consonant before the vowel. And what he found was that partly because of the acoustic properties of the consonants (how it influences the vowel), some consonants were more likely to be confused than others. So the boxes from the upper left to the lower right indicate what you'd expect: they did recognize the consonants to be what they were. The other numbers in the table show that sometimes speakers misperceived the consonant. In particular they perceived a /p/ as being a /t/ when it occurs before the /i/ vowel.

Listener: Sound Change

Table 22.3 Examples of sound changes involving large changes in place of articulation

Sound change	Language	Example	Origin, root
k > t, ʧ, ʃ, s/ __ i, j	English	*chicken* ['ʧɪkən]	*cocc* + diminutive
k > t, ʧ, ʃ, s/ __ i, j	English	*church* [ʧɚʧ]	kirke
k > t, ʧ, ʃ, s/ __ i, j	French	*racine* [ʁasin]	Gallo-Roman
		'root' < ratsinə̯	radi'kiːna
k > p / __ u, w	Classical Greek	hippos 'horse'	PIE *ekwos
k > p / __ u, w	West Teke	pfuma 'chief'	PB *-kumu
p > t / __ i, j	E. Bohemian Czech	tɛt 'five'	pʲɛt
p > t / __ i, j	Genoese Italian	ʧena 'full'	pjeno
p > t / __ i, j	Zulu	-ʧʰa 'new'	PB *pia

FIGURE 251

They also perceived the /k/ to be a /t/ before a /i/ vowel. And with a pretty high percentage, they interpreted a /k/ to be a /p/ before the /u/ vowel.

And sure enough, Ohala shows, if you look at language changes, this is what you typically find [Figure 251]: that /k/ changes to a /t/ in front of an /i/ vowel, /k/ changes to a /p/ in front of an /u/ vowel, and a /p/ changes to a /t/ in front of an /i/ vowel. So in other words, in the vowel contexts where perceivers are most likely to misperceive the consonant, this is where you actually find sound changes attested in the world's languages. So this suggests that the kind of perception problems that Ohala identified is a source of variation, could generate variation, and that variation is a source of language changes like these.

So now let's look at grammatical change. Now we're looking at things that I talked about this this morning [Lecture 9]. Most of us think of grammar in terms of starting from linguistic form and describing how you use a particular linguistic form. That's the way reference grammars are written. It's probably the way you're mostly taught how to use a language as a second language. However, what do the native speakers do? They have a language, and they have to start from the experiences they want to communicate and then they have to verbalize them in particular ways.

Speaker: Grammatical Change

Variation in verbalization: scene A6 from the Pear Stories

1	[3.3 [.85] A-nd u-h [1.5]] and then he gets down out of the tree,
2	[1.6? and [.5]] anyway,
	he comes down with a load of pears,
4	[1.4 [.55 {laugh}] . . . a--nd [.35]] he walked down the ladder,
6	[.5] and he walks down the [.75] ladder,
7	[2.25 [.6] tsk [.1] A--nd [.75]] he-- [.35] was going up and down the ladder,
8	and comes down,
9	he comes off of the ladder,
10	and then he'll walk down the ladder,
11	[.4] climbs down the ladder,
12	[.85] /the whole idea/ he picked pears came down the ladder,
15	[2.65 [1.4] A--nd [.8]] he went down the ladder,
17	[1.05? [.35] and the--n . . u--m . .] going . . down off the ladder,
18	[1.4 [.9] tsk And then . .] climbing very carefully . . down the [.2] the ladder,
19	And he comes down,
	. . from the ladder,
20	[.6] So he didn't have to go down to the ground,

FIGURE 252

These examples are taken from a study I did of how different speakers verbalized this film called the Pear film that has been used for experimental study of language production and language verbalization for many years [Figure 252]. This is one scene that I labeled A6. And if you've being reading the screen while I've been talking, you'll see that these different speakers all verbalize the same thing in the movie with different grammatical constructions, different verbs, different noun phrases and so on. No two expressions are alike. So in fact, when you look at what speakers do in actual language use, there is a lot of variation being generated at the grammatical level, where, like any other construction grammarian, I take grammar to mean the relationship between meaning and form.

So we see that there is a lot of variation going on. This morning I talked about what the consequences of the facts of variation are and how we represent what speakers know about their language. Today this afternoon I want to talk about what this means about how languages change. And it's basically the same story that I presented to you about sound change. Just like speakers pronounce the same phoneme in different ways and that can shift over time, speakers use different words and different constructions to express the same scene and that can change over time.

Speaker: Grammatical Change

Variation in the verbalization of PUT in the Pear Stories

	put	Other verb	Other verbs used	Object being PUT	Instrument
C5	15	–		singular	hand
A5	8	2	*drop, stuff*	distributive	hand
E5	8	4	*load, throw, toss, pour*	plural	hand
A7	9	13	*empty, dump, tumble, drop, place, deposit*	plural	apron
G3	1	6	*deposit, dump, empty, unload*	plural	apron

FIGURE 253

So now let's consider, for example, the verb *put* [Figure 253]. Ok, this is what they call a very general verb in English that means PUT. So what I did here was I took every scene in the Pear film where at least one speaker uses the verb *put* to express that relationship. And then I also looked to see what are the other verbs the speakers used. You can see that for the scenes where some speakers used *put*, other speakers used a lot of different verbs. So the first thing we should note is that with the exception of the top scene listed, the scenes evoke different verbs. Every other scene uses multiple verbs: *put* and some other verbs. I have now divided here what other verbs are used by the different scenes. And something I want to mention again, a point that I made this morning, is that if you look at the usage you can see that the verb *put* is more likely to be used in the upper scenes in the table, and other verbs are likely to be used in the lower scenes. If you look at the actual actions that are performed, you can see they are rather different. So the scene that always has *put* was a single object with a hand being used to place the object. *Drop* and *stuff*, that *put* is replaced by in the other scene, is distributive: multiple actions, not just a single object, but multiple objects, multiple pears for those of you who saw the film this morning. Likewise with E5, there it's plural objects, so they have multiple pears at once. And then the last two scenes—where this pearpicker had an apron that

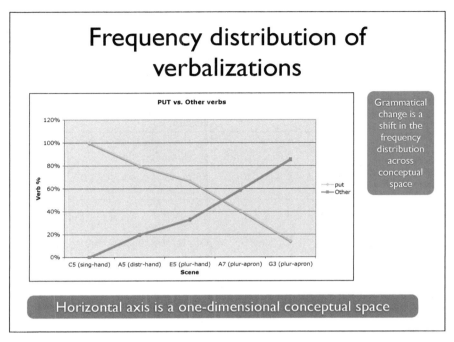

FIGURE 254

he put the pears in, and then he dumped them out into the basket—some people describe that as *put*, but others used all those other verbs listed on the screen. In fact more people use the other verbs than *put*.

So we can look at the frequency distribution of these verbalizations where, now I'm just going to be crude and divide between the verb *put* and the other verbs. This is not in your handout. And you can see that you can arrange these scenes depending where the most put-like scene is [Figure 254]—the single object being placed with the hand—and as soon as you go to multiple objects and you stop using your hands, then the caused change of location is verbalized with other verbs. So you can think of this horizontal axis as a one-dimensional conceptual space. So this is a single semantic dimension. It's a bit of a simpli-fication of course. But we're treating it as a single semantic dimension which essentially determines the likelihood that a speaker will use the verb *put* as opposed to some other verb.

Now I'm going to suggest that just like with the Queen of England using vowels, grammatical change is a shift in that frequency distribution across the conceptual space. So when we say that in a language that a certain verb comes to mean PUT, what we really mean is: the frequency distribution on the right hand side starts shifting to the left hand side. And the old PUT

Speaker: Grammatical Change

Pear Stories verbs and etymology of PUT in Indo-European

Pear Stories	Indo-European PUT verb	Source/related verb in older language
throw, toss	Modern Greek *vazo*	Ancient Greek *bállō* 'throw', occasionally 'put'
	French *mettre*, Italian *mettere*, etc.	Latin *mittere* 'let go, throw', Late Latin 'put'
	Modern Irish *cuirim*	Old Irish *cuirim* 'throw, put'
stuff	English *put*	Old English *potian* 'thrust, push'
place	Dutch *plaatsen*	Dutch *plaats* 'place [n.]'

Croft, "The origins of grammaticalization in the verbalization of experience", *Linguistics* (2010)

FIGURE 255

verb, its frequency gets suppressed and this new PUT verb comes to be used even for the most prototypical examples of PUT. And at that point, a linguist would say the verb has changed meaning. But it's a very gradual process and it should be given a fine-grained semantic analysis like the one represented by this graph.

And indeed, if you look at the etymology of *put*, that's what you find [Figure 255]. So, with *put* and several other verbs in the paper that is cited at the bottom, I took a large comparative dictionary of Indo-European, a standard reference source. And for *put* and a lot of other verbs—*go, come, see* and so on that I found in this Pear film—I looked at the other verbs that speakers used to describe the same scenes, and I compared it to the verbs that were the etymological sources of *put* and other verbs. And in general, I found what you see here on the slide, which is that if you look at other verbs the speakers use—*throw, toss, stuff, place*—those are the verbs that are the sources of *put* in the history of the Indo-European family, where we know the history probably the best.

And you can see the examples of modern European verbs meaning PUT in the second column and their etymological source and the meaning they have in the last column. So this evidence and other evidence that I present in this paper suggest that in fact the kind of grammatical changes we see—lexical changes, grammaticalization processes—originate in the variation that is generated in the process of verbalizing your experience. So it does originate in language use.

The hearer also plays a role in grammatical change. So now, the kind of grammatical changes I'm going to illustrate are examples that are similar to the examples that John Ohala had, the perceptual changes that underlie changes like /pi/ to /ti/ and /ku/ to /pu/ that we saw before. So basically those came because the sort of reconstruction from the phonetic signal of /pi/ is actually acoustically rather difficult. So listeners reconstruct it as /ti/ instead of /pi/, and if enough speakers do that for long enough, then we say there's been a sound change from /p/ to /t/ before the /i/ vowel.

Well, basically the same kind of process is going on when you look at the relationship between form and meaning. Once again, like a construction grammarian and cognitive linguist, I take grammar to be the relationship between form and meaning. So if you are a listener and you are interpreting an utterance that someone just produced, which is a complex combination of words and constructions, it's not easy to reconstruct what the original words' and constructions' meanings were. Utterance meaning in context is unique and different from prior uses of the same constructions that were replicated. Speakers' verbalization of experience is highly variable. We just saw that. And most important is: the hearer cannot read the speakers' mind. That's why we use language to communicate. But the hearer has to read the speakers' mind in order to interpret the utterance. So the hearer might make some changes. In particular, they might reanalyze the relationship between form and meaning in a construction. Those of you who were here this morning, you heard Melissa Bowerman talk about the children learning these resultative verb compounds in Chinese, and talking about how children have to figure out how to essentially attribute parts of the meaning of the event to the first verb and the second verb in the compound. And that was a difficult process for the child.

One process we can observe is one I called "hyperanalysis" [Figure 256]. These terms were taken from Ohala's terminology for the sound changes he uses. I elaborated the system but I'm going to give you just two examples here. In hyperanalysis, a speaker overanalyzes the meaning in an utterance. So if you consider the morpheme here [*m-*], that morpheme in the first sentence indicates a locative relationship. This is a Bantu language and in Bantu languages nouns belong to different classes, and locative meaning is expressed by classes 16 through 18. So you have class 18 which is really essentially a prefix meaning 'in'. And then the verb also agrees with this [*mw-*]. It's a very unusual construction across languages.

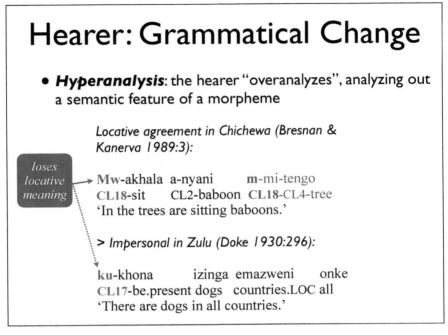

Hearer: Grammatical Change

- **Hyperanalysis**: the hearer "overanalyzes", analyzing out a semantic feature of a morpheme

    Locative agreement in Chichewa (Bresnan & Kanerva 1989:3):

    loses locative meaning → Mw-akhala a-nyani   m-mi-tengo
    CL18-sit   CL2-baboon CL18-CL4-tree
    'In the trees are sitting baboons.'

    > Impersonal in Zulu (Doke 1930:296):

    ku-khona   izinga emazweni   onke
    CL17-be.present dogs   countries.LOC all
    'There are dogs in all countries.'

FIGURE 256

Well, apparently it's not a terribly stable construction. Locative meaning is expressed in the phrase "in the trees". It's also expressed in the verb. It's expressed in two different places. And speakers of related Bantu languages reanalyzed this. So they essentially analyze out the locative meaning from the verb prefix, and the verb prefix is now used for various kinds of so-called "impersonal" constructions such as the existential construction you see on the bottom: "There are dogs in all countries." So that's a case where essentially the speaker had this complex construction, essentially reanalyzed where the locative meaning was expressed in this construction, and reinterpreted the initial prefix on the verb as not having a locative meaning, and instead it has what they call an impersonal meaning.

You can also get the other way around [Figure 257]. So the hearer "underanalyzes" a construction and attributes some contextual semantic feature to the morpheme. This is a pattern that has been observed by John Bybee and her colleagues and by Martin Haspelmath. This is where you have a present tense in a language. A present tense is often replaced by a progressive. It's happening in English now: we use the progressive to describe an event that takes place at the present moment in many different contexts, and it appears to be extending its use. That means the simple present gets more and more

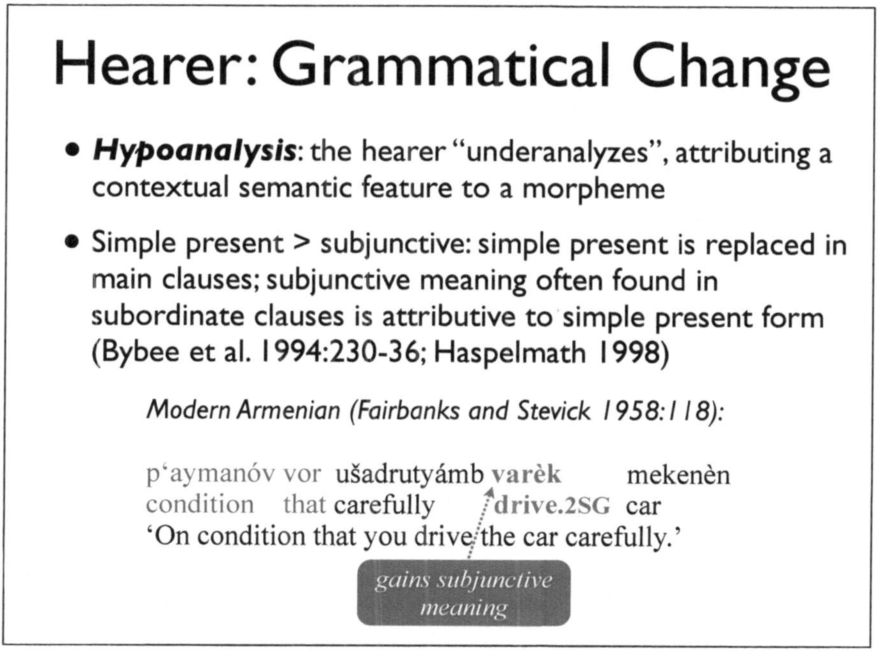

Hearer: Grammatical Change

- **Hypoanalysis**: the hearer "underanalyzes", attributing a contextual semantic feature to a morpheme

- Simple present > subjunctive: simple present is replaced in main clauses; subjunctive meaning often found in subordinate clauses is attributive to simple present form (Bybee et al. 1994:230-36; Haspelmath 1998)

Modern Armenian (Fairbanks and Stevick 1958:118):

p'aymanóv vor ušadrutyámb **varèk**   mekenèn
condition   that carefully   drive.2SG car
'On condition that you drive the car carefully.'

gains subjunctive meaning

FIGURE 257

restricted in its use. One context where the simple present tense has survived is in a subordinate clause. What happens in some languages is essentially they assume that this subordination is part of the meaning of that present tense, because it's not being used elsewhere for present tense meaning. And therefore, the verb form gets reanalyzed as a subjunctive—an indication of a subordinate clause meaning. So that form there [*varèk*] gains subjunctive meaning that it didn't have before, because it has been restricted to subjunctive contexts.

These are just two examples of how grammatical change can take place as a result of reanalyzing the relationship between form and meaning in constructions or in utterances. So now I'd like to conclude by taking this evolutionary model and taking a slightly larger perspective. I've focused on linguistic form and how speakers essentially try to deal with linguistic form in language use and end up changing the language in the process—ending up getting language change started. So now I'd like to embed this view of what's going on with language use into a larger model of language and speakers in particular.

Now this evolutionary model has been around for a long time. There is a famous quotation from Darwin, the founder of evolutionary biology, where he points out the parallelism [Figure 258]. And we talked about that already. As

---

Language and evolution

- The close relationship between language and evolution was a commonplace in the 19th century:

  The formation of different languages and of distinct species, and the proof that both have been developed through a gradual process, are curiously parallel...
  (Charles Darwin, *The Descent of Man*)

- In the past decade or so, evolutionary models of language have been proposed in linguistics

- What happened in the century in between?

FIGURE 258

I said, in the past decade or so, evolutionary models have been proposed by myself, by Salikoko Mufwene, and a number of other linguists.

But there is a whole century where nothing much happened in this domain. And that's because language has traditionally been conceived of as a uniform system of synchronic rules [Figure 259]. This [tool] is one you all may be familiar with, since most of you are second language learners of English, and maybe teachers of English as a second language. It's kind of the prescriptive view where you tell people how they are supposed to speak. There is a fairly narrow interpretation of this, which is there is only one right way to speak. And you even get some hints of this in certain linguistic theories which reject a view of language as being essentially variable.

This corresponds to the view in biology that's called "essentialism" [Figure 260]. The idea here is that a particular biological species is defined by certain essential features. So if you want to identify a particular tree species like the one that's illustrated on the right, a tree from California, you look at the essential features which are described in this fine print here, which of course you don't need to worry about; this is just an illustration.

There are problems with this view. This is what Darwin was challenging. Species vary tremendously across individuals in their essential features, and so do languages. This is the whole point behind the usage-based, variationist view

Two views of language (1)

- Language has been traditionally conceived of as a **uniform system of synchronic rules**

- This approach, which has a long tradition, we call the "prescriptive grammar" view of language

- Nonvariationist approaches to language (e.g. generative grammar) sometimes tends toward prescriptivism

FIGURE 259

"Prescriptive grammar" view = essentialism in biology

- Essentialism in biology is the idea that a species is a **type** defined by **essential features**

Calocedrus decurrens (Torrey) Florin 1956. Resinous, aromatic tree 18–46(57) m tall and 90–150(360) cm dbh. Tapering, irregularly angled trunk and narrow, columnar crown, becoming open and irregular. Bark light or reddish-brown, thick, fibrous, deeply and irregularly furrowed into shreddy ridges. Twigs much-branched and flattish, with wedge-shaped joints longer than broad; composed of scalelike leaves. Leaves evergreen, shiny, opposite in 4 rows, 3–14 mm long, scalelike, including long-decurrent base, rounded abaxially, apex acute (often abruptly), usually mucronate, the side pair keeled, long-pointed, overlapping the next pair, extending down twig; aromatic when crushed. Pollen cones red-brown to light brown. Seed cones cones red-brown to golden brown, 14–25 mm long (including wings), oblong-ovate when closed, pendant at end of slender, leafy stalk, proximal scales often reflexed at cone maturity, median scales then widely spreading to recurved, distal scales erect. Seeds 4 or fewer in cone, paired with 2 unequal wings. 2n= 22 (Little 1980, Thieret 1993).

FIGURE 260

Population definition of a species

- A set of individuals that
interbreed, *i.e. they are
defined by their relationship to each other*

- The population is
(relatively) *reproductively isolated* from other
populations

- The defining relationship is also the process by
which replication occurs in the population

FIGURE 261

Two views of language (2)

- There is another,
informal view of
language, which is more
suited to the facts of
language and is
compatible with
population thinking and
the evolutionary
framework

- GAS formalizes this
"Story of English" view
of language as a
historical process

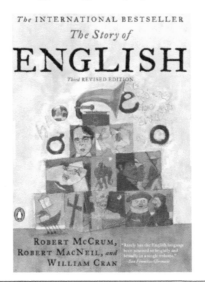

FIGURE 262

of language. Also, species evolve and change essential features, and there is no sharp dividing line. And that's true of languages as well. As long as the speech community is cohesive, you can see evolution. So Middle English is not the same language as Early Modern English: we'd have great difficulty understanding it even if you are a native speaker of Modern English. But you can't really draw a line and say, in 1586 Middle English ended and Early Modern English began.

So this notion of language having an essential type is really ultimately misleading. So what do we replace this with? And this is the notion of a "population" [Figure 261]. This is actually not so much Darwin but his successors who had this insight. A population is what David Hull described as a historical entity bounded in space and time. So, in biology, the species exists over a particular space—a geographical area—and a particular time interval. And it is bounded in time and space. And it eventually ends by extinction or by splitting into two new species.

So what is it that defines a species then, if it is this historical entity? Well, a standard definition now is a set of individuals that interbreed. So if two birds in this case interbreed, then they are part of the same species. So in other words they are defined by their relationship to each other. They are not defined by some essential features. A population is reproductively isolated from other populations. It's that these birds reproduce among themselves; they don't reproduce with other birds. That's what distinguishes their species from another species. And critically, this relationship that defines the species population is also the process by which replication occurs. That's replication in biology.

So everything that I've just told you is also true of language. So there is another informal view of language, which we can call "the Story of English" after this famous TV series in the United States and the book that came out of it, that's more compatible: and that's the idea that English is a historical entity [Figure 262]. And the general analysis of selection that I presented to you formalizes this "Story of English" view of language as a historical process.

So a language exists over a particular time and space [Figure 263]. Here is a language family. And it will end where it becomes extinct.

And we can have a population definition of a speech community [Figure 264]. So the speech community is a set of individuals that conversationally interact. They talk to each other. So in other words, what makes people a member of a speech community is not anything inherent about themselves, in fact, not even whether they are what we call native speakers, but whether they are part of the speech community. They talk to each other. That population is relatively communicatively isolated from other populations. So for instance, in Europe, we used to speak of a single language called Serbo-Croatian when the country of Yugoslavia existed. Now they generally really don't like each other. They have

A language…

- Exists over a particular time and space

- And is bounded in time and space by its eventual end (breakup or extinction)

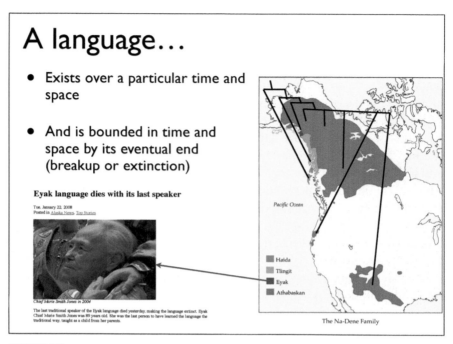

Eyak language dies with its last speaker

Tue. January 22, 2008
Posted in Alaska News, Top Stories

Chief Marie Smith Jones in 2004

The last traditional speaker of the Eyak language died yesterday, making the language extinct. Eyak Chief Marie Smith Jones was 89 years old. She was the last person to have learned the language the traditional way, taught as a child from her parents.

Pacific Ocean

■ Haida
■ Tlingit
■ Eyak
■ Athabaskan

The Na-Dene Family

FIGURE 263

Populations in language

- ***Speech community***: population of speakers, communicatively relatively isolated

- ***Language***: population of utterances produced by speakers of the speech community

- ***Lingueme pool***: population of variants of linguistic variables

  ★***Grammar***: what a speaker knows about her language, derived from language use around her (as in Lecture 9)

FIGURE 264

split into separate countries. They don't talk to each other. Given enough time, their languages will diverge, because now they are separate languages and they are communicatively isolated. And that defining relationship—talking to each other—is the process by which replication occurs. That's what we described in the whole first part of this talk. Replication happens every time we speak. Every time we talk, we replicate linguistic structure.

So the populations we find in language are: the speech community, this population of speakers who are communicatively relatively isolated. So language: what's a language in this sense? Well, I'm going to take a language to be the population of utterances produced by those speakers. So we can think of English as essentially this gigantic corpus of all the utterances that we think of as being English that have been produced in the history of English until English comes to be extinct or splits up. We can then talk about what we'll call the "lingueme pool" (this is following the term "gene pool" in biology)—a term that will sound strange to you. It's a population of variants of linguistic variables. So you look at particular linguistic forms and their variants; this is what sociolinguists do all the time, this is what they analyze. This is just a different name for that, showing how it fits into the evolutionary model. So then what's a grammar? A grammar—again, we're thinking of this in terms of knowledge that speakers have about their language—it's what a speaker knows about her language, derived from the language use around her. So this is the usage-based model of grammar, now embedded in this model of speaker populations and language as a population of utterances and lingueme populations.

So, to conclude, looking at language and change in grammar. So in conversation, speakers replicate variants that they have been exposed to, as processed and stored in their minds. Their choice of variants—this means their choices of variants to replicate, to produce—depends on the experience they are communicating, including how they construe it; the social context of their conversation, like for instance the social status and roles of interlocutors; the social domain in which the conversation occurs, and so on. But there is a constant feedback between the speaker's cognition and their communicative interaction. Language use influences speaker knowledge about their language, and then speaker knowledge obviously influences their language use; it determines their language use. Also over time, an individual speaker's social activities and goals change, and the social structures that determine speaker status/role and the domains of language use also change—remember, I talked about the constantly evolving environment of language use. So this cognition and social interaction feedback process, combined with the evolving social system, results in a constantly evolving linguistic system, or more precisely, a constantly evolving population of utterances that are embedded in their social context of use. And that's where I'm ending my lectures for today. Thank you.

About the Series Editor

Fuyin (Thomas) Li received his Ph.D. in English Linguistics and Applied Linguistics from the Chinese University of Hong Kong in 2003. He is currently a full Professor of linguistics at Beihang University, Beijing. He is the founding editor of *Cognitive Semantics*, a peer reviewed international journal, http://cosebrill.edmgr.com/; the organizer of China International Forum on Cognitive Linguistics, http://cifcl.buaa.edu.cn/; the editor of the following series: *The Eminent Linguists' Lecture Series* (Beijing: Foreign Language Teaching and Research Press); *Compendium of Cognitive Linguistics Research* (New York: Nova Science); and *Distinguished Lectures in Cognitive Linguistics* (DLCL, Brill, the Netherlands), http://www.brill.com/cn/products/series/distinguished -lectures-cognitive-linguistics. He was the organizer for ICLC-11, 2011.

His main areas of expertise include Talmyan cognitive semantics, event grammar, Causality, etc. His representative works include, Chinese version of *Toward a Cognitive Semantics*, Volume I & II (2017, Beijing: PUP), originally published in English by Leonard Talmy, 2000, MIT; *Metaphor, Image, and Image Schemas in Second Language Pedagogy* (2009, Köln, Germany: LAP LAMBERT Academic Publishing); and journal articles publish ed in English and Chinese.

His overseas experiences include visiting and research at University of Canterbury, University of Otago, University of Malaga, The Chinese University of Hong Kong, UC Berkeley, MIT, The State University of New York at Buffalo, University of Edinburgh, University of Leuven, etc.

Personal homepage: http://shi.buaa.edu.cn/thomasli/zh_CN/index.htm

Websites for Cognitive Linguistics and CIFCL Speakers

All the websites were checked for validity on 20 January 2019.

Part 1 Websites for Cognitive Linguistics

1. http://www.cogling.org/
   Website for the International Cognitive Linguistics Association, ICLA

2. http://www.cognitivelinguistics.org/en/journal
   Website for the journal edited by ICLA, *Cognitive Linguistics*

3. http://cifcl.buaa.edu.cn/
   Website for China International Forum on Cognitive Linguistics (CIFCL)

4. http://cosebrill.edmgr.com/
   Website for the journal *Cognitive Semantics* (*ISSN 2352–6408 / E-ISSN 2352–6416*), edited by CIFCL

5. http://www.degruyter.com/view/serial/16078?rskey=fw6Q2O&result=1&q=CLR
   Website for the Cognitive Linguistics Research [CLR]

6. http://www.degruyter.com/view/serial/20568?rskey=dddL3r&result=1&q=ACL
   Website for Application of Cognitive Linguistics [ACL]

7. http://www.benjamins.com/#catalog/books/clscc/main
   Website for book series in Cognitive Linguistics by Benjamins

8. http://www.brill.com/cn/products/series/distinguished-lectures-cognitive
   -linguistics
   Website for Distinguished Lectures in Cognitive Linguistics (DLCL)

9. http://refworks.reference-global.com/
   Website for online resources for Cognitive Linguistics Bibliography

10. http://benjamins.com/online/met/
    Website for Bibliography of Metaphor and Metonymy

11.   http://linguistics.berkeley.edu/research/cognitive/
       Website for the Cognitive Linguistics Program at UC Berkeley

12.   https://framenet.icsi.berkeley.edu/fndrupal/
       Website for Framenet

13.   http://www.mpi.nl/
       Website for the Max Planck Institute for Psycholinguistics

Part 2   Websites for CIFCL Speakers and Their Research

14.   CIFCL Organizer
       Thomas Li, thomasli@buaa.edu.cn; thomaslfy@gmail.com
       Personal homepage: http://shi.buaa.edu.cn/thomasli
       http://shi.buaa.edu.cn/lifuyin/en/index.htm

15.   CIFCL 18, 2018
       Arie Verhagen, A.Verhagen@hum.leidenuniv.nl
       http://www.arieverhagen.nl/

16.   CIFCL 17, 2017
       Jeffrey M. Zacks, jzacks@wustl.edu
       Lab: dcl.wustl.edu
       Personal site: https://dcl.wustl.edu/affiliates/jeff-zacks/

17.   CIFCL 16, 2016
       Cliff Goddard, c.goddard@griffith.edu.au
       https://www.griffith.edu.au/griffith-centre-social-cultural-research/our-centre/
       cliff-goddard

18.   CIFCL 15, 2016
       Nikolas Gisborne, n.gisborne@ed.ac.uk

19.   CIFCL 14, 2014
       Phillip Wolff, pwolff@emory.edu

20.   CIFCL 13, 2013 (CIFCL 03, 2006)
       Ronald W. Langacker, rlangacker@ucsd.edu
       http://idiom.ucsd.edu/~rwl/

21.   CIFCL 12, 2013 (CIFCL 18, 2018)
       Stefan Th. Gries, stgries@linguistics.ucsb.edu
       http://www.stgries.info

22.   CIFCL 12, 2013
       Alan Cienki, a.cienki@vu.nl
       https://research.vu.nl/en/persons/alan-cienki

23.   CIFCL 11, 2012
       Sherman Wilcox, wilcox@unm.edu
       http://www.unm.edu/~wilcox

24.   CIFCL 10, 2012
       Jürgen Bohnemeyer, jb77@buffalo.edu
       Personal homepage: http://www.acsu.buffalo.edu/~jb77/
       The CAL blog: https://causalityacrosslanguages.wordpress.com/
       The blog of the UB Semantic Typology Lab: https://ubstlab.wordpress.com/

25.   CIFCL 09, 2011
       Laura A. Janda, laura.janda@uit.no
       http://ansatte.uit.no/laura.janda/

26.   CIFCL 09, 2011
       Ewa Dabrowska, ewa.dabrowska@northumbria.ac.uk

27.   CIFCL 08, 2010
       William Croft, wcroft@unm.edu
       http://www.unm.edu/~wcroft

28.   CIFCL 08, 2010
       Zoltán Kövecses, kovecses.zoltan@btk.elte.hu

29.   CIFCL 08, 2010
       (Melissa Bowerman: 1942–2011)

30.   CIFCL 07, 2009
       Dirk Geeraerts, dirk.geeraerts@arts.kuleuven.be
       http://wwwling.arts.kuleuven.be/qlvl/dirkg.htm

31.   CIFCL 07, 2009
      Mark Turner, mark.turner@case.edu

32.   CIFCL 06, 2008
      Chris Sinha, chris.sinha@ling.lu.se

33.   CIFCL 05, 2008
      Gilles Fauconnier, faucon@cogsci.ucsd.edu

34.   CIFCL 04, 2007
      Leonard Talmy, talmy@buffalo.edu
      https://www.acsu.buffalo.edu/~talmy/talmy.html

35.   CIFCL 03, 2006 (CIFCL 13, 2013)
      Ronald W. Langacker, rlangacker@ucsd.edu
      http://idiom.ucsd.edu/~rwl/

36.   CIFCL 02, 2005
      John Taylor, john.taylor65@xtra.co.nz
      https://independent.academia.edu/JohnRTaylor

37.   CIFCL 01, 2004
      George Lakoff, lakoff@berkeley.edu
      http://georgelakoff.com/